MONTESQUIEU AND BURKE

MODERN LANGUAGE STUDIES

J. Boyd, J. Seznec, P. E. Russell, *General Editors*

MONTESQUIEU AND BURKE

By C. P. COURTNEY

FELLOW OF CHRIST'S COLLEGE, CAMBRIDGE
LECTURER IN FRENCH IN THE UNIVERSITY OF CAMBRIDGE

BASIL BLACKWELL
OXFORD
1963

First printed in 1963

Printed in Great Britain for BASIL BLACKWELL & MOTT, LTD.
by A. R. MOWBRAY & Co. LIMITED in the City of Oxford
and bound at the KEMP HALL BINDERY

PREFACE

IT is often asserted that Edmund Burke was Montesquieu's greatest English disciple; but the exact relations of these two thinkers have not hitherto been worked out in any detail. Although there are many studies of Montesquieu's connections with England, these normally show more interest in Montesquieu's English sources than in his influence in that country; and Burke scholars have, on the whole, been more concerned with Burke and Rousseau than with Burke and Montesquieu. The following study attempts to provide a fuller account of the influence of Montesquieu on Burke than has hitherto been available.

This book is a slightly revised form of a doctoral dissertation submitted in 1959 in the University of Oxford. Since then, and indeed since this book went to press, a number of important studies on Montesquieu and on Burke have appeared. On Montesquieu the most important is Mr. Robert Shackleton's *Montesquieu, A Critical Biography* (Oxford, 1961), in which the reader will find, among other things, a fuller account of Montesquieu's visit to England than I have given below. On Burke the most important publication is the new edition of the *Correspondence* under the general editorship of Professor T. W. Copeland, and of which three volumes have now appeared. Two important works on Burke not mentioned in my bibliography are Professor T. H. D. Mahoney's *Edmund Burke and Ireland* (Oxford, 1960) and Father F. Canavan's *The Political Reason of Edmund Burke* (Duke University, 1960).

I am indebted to the Queen's University of Belfast, the University of Sheffield, and the Centre National de la Recherche Scientifique for financial help which made my researches possible; and to the University of Sheffield for a generous grant towards publication. I am also grateful to Sir Basil Blackwell and his board of editors for publishing this work in Modern Language Studies.

I wish to thank Earl Fitzwilliam for permitting me to make use of unpublished material from the Burke and Rockingham papers in the Central Library, Sheffield, and the Northamptonshire Record Office. I am grateful to the Librarian and staff of the Sheffield Central Library for placing manuscripts and photostats at my disposal.

I am greatly indebted to Mr. Robert Shackleton for his advice and encouragement throughout the whole preparation of this work;

to the Principal of Lady Margaret Hall for guidance in my study of Burke and eighteenth-century politics; and to Professor L. A. Bisson, Professor Fraser Mackenzie, Professor S. Skalweit, and Professor T.W. Copeland for help at various stages of my research. I am particularly grateful to Dr. Robert A. Smith for reading the typescript and proofs and offering constructive criticism; and I wish to thank Mr. J. P. Short and Dr. J. E. S. Hayward who helped to read the proofs and made many helpful suggestions.

C. P. C.

SHEFFIELD, 1962

CONTENTS

ABBREVIATIONS

Corr.	*Correspondence of the Right Hon. Edmund Burke,* ed. Earl Fitzwilliam and Sir R. Bourke, 4 vols., 1844.
EHR	*English Historical Review.*
E.L.	Montesquieu, *De l'Esprit des lois.*
Fitzwilliam MSS. (N.R.S.)	Correspondence of E. Burke deposited by Earl Fitzwilliam with the Northamptonshire Record Society, Delapré Abbey, Northampton.
Fitzwilliam MSS. (Sheffield).	Correspondence of E. Burke and of the second Marquis of Rockingham deposited by Earl Fitzwilliam in the Central Library, Sheffield.
FS	*French Studies.*
Œuvres (Nagel)	*Œuvres complètes de Montesquieu,* ed. A. Masson (Les Editions Nagel), 3 vols., 1950–55.
Œuvres (Pléiade)	Montesquieu, *Œuvres complètes,* ed. R. Caillois (Bibliothèque de la Pléiade), 2 vols., 1949–51.
P.H.	*The Parliamentary History of England,* ed. W. Cobbett and J. Wright, 36 vols., 1806–20.
PMLA	*Publications of the Modern Languages Association of America.*
RMM	*Revue de métaphysique et de morale.*
Works	*The Works of Edmund Burke* (Bohn's British Classics), 8 vols., 1854–89.

Note: Unless otherwise specified London is the place of publication of all works with titles in English, and Paris of those with titles in French.

INTRODUCTION

IN one of his earliest writings Burke refers to Montesquieu as 'the greatest genius which has enlightened this age';[1] and in one of his late works he concludes with a magnificent eulogy of Montesquieu as 'a genius not born in every country, or every time'.[2] However, Burke did more than simply admire the great French thinker: he found in him sustenance for his own thought; and, indeed, it has long been commonplace to consider Burke as Montesquieu's disciple.[3] The purpose of the present study is to examine in some detail the nature and extent of this influence of one great thinker on another.

Any study of the thought of Edmund Burke must face the problem of the protean nature of Burke's activities. He is writer, politician, propagandist, orator, and philosopher; and his subject matter is as wide and varied as such combined careers would suggest, ranging from America to India, and from polite literature to political philosophy. The consequence of this is that anyone who wishes to see Burke steadily and to see him whole cannot hope to do so by approaching him merely from the standpoint of one narrow specialized discipline. This has perhaps not always been sufficiently understood by Burke scholars, and it is all too common to find studies of his thought consisting of a rather rigid systematizing of *obiter dicta* culled in a haphazard fashion from different parts of his writings and speeches with a complete disregard of chronology and of the practical nature of the political issues with which Burke was dealing. Such accounts of his thought normally assume *a priori* that Burke never changed his mind on anything, that he was perfectly consistent throughout his long and varied career, and that we only have to look and we shall find in him a systematic philosophy. Such studies, by disregarding the active politician, and by forgetting that politicians are rarely, if ever, disinterested philosophers, tend to idealize Burke, to see in him nothing but the sublime and beautiful philosopher of liberalism and conservatism, whose wisdom on England, Ireland, America, India and France, would have made a

---

[1] *Abridgment of English History* (1757), *Works*, vi, p. 297.
[2] *Appeal from the New to the Old Whigs* (1791), *Works*, iii, p. 113.
[3] The fullest account of Montesquieu's influence on Burke is in F. T. H. Fletcher, *Montesquieu and English Politics, 1750–1800*, 1939. Cf. R. S. Crane, 'Montesquieu and British Thought', *Journal of Political Economy*, 49 (1941), pp. 592–600. The following general studies mention *passim* Montesquieu's influence: J. Morley, *Burke*, 1879; R. H. Murray, *Edmund Burke*, Oxford, 1931; B. Newman, *Edmund Burke*, 1927. Cf. also, C. E. Vaughan, *Studies in the History of Political Philosophy*, 2 vols., Manchester, 1925.

new heaven and a new earth if it had not been for the influence of
evil men like George III, Lord North, Warren Hastings, and the
French revolutionaries. Such studies usually select from Burke
those passages that will confirm the students' own prejudices: thus
positivists see in him a positivist, conservatives a conservative, and
Catholics regard him as a writer in the tradition of Aquinas.[1] If, on
the other hand, we turn away from political philosophers to historians, we shall find a picture of Burke which is so different that we
might wonder whether we are still dealing with the same person.
To them he is often merely a crafty politician, an Irish adventurer
who curried favour with the great, and whose private life was
involved in financial scandals. They believe that on most of the
great political problems of the time he was lacking in the wisdom of
a Chatham, a Warren Hastings, or a Pitt; and they show little
interest in his interpretation of the French Revolution.[2]

It is obvious that our opinion of Burke will depend to a large
degree on the approach we make to him. It is, however, unfortunate
that Burke should be studied merely from the standpoint of the
political philosopher or the historian, and thus have the narrowness
of modern specialization imposed on him. He lived in an age when
specialization was less intense than it is to-day, and when one mind
could embrace many subjects. Perhaps the most satisfactory
approach to Burke is through the chronology of his career. Up to
1765 he was primarily a literary man with a bent for history and
philosophy. In these years he wrote the *Vindication of Natural
Society* (1756), the *Sublime and Beautiful* (1757), the *Abridgment of
English History* (1757); and from 1758 to about 1766 he was editing
the *Annual Register*.[3] It is true that during these years his activities
were not exclusively literary, for in 1759 he became secretary to
William Gerard Hamilton, who was a Commissioner at the Board
of Trade; and when in 1761 Hamilton became Chief Secretary in
Ireland, Burke accompanied him to Dublin. In this capacity Burke
spent the parliamentary sessions 1761-2 and 1763-4 in Ireland, during
which time he was engaged to some extent in practical political

[1] For the positivists' interpretation of Burke see the following studies: L. Stephen, *History
of English Thought in the Eighteenth Century*, 2 vols., 1876; J. MacCunn, *The Political Philosophy
of Burke*, 1913. In the same tradition is A. Cobban, *Edmund Burke*, 1929. For a conservative's
interpretation see R. Kirk, *The Conservative Mind*, 1954. For a Catholic interpretation see
P. J. Stanlis, *Edmund Burke and the Natural Law*, Michigan, 1958.

[2] For the historians' point of view see: R. Pares, *King George III and the Politicians*, Oxford,
1954; Sir Lewis Namier, *Monarchy and the Party System*, Oxford, 1952; K. Feiling, *Warren
Hastings*, 1954; D. Wecter, *Edmund Burke and His Kinsmen*, Boulder, 1939.

[3] For dates of Burke's editorship of the *Annual Register* see D. C. Bryant, 'New Light on
Burke', *The Quarterly Journal of Speech*, 39 (1953), pp. 351-2.

problems.[1] However, his interests were still primarily literary; and his quarrel with Hamilton, leading to their separation early in 1765, was mainly because Hamilton would not allow him enough time for literary activities.[2] The work which he wrote while in Ireland, *Tracts on the Popery Laws*, is the work of a young man who is still more interested in writing and philosophy than in practical political issues.[3] Perhaps the best description of Burke during this pre-political part of his career is that of Horace Walpole, who in 1761 referred to him in the following terms:

> He is a sensible man, but has not worn off his authorism yet, and thinks there is nothing so charming as writers and to be one.[4]

Our approach to these early works will be quite straightforward: they are literary works with a bent towards history and philosophy. In examining them for influences of Montesquieu it will be sufficient to apply the normal comparativist technique of analysis, comparison, and elimination of common sources.[5]

When in July 1765 Burke, at the age of thirty-six, became secretary to the Marquis of Rockingham, recently appointed head of a new administration, he was apparently making a break with his previous career. Henceforth his main interest was to be politics, and literature was to take a secondary place. In 1765 he was so little known to the political world that one of his own leaders, the Duke of Newcastle, was ready to believe the story that he was a Papist whose real name was O'Burke and who had been educated as a Jesuit at St. Omer.[6] His enemies despised him at first as a mere literary man with no knowledge of practical politics:

> Mr. Bourk, descended from a garret to the head of our administration, is a metaphysician, a man of learning and imagination; a garret is a very proper situation for those who mean to read the stars, but the springs which decide on the fate of nations, lay nearer the earth.[7]

However, contrary to the expectations of such critics, Burke proved himself an efficient politician, employing his time debating, organizing, and writing political pamphlets. It is one of the paradoxes of his career that it was only when he apparently abandoned literature for politics that he began to write pamphlets which, like those of

---

[1] See below, chap. ix. [2] *Corr.*, I, p. 46 seq.
[3] See below, chap. iii, pp. 56–7; chap. ix, pp. 170–1.
[4] H. Walpole, *Correspondence*, ed. W. S. Lewis, New Haven, 1937 seq., ix, p. 380.
[5] This is the plan followed in chap. iii, below.
[6] *Historical Manuscripts Commission*, 12th Report, Appendix, Part x (Charlemont MSS.), pp. 148–9.
[7] Quoted in D. A. Winstanley, *Personal and Party Government*, 1760–1766, Cambridge, 1910, p. 243.

Milton, have become classics of English literature. If his career had
ended in 1765 he would be remembered by specialists for the
Sublime and Beautiful, and as editor of the *Annual Register*; but he
would not be considered a literary figure of the highest order. It
was only when he became a politician that Burke found full scope
for his talents. He became great not only as a writer, but also as an
orator, thus achieving another ambition, which dated from his
undergraduate days, when he founded the college debating club.[1]
To his political writings and speeches Burke also brings his early
interest in philosophy, and he has a marked tendency, perhaps
encouraged by his love of oratory, to generalize, and to formulate
maxims of general political wisdom. It is tempting for the student
to approach these works, full of literary and oratorical charm, and
replete with generalizations, as if they were disinterested works of
literature or philosophy. It must be understood, however, that such
an approach will only lead to the dangers already described above,
and that Burke's political writings and speeches are always made in
response to definite practical issues, which it is the duty of the student
to understand before attempting to judge the wisdom or unwisdom
of the solutions offered by Burke. It is also important to remember
that, apart from three brief periods of office, Burke spent his political
career in opposition.[2] His attitude to political problems was thus
coloured by the belief that if he and his friends were in office they
would be more successful than the ministry they opposed. This is
natural in an opposition politician, and in no way dishonourable so
long as it does not degenerate into factious opposition intended
merely to embarrass the government. We shall see that Burke's
political writings are largely devoted to illustrating his belief that
the policy initiated by the short Rockingham administration of
1765–66 was the right one, and that almost everything then or since
proposed by anyone else was wrong. Burke's political philosophy
is very often, in the last analysis, an idealization and rationalization of
the policy of Lord Rockingham and his friends.[3] It is too often
assumed, however, that Lord Rockingham and his supporters were
mere nonentities to whom Burke gave a political programme and
philosophy. The evidence is rather the other way, that it was men
like Rockingham, Newcastle and Dowdeswell who in 1765 and

---

[1] Founded 1747: the Minute Book is in A. P. I. Samuels, *Early Life, Correspondence and
Writings of E. Burke*, Cambridge, 1923, pp. 225–96.
[2] The three periods are: July, 1765–July, 1766; March–July, 1782; April–December, 1783.
[3] Cf. L. S. Sutherland, 'E. Burke and the first Rockingham administration', EHR, 47
(1932), pp. 46–72; Pares, op. cit., p. 84.

1766 formulated policy; and it was the rôle of Burke—a newcomer to politics—to give this policy literary form and elevate it to the rank of a philosophy. As Burke became older and more experienced he probably played a correspondingly greater part in policy-making; but it is a mistake to disregard Lord Rockingham and his friends, to whom Burke himself always looked up as superiors.

It is obvious that in dealing with Burke's political works the problem of the influence of Montesquieu becomes more complicated than in the earlier writings. His reading of Montesquieu and other political philosophers did not furnish him with a ready-made answer to the political problems of the eighteenth century; but, on the other hand, when he gave literary and philosophical expression to the policy he and his colleagues had been following, he found it useful and inspiring to exploit and adapt the wisdom of political philosophers he admired. Burke is never a servile imitator, and we shall see that the use he makes of Montesquieu, in his political works, usually amounts to making a free adaptation, for his own purpose, of something he has learned from the study of Montesquieu's writings. We shall also see that while Burke may admire and imitate some of Montesquieu's ideas, he is not afraid to disagree with him in others. The most interesting case of this is the problem of the nature of the British constitution and its working, on which Montesquieu was considered a great authority in the eighteenth century. Burke's essential ideas on this subject have their origin in the experiences of Lord Rockingham and his friends in 1765–66, and not in Montesquieu or any other political philosopher.[1]

It will not suffice to treat Burke before 1765 as simply a literary man, and after that simply as a politician. There is a break in 1765, but there is also continuity, resulting in an enriching of Burke's total activities, as he brings his philosophical and literary mind to practical politics. A special problem, however, is presented by his writings on the French Revolution. He is reproached by historians for his ignorance of the real nature of the Revolution and, at the same time, it is in his writings on the Revolution that Burke offers most to political philosophers eager to systematize his thought. We shall see that Burke was not entirely ignorant of France, and that during his visit there in 1773 he saw a great deal of French life and French society.[2] He tended, however, to idealize much of what he saw, especially the nobility and clergy; and he overestimated the part played in the Revolution by the French *philosophes*. The Revolution

---

[1] See below, chaps. iv and vi.   [2] See below, chap. ii.

presented itself to him very largely as a set of ideas, formulated in France by writers like Rousseau, and propagated in England by Richard Price and other radicals. Burke chose to meet the English exponents of the revolutionary philosophy on their own ground, and thus his writings on the Revolution are largely devoted to refuting what he considered a false political philosophy. It might seem to follow that our approach to this part of his works should be simply the normal approach to any political theorist. This is, however, only partly true, for although Burke's writings on the Revolution contain a great deal of what might appear to be pure theory, much of what he says has its origin in his experience of twenty-five years spent in politics. His dislike of radicalism is the outcome of his long service with the aristocratic Rockingham connection, and not merely something he discovered in political theorists. However, the terms in which he combats the revolutionary philosophy are largely inspired by his study of political philosophy, though it is certain he did not compose his works on the Revolution with the works of philosophers open on his desk. He drew on a rich and well-stored mind, and on his personal knowledge of France and of English politics. Burke put into his writings on the French Revolution the wisdom of a lifetime, and what he had learned from Montesquieu was by then so thoroughly assimilated that the problem of tracing an influence is extremely difficult. The writings on the French Revolution are best approached, at least for our purpose, through Burke's earlier works, thus enabling us to trace the development of his mind.[1]

By following the development of Burke's career we shall avoid the pitfall, which would be almost inevitable in a thematic treatment of his works, of attributing to the influence of some political philosopher an idea which has a much humbler and more practical origin. In this study we are concerned with the problem of the origin of Burke's ideas. We have, however, refused to be hypnotized by Burke's oratory or his generalizations into believing that he is always writing on the elevated plane of pure political theory. His sources—at least after 1765—are not to be found simply by searching the writings of earlier political philosophers, but rather by adopting an approach which will take into account the contribution both of his experience as a politician, and of his interest in literature and philosophy. Thus, though our task in the following pages is to examine the influence of Montesquieu on Burke, we shall find it

[1] On Burke and the French Revolution see below, chap. viii.

necessary, if we wish to discover the source of Burke's ideas, to follow him in the rough-and-tumble of eighteenth-century parliamentary politics, as well as to consider his knowledge of political theory.

The approach to Burke which we have here outlined is possibly over-ambitious, as it is difficult to make oneself as protean as Burke. It is clear, however, that it is the only approach that can attempt to do justice to Burke; and it is the only method that can be used to discover what he owes Montesquieu and what he found elsewhere. Any other method would examine not the influence of Montesquieu on Burke, but on a truncated Burke, who would probably be simply the projection of the student's own political opinions and prejudices. In our study of the influence of Montesquieu on Burke we shall find an interesting meeting of theory and practice; and in examining how they mingled in his mind we are perhaps coming close to the creative process which gave birth to Burke's greatest works.

MONTESQUIEU AND BURKE

CHAPTER I

MONTESQUIEU AND ENGLAND

NO French writer was more highly esteemed or more influential in England in the eighteenth century than Montesquieu.[1] In this chapter it will be of interest to consider briefly some aspects of his career relevant to our study of his influence on his greatest British disciple. We shall consider especially Montesquieu's contacts with British people, and his famous visit to England from 1729 to 1731. We shall also consider, as a necessary preliminary to the chapters that follow, his more important contributions to eighteenth-century thought and their significance for England.

Details of Montesquieu's life were most readily available to the English public in the *Eloge de Montesquieu* written by D'Alembert for the fifth volume of the *Encyclopédie* (1755) and prefixed to most editions of the complete works of Montesquieu, beginning with the great edition of 1758.[2] It was a life which was, on the whole, remarkably peaceful and free from unusual events. Montesquieu spent most of his time living at his native château in La Brède, near Bordeaux, combining the life of a scholar and man of letters with that of a provincial *seigneur*. This was interrupted seriously only once: during the years of his travels, which lasted from 1728 to 1731. Otherwise the only interruptions were visits to Paris, where he enjoyed fashionable and learned society.

Charles-Louis de Secondat was born in La Brède on January 18, 1689. He was the eldest son of Jacques de Secondat, who had married Marie-Françoise de Pesnel, a lady whose family was of English origin.[3] Montesquieu thus had some English blood in his veins, and it has been noted that he was born in the month of the Bill of Rights which proclaimed that English liberty of which he was to become the great exponent.[4] However, by temperament Montesquieu was Gascon, by education French, and by outlook—at least after his travels—he was cosmopolitan. He received his early education from

---

[1] For eighteenth-century British opinion of Montesquieu see F. T. H. Fletcher, *Montesquieu and English Politics*, 1750–1800, 1939, chap. i.

[2] *Œuvres de M. de Montesquieu*, 3 vols., Amsterdam and Leipzig.

[3] P. Barrière, *Un grand Provincial : Montesquieu*, Bordeaux, 1946, p. 6.

[4] J. Dedieu, *Montesquieu*, 1943, p. 6.

the Oratorians of Juilly, and then studied law at Bordeaux and Paris, becoming *conseiller* in the parlement of Guyenne in 1714. Two years later, on the death of an uncle, he inherited the title of baron de Montesquieu and the office of *président à mortier*. He retained this office until 1726 when, before setting out on his grand tour, he sold it.

During these years, before his travels, Montesquieu was becoming a celebrity in Bordeaux and Paris. In Bordeaux he was well known as an eminent *président à mortier* and for his studies in science and philosophy which he carried on in association with the local Académie des sciences, of which he became a member in 1716. Of works written at this time only two[1] were published before the collected edition of his works published in Paris in 1796, a year before Burke's death.[2] In this 1796 edition were published for the first time some of Montesquieu's early scientific essays; but it is clear that the English reading public of Burke's generation knew practically nothing of Montesquieu's early philosophical and scientific works. It is worth noting, however, that Montesquieu's connection with the Académie des sciences of Bordeaux, and his interest in science won him the friendship of Martin Folkes, and secured his election, while in England, to the Royal Society, of which Folkes was vice-president.[3]

The most important work written by Montesquieu before his tour was the *Lettres persanes*, published in 1721 and translated into English in the following year.[4] At this time Montesquieu became a more frequent visitor to Paris, where his company was much sought in the salons of Mme de Lambert, Mme de Tencin, and others. In the salons he met the most fashionable company and the most eminent men of letters and scholars of the day. It was about this time that Montesquieu wrote the *Dialogue de Sylla et d'Eucrate*, which, it is said, he read to the club de l'Entresol;[5] and, in a more frivolous vein, he wrote the *Temple de Gnide, Céphise et l'Amour* and the *Voyage à Paphos*.[6] But he still continued his more serious

---

[1] *Projet d'une histoire physique de la terre ancienne et moderne*, in *Mercure de France* and *Journal des Savants*, 1719; *Discours prononcé à la rentrée du parlement de Bordeaux* . . . 1725, Geneva and Paris, 1772.   [2] *Œuvres de Montesquieu*, 5 vols., An IV—1796.   [3] *Œuvres* (Nagel), iii, p. 940.
[4] *Persian Letters*, translated by *John Ozell*, 1722; 6th. edition, Edinburgh, 1773. The first French edition was: *Lettres persanes*, 2 vols., Cologne [= Amsterdam], 1721. Also, *The History of the Troglodytes* [Lettres 11–14 translated], Chelmsford, 1766.
[5] Louis Vian, *Histoire de Montesquieu*, 1878, p. 70.
[6] The *Temple de Gnide*, first pub. in the *Bibliothèque française*, Amsterdam, 1724, was translated as *The Temple of Gnidus*, 1767. The *Voyage à Paphos* was first pub. in *Mercure de France*, 1727; *Céphise et l'Amour* first pub. (with ed. of *Le Temple de Gnide*) 1725. *Le Dialogue de Sylla et d'Eucrate* was first pub. in *Mercure de France*, 1745; also pub. with *Romains*, 1748.

studies, which after 1721 were mainly on philosophical subjects. However, none of these serious works appears to have been readily available to English readers in the eighteenth century.[1] It is clear from the *Lettres persanes* that Montesquieu had become interested in England, or at least in English history.[2] But his early works show no trace of any important English influence; his main interest is in the great writers of classical antiquity, and especially in the Stoics and Cicero. His closest connections with England at this time were personal. He was a friend of James Fitzjames, Duke of Berwick, the natural son of James II and Arabella Churchill. Berwick was commandant in Guyenne from 1716 to 1719, and Montesquieu's correspondence shows close friendship not only with Berwick, but also with a number of Berwick's relatives, especially François de Bulkeley, Berwick's brother-in-law. When Berwick died in 1734 Montesquieu composed an *Eloge* later published in Berwick's memoirs.[3]

The year 1728 was an important one for Montesquieu. He was elected to the Académie Française;[4] and, having sold his office of *président à mortier*, he set out on what might be called his grand tour. This tour, among other things, brought him into closer contact than hitherto with English people and English ideas. A great deal of the early part of his tour was spent in countries on the continent in the company of James, first Earl Waldegrave, who was a nephew of the Duke of Berwick, and who in 1728 was British ambassador to Vienna. In Venice Montesquieu met the notorious financier John Law, and had a discussion with him on financial problems.[5] In Hanover Montesquieu was presented to King George II, and he met Charles, second Viscount Townshend.[6] At the Hague he had a letter of introduction from Waldegrave to the British ambassador, Lord Chesterfield; and it was Lord Chesterfield's yacht that brought Montesquieu to England in October 1729.[7] He remained there until early in 1731,[8] thus devoting half of the duration of his tour to England.

It has never been denied that Montesquieu's stay in England was

---

[1] The *Traité des devoirs*, in *Bibliothèque française*, 1726, was probably little known in England.
[2] Lettre 104.
[3] J. Fitzjames, Duke of Berwick, *Memoires ... écrits par lui-même*, 2 vols., 1778; translated as *Memoirs of the Marshal Duke of Berwick*, 2 vols., 1779.
[4] In this year was published *Discours prononcé par M. de Montesquieu, lorsqu'il fut reçu à l'Académie françoise;* translated in the *Miscellaneous Pieces of M. de Secondat*, 1759.
[5] *Œuvres* (Pléiade), i, pp. 571–4.   [6] Ibid., i, p. 844.
[7] Ibid., i, pp. 873–5.
[8] He was back in Bordeaux by May, 1731; Cf. *Œuvres* (Nagel), iii, p. 945.

an important formative influence on his life; but it is unfortunate that his own full account of his stay has been lost,[1] and that all that survives is the *Notes sur l'Angleterre*. It is quite certain, however, that during the time he spent in England he met important and interesting people, and had plenty of time to study English life and government. His son tells us,

M. de Montesquieu eut le temps d'approfondir la nature du gouvernement, de former des liaisons intimes avec tous les hommes célèbres d'alors, avec tous ceux qui ont depuis joué de grands rôles.[2]

We find Montesquieu moving in aristocratic circles during his stay in England. Lord Chesterfield presented him to the King, Queen, and Prince of Wales at Kensington Palace, and he was on intimate terms with John, Duke of Montagu, Charles Lennox, Duke of Richmond, Lord Hervey (Pope's Sporus) and Lady Hervey, Sarah, Dowager Duchess of Marlborough, William Pulteney, Lord Bath, and possibly also with John Carteret, Lord Granville.[3] He also knew Lady Mary Wortley Montagu.[4] He was acquainted with Andrew Mitchell, later ambassador to Berlin, and with Martin Folkes, already mentioned.[5] No doubt Montesquieu met many other celebrated Englishmen; but of this there is no record. It is worth noting, however, that Montesquieu already knew Lord Bolingbroke, having met him several years earlier.[6] It is known that Montesquieu, while in England, studied Bolingbroke's opposition paper *The Craftsman*.[7] We also know that Montesquieu attended debates in Parliament, where he had an opportunity of seeing the British form of government in action.[8] This was to have important consequences when he wrote the *Esprit des lois*.

When Montesquieu returned to France from England, he did not sever his relations with the latter. He had greatly admired the English gardens of William Kent, and he began to lay out part of the grounds of La Brède in the English style. Also, more important,

[1] Extant in 1818, since possibly destroyed; Cf. Ibid. iii, 1575.
[2] *Mémoire pour servir à l'éloge historique de M. de Montesquieu*, in Vian, op. cit., pp. 396–407; see p. 401. For more recent accounts of Montesquieu in England see: J. C. Collins, *Voltaire, Montesquieu and Rousseau in England*, 1908; W. Stewart, 'Montesquieu et l'Angleterre', *Deuxième Centenaire de l'Esprit des lois*, Bordeaux, 1949, pp. 173–226.
[3] Evidence for these friendships is found in the correspondence, *Œuvres* (Nagel), vol. iii.
[4] R. Shackleton, 'Montesquieu's correspondence: additions and corrections', FS, 12 (1958), pp. 324–45.   [5] *Œuvres* (Nagel), iii, pp. 988, 1429.
[6] M.-J. Durry, *Autographes de Mariemont, première partie : avant 1800*, 2 vols., 1955, ii, pp. 499–500.
[7] R. Shackleton, 'Montesquieu, Bolingbroke, and the separation of powers', FS, 3 (1949), pp. 25–38.
[8] *Œuvres* (Pléiade), i, pp. 879–883.

not long after his return he wrote a short essay on the English form of government, later to become the most famous chapter in the *Esprit des lois*.[1] He kept up his correspondence with his English friends, and especially with Martin Folkes.

In 1734 Montesquieu published the *Considérations sur les causes de la grandeur des Romains et de leur décadence*.[2] This great work, an earnest of the greater work that was to come, was almost immediately translated into English.[3] It was, however, with the publication of the *Esprit des lois* in 1748 that Montesquieu became an important influence on English thought.[4] The work was translated by the eminent translator and lawyer Thomas Nugent, who was probably a relative of Burke's wife, and therefore possibly known to Burke.[5] Particular interest was shown in the chapters of the *Esprit des lois* dealing with the British constitution, and in the eighteenth century at least two separate translations of Book XI, chapter 6, and Book XIX, chapter 27, were published.[6] After the publication of the *Esprit des lois* one of Montesquieu's main tasks was defending it against attacks, mainly from religious bodies, and in 1750 he published the *Défense de l'Esprit des lois*.[7] He also entered into correspondence with the Duc de Nivernais, who was French ambassador to Rome, in an attempt to keep the *Esprit des lois* from being placed on the Index, an attempt which failed.[8] A few more works came from his pen before his death, notably *Lysimaque*[9] and the *Essai sur le goût*, the latter being published in the *Encyclopédie* in 1757.[10]

During the last years of his life we find Montesquieu in correspondence with a large number of Englishmen who admired his work. Most notable among these correspondents are David Hume, Bishop Warburton, Thomas Blackwell (Rector of the University of Aberdeen), Charles Yorke, and William Domville. The last-mentioned was, with Bulkeley, responsible for seeing Nugent's

---

[1] E.L., xi, 6. Evidence for this statement is found in his son's memoir, Vian, op. cit., pp. 401–2.

[2] Amsterdam, 1734.

[3] *Reflections on the Causes of the Grandeur and Declension of the Romans*, 1734.

[4] 2 vols., Geneva.

[5] *The Spirit of the Laws*, 2 vols., 1750. In his will (Principal Probate Registry, Somerset House, proved April 27, 1772) Nugent left £50 to Dr. Christopher Nugent, Burke's father-in-law, to be disposed of in charity.

[6] *Two Chapters of a Celebrated French Work entitled 'De l'Esprit des lois'*, Edinburgh, 1750; *A View of the English Constitution, by Baron de Montesquieu* [translated by F. Maseres], 1781.

[7] Geneva, 1750.

[8] For Montesquieu and Nivernais, see E.-A. Blampignon, *Le Duc de Nivernais*, n.d.

[9] *Mercure de France*, 1754; translated as *Lysimachus*, in *Miscellaneous Pieces*, 1759.

[10] Translated as *An Essay on Taste*, in *Miscellaneous Pieces*, 1759.

translation through the press.[1] With these correspondents, and especially with Hume and Domville, Montesquieu discussed the nature of the British constitution.[2] He also had, at this period of his life, many personal contacts with Englishmen. He was visited by Charles Yorke's brother, Philip Yorke;[3] and at dinner parties given by the British ambassador, Lord Albemarle, he met many distinguished English guests.[4] It is particularly interesting to note that Montesquieu knew many Irishmen. Considering the large number of Irish exiles living in France at this time this is not surprising.[5] Montesquieu tells us he was taught English by an Irishman,[6] and we know that his secretary Florence Fitzpatrick was Irish.[7] Many Irish families had settled in Bordeaux, and with one of the most celebrated of these, that of John Black, father of Joseph Black the chemist, Montesquieu was acquainted.[8]

Shortly before his death Montesquieu was visited by one of the most cultured and widely travelled Irish gentlemen of the century, Lord Charlemont, who was later a close friend of Burke. The meeting of Montesquieu and Lord Charlemont, known to all students of Montesquieu for its intimate picture of the President, took place at La Brède in 1754. Charlemont was Montesquieu's guest for three nights; and the two met again, in Paris, shortly before Montesquieu's death in February 1755.[9] At the time of his death, Montesquieu, we are told,[10] was attended by the daughter of an Irishman called Clarke, who procured for him the ministration of Father Routh, an Irish Jesuit. The abbé Routh's letter, in which he tells how Montesquieu died a Christian, is well known to biographers of Montesquieu.[11] It is not so well known that Routh gave a copy of this letter to his friend Daniel O'Conor, an Irishman serving in the Irish Brigade, who sent the letter to his brother

---

[1] *Œuvres* (Nagel), iii, pp. 1195–6, 1235.   [2] Ibid., iii, pp. 1245, 1217–22, 1230–31.
[3] Ibid., iii, pp. 1380, 1398, 1482.
[4] Cf. F. Hardy, *Memoirs of Lord Charlemont*, 2 vols., 1812, i, p. 69.
[5] See below, chap. ii.
[6] *Œuvres* (Pléiade), i, p. 679.
[7] R. Shackleton, 'Les Secrétaires de Montesquieu', in *Œuvres* (Nagel), ii, pp. xxxv–xliii; Cf. Hardy, op. cit., i, pp. 66–7.
[8] There was a John Black–Montesquieu correspondence, some of which is summarized in Black's account books in the P.R.O. of Northern Ireland. On Joseph Black and his father see the *Dictionary of National Biography*.
[9] Hardy, op. cit., i, p. 68.
[10] James Roche, *Critical and Miscellaneous Essays of an Octogenarian*, Cork, 1851, 2 vols., i, pp. 220–21.
[11] For the text and recent discussion of this letter see O. R. Taylor, 'Bernard Routh et la mort de Montesquieu', FS, 3 (1949), pp. 101–21. On the interpretation of this Cf. R. Shackleton, 'La religion de Montesquieu', *Actes du Congrès Montesquieu*, Bordeaux, 1956.

Charles, the eminent antiquarian and historian.[1] Charles O'Conor was a friend of Burke, and as the latter usually reproached contemporary French writers with atheism, it is by no means irrelevant that we should note that he had access to a source which assured him that Montesquieu was a Christian.[2] He certainly would have found the abbé Routh's letter more informative than the only notable obituary to appear in England on Montesquieu, that written by Lord Chesterfield for the *Evening Post*.[3]

Eighteenth-century readers were unfortunate in being deprived of some of Montesquieu's most intimate writings, especially the *Pensées* and the Correspondence;[4] and also the *Voyages*, *Spicilège*, and the early philosophical works.[5] But all the major works were readily available in the eighteenth century, and, moreover, as we have been noting, most of them were also translated into English.[6] It will be worth considering the importance of some of these works which were readily available in England.

The *Lettres persanes* was the first important work of Montesquieu, and it made an immediate appeal to the English reading public.[7] The story of the Persian travellers residing in Paris and relating all they saw there, as well as the voluptuous story of the seraglio, was very much in the taste of the time. Its scathing indictment of French society at the time of the Regency was a masterpiece of satire in the tradition of La Bruyère, and it offered English readers no very flattering account of the French nation. The work also contains Montesquieu's reflections on a multitude of subjects, revealing an active and enquiring mind. In religion he is very much a man of his age: he is violently anti-clerical, dislikes dogma and mystery, and, while not an atheist, insists mainly on the moral and social value of religion, believing that the best way to serve God is 'de vivre en bon citoyen', and 'd'observer les règles de la société, et les devoirs de l'humanité'.[8] In politics he hates despotism, by which he

---

[1] C. O'Conor, *Memoirs of the Late Charles O'Conor*, vol. i, Dublin, n.d., p. 276 seq.

[2] For Burke and O'Conor see below, chap. ii, pp. 31–2.

[3] Feb., 1755, reprinted in Chesterfield's *Letters*, ed. Bonamy Dobrée, 6 vols., 1932, pp. 2136–2137.

[4] A few letters and *pensées* were in fact published in the eighteenth century: *Lettres familières du président Montesquieu*, n.p. [Florence], 1767; *Pensées de Montesquieu adressées à son fils*, Brussels, 1786. The *Lettres familières* are also in *Œuvres*, 3 vols., London, 1767.

[5] A few scientific *discours* were published in *Œuvres*, 5 vols., An IV–1796.

[6] In 1777 there appeared the *Complete Works of M. de Montesquieu*, 4 vols., containing all the works previously translated and, in addition, a translation of the *Lettres familières*.

[7] Apart from translations it was imitated in Lord Lyttelton's *Letters from a Persian in England to his Friend at Ispahan*, 1735.

[8] Lettre 46.

means in particular the despotism of Louis XIV, and he admires
republics on the ancient model; but he has serious reserves about
monarchy, which is 'un état violent, qui dégénère toujours en
despotisme ou en république'.[1] He is particularly interested in the
relations of politics and morality, and his ideas on this are best
illustrated in the story of the Troglodytes. This part of the *Lettres
persanes* was, as we noted, translated separately into English. The
story is related by Usbek, who had received a letter posing the
problem:

> Je t'ai souvent ouï dire que les hommes étaient nés pour être vertueux, et que la
> justice est une qualité qui leur est aussi propre que l'existence. Explique-moi, je
> te prie, ce que tu veux dire.[2]

Usbek relates how the Troglodytes founded a state on the principles
of selfishness and force:

> Ce peuple...ne consulta plus que son naturel sauvage; tous les particuliers
> convinrent qu'ils n'obéiraient plus à personne; que chacun veillerait uniquement à
> ses intérêts, sans consulter ceux des autres.[3]

Montesquieu was simply reformulating the problem which Hobbes
had considered in *Leviathan*; but from similar premises Montesquieu
reaches different conclusions from Hobbes: unlike Hobbes he does
not believe that a state can be based on force and selfishness, and he
shows that the logical conclusion from such premises is not order,
but chaos and destruction.[4] However, two families survive from
this destruction, and, using them, Montesquieu constructs another
story, in which the Troglodytes now form a state on exactly the
opposite principles: on humanity, justice and virtue, children and
parents being bound together by love, and their manners made
gentler by religion. The result is perfect bliss; indeed, too perfect
for this world, and Montesquieu introduces a more realistic note
when he relates that the Troglodytes wished to appoint a king,
which was a sign that they were no longer able to be virtuous of
their own accord, and required authority be be imposed on them
from without.

Montesquieu is fundamentally a realist: he does not believe that a
Utopia, where everyone is perfect, is practicable. While he stresses
the importance of virtue and self-restraint in the state, his approach

---

[1] Lettre 102.   [2] Lettre 10.   [3] Lettre 11.
[4] Cf. A. S. Crisafulli, 'Montesquieu's story of the Troglodytes: its background, meaning
and significance', PMLA, 58 (1943), pp. 372–92; P. Dimoff, 'Cicéron, Hobbes et Montesquieu', *Annales Universitatis Saraviensis*, 1 (1952), pp. 19–47.

to politics is empirical and conservative. He believes that the best form of government is that which 'va à son but à moins de frais; de sorte que celui qui conduit les hommes de la manière qui convient le plus à leur penchant et à leur inclination est le plus parfait'.[1] He does not envisage a radical change in society as practicable or desirable. He ridicules idle speculations on the state of nature and the hypothetical origin of society.[2] He advises great caution in changing laws:

Il est quelquefois nécessaire de changer certaines lois. Mais le cas est rare, et, lorsqu'il arrive, il n'y faut toucher que d'une main tremblante.[3]

Montesquieu never abandons this empirical and conservative standpoint.

It was with the publication of the *Considérations sur les causes de la grandeur des Romains et de leur décadence* in 1734 that Montesquieu first became a major figure in European thought. This work is one of the greatest importance in the history of historiography, and in it we find Montesquieu in possession of the historical method which he was to develop further in the *Esprit des lois*.[4] In the *Romains* he reveals to his contemporaries a new conception of how history should be written. History is no longer, as with Bossuet, to be a branch of theology, where the historian relates events to final causes; nor is it to be simply a narrative of events produced by mere chance or fortune. Montesquieu shows how history can be made scientific, how the historian can find in history general laws of change; and it is as a scientist, with a scientist's interest in inductive laws, that he approaches history:

Comme les hommes ont eu dans tous les temps les mêmes passions, les occasions qui produisent les grands changements sont différentes, mais les causes sont toujours les mêmes.[5]

Thus behind particular examples of change there lie general laws; and it is the object of the historian to discover these laws:

Ce n'est pas la fortune qui domine le monde...Il y a des causes générales, soit morales, soit physiques, qui agissent dans chaque monarchie, l'élèvent, la maintiennent, ou la précipitent; tous les accidents sont soumis à des causes; et, si le hasard d'une bataille, c'est-à-dire une cause particulière, a ruiné un état, il y avait une cause générale qui faisait que cet état devait périr par une seule bataille: en un mot, l'allure principale entraîne avec elle tous les accidents particuliers.[6]

---

[1] Lettre 80.   [2] Lettre 94.   [3] Lettre 129.
[4] The method is already present to some extent in the *Lettres persanes*, Lettres 113–124.
[5] *Romains*, chap. 1.
[6] Ibid., chap. 18.

This gives the essence of Montesquieu's historical method at the time of writing the *Romains*: here we have his conception of physical and moral causation, his understanding of the continuity of historical experience, and his distinction between cause and occasion.

The best illustration in this work of Montesquieu's historical method is his masterly account of the causes of the decline of Rome.[1] The extension of the Empire by military conquest, and the establishment of large armies at a long distance from Rome brought about a difference in both generals and soldiers, both losing the spirit of citizenship, and feeling no compulsion to obey the central authority. The second cause was the admission to Roman citizenship of the conquered races, destroying the unified spirit of Rome, and rendering laws originally designed for a small republic unsuitable for this large and heterogeneous empire. Rome, indeed, contained the seeds of its own destruction: its laws were those of a small republic that was constantly expanding, but once this expansion had taken place the original laws were no longer suitable, and decline followed. Montesquieu feels that his analysis of the decline of Rome has enabled him to arrive inductively at a general historical law, valid at all times, regarding the relation of a government to its size.[2] Turning, for example, to the canton of Berne in his own day, a small state aiming at expansion, he feels competent to predict, in the light of the historical law he has discovered, that if it achieves expansion it will, like Rome, necessarily perish.[3]

The importance of Montesquieu's contribution to historiography can be seen by comparing his ideas to those of his contemporaries.[4] The Cartesian spirit of the seventeenth century was generally unfavourable to history, which it regarded as incapable of acquiring the status of certain knowledge. The age was not, however, without its achievement in history, though history, if it is not antiquarian scholarship—in which the seventeenth century was unusually great —is subordinated to theology or political controversy. This is true of great historians like Bossuet and Clarendon; and it is not until the historical works of Voltaire and Montesquieu appear that history becomes a great art in its own right. Also, before the middle of the

---

[1] *Romains*, chap. 9.
[2] Ibid., chap. 9. Cf. R. B. Oake, 'Montesquieu's analysis of Roman History', *Journal of the History of Ideas*, 16 (1955), pp. 44–59.
[3] *Romains*, chap. 9.
[4] On eighteenth-century historiography see: J. B. Black, *The Art of History*, 1926; E. Fueter, *Geschichte der neueren Historiographie*, Munich and Berlin, 1936; F. Meinecke, *Entstehung des Historismus*, 2 vols., Munich and Berlin, 1936; E. Cassirer, *The Philosophy of the Enlightenment*, translated by F. C. A. Koelln and J. P. Pettegrove, Princeton, 1951.

eighteenth century, fertilizing ideas are found in the writings of Hume and Bolingbroke, though it is not until slightly later in the century that the British historians make any important advances in practice.[1] It was in 1757 that Burke wrote his *Abridgment of English History*, and it is therefore of particular interest to us to consider the significance of Montesquieu for English historiography up to that date. Before 1757 Voltaire and Montesquieu were the most influential writers in eighteenth-century historiography; and English historians would also have learned much from Hume and Bolingbroke. It is important that we should distinguish the contribution of Montesquieu from that of his most influential contemporaries.

Bayle, in his *Dictionnaire historique et critique*,[2] had done much to answer the Cartesian objections to history, by showing how to distinguish between unreliable tradition and sound historical fact. In Voltaire's *Charles XII* (1731) this lesson has been learned, and Voltaire achieves a high degree of accuracy in his documentation. He also makes history urbane, freeing it from pedantic set speeches, genealogies and portraits in the classical tradition. But his greatest achievements in history are in the *Siècle de Louis XIV* (1751) and in the *Essai sur les mœurs* (1756), where he makes history more than mere political and military history, and attempts to write an account of civilization in all its manifestations, aiming at a type of history that will achieve the object of disentangling from events the history of *l'esprit humain*.[3] Voltaire has, however, some shortcomings which, on final analysis, make him inferior as historian to Montesquieu. Although he is not ignorant of the interplay of physical and moral causes, he does not apply this consistently to history, leaving much to mere chance, and often attributing important events to trivial causes. He also tends to use history merely as a means of illustrating his prejudices against religion and the Middle Ages. In the *Esprit des lois* Montesquieu uses his historical method to trace institutions and laws to their sources. Voltaire's lack of a consistent historical method, and his prejudice against the Middle Ages, made it impossible for him to rival Montesquieu in this field.

When we turn to Hume and Bolingbroke we find that they are separated from Montesquieu's conception of history in the same

---

[1] Hume's *History of England*, 6 vols., did not start to appear until 1754, and was completely published by 1762; Gibbon's *Decline and Fall*, 6 vols., was pub. 1776–88; Robertson's *History of Scotland*, 2 vols., was pub. 1759.   [2] First published, Rotterdam, 1697.
[3] For Voltaire's ideas on history see especially the *Avant-propos* to the *Essai sur les mœurs*, *Œuvres complètes de Voltaire*, ed. L. Moland, 52 vols., 1877–85, xi, pp. 157–64.

way as Voltaire. Hume conceives of history as data to which the historian must apply the experimental method in order to discover general truths about human nature: 'Its chief use is only to discover the constant and universal principles of human nature'.[1] However, we do not find in Hume a method which is really scientific, for he believes that a great deal in history depends on chance or 'secret and unknown causes'.[2] Such causes as can be discovered are usually moral causes, which he thinks more important than physical ones.[3] The result is that in practice Hume, like Voltaire, has little idea of the continuity of historical experience, and he tends to read his own prejudices into history. It is true that in parts of the *History of England* he has to deal with the problem of the origins of institutions; but here he borrows freely from Montesquieu.[4]

In Bolingbroke's works it is usually possible to find, in one form or another, expression of most ideas current in the century. He understands the possibility of writing history in a way that traces every event to a cause so as to make a chain of causality.[5] But he also thinks that history should be didactic and utilitarian: it should be 'philosophy teaching by examples',[6] and it should enable us to 'rise from particular to general knowledge'.[7] His own short historical essays are written for the purposes of political propaganda. His contribution to historiography amounts, therefore, to a few general precepts, which are better expressed, and further developed, in Voltaire and Hume.[8]

The originality of Montesquieu's ideas on historiography is quite clear when we compare him with Bolingbroke, Hume and Voltaire. It is not to be denied, however, that Montesquieu is in many ways anticipated by other writers. He is anticipated especially by Vico, Doria and Giannone,[9] though this is hardly of much importance for our study, since these Italian writers were little known in England

---

[1] *Enquiries*, ed. L. A. Selby-Bigge, 2nd edition, Oxford, 1951, p. 83. (*Enquiries* first pub. in 1748).

[2] *Rise and Progress of the Arts and Sciences* (1741), in *Essays Moral, Political and Literary*, ed. T. H. Green and T. H. Grose, 2 vols., 1875, i, p. 176.

[3] *Of National Characters* (1748), in *Essays Moral, Political and Literary*, i, pp. 244–58.

[4] *History of England*, 6 vols., 1754–62, i, p. 397 seq.

[5] *Letters on the Study and Use of History*, 2 vols., 1752, i, pp. 40–42.

[6] Ibid., i, pp. 57–8.

[7] Ibid., i, p. 58.

[8] The relation between the three is not very clear; see: Black, op. cit., p. 31; Meinecke, op. cit., i, p. 78. It is sufficient for our purpose to note that all three had expressed their views on history before Burke wrote his *Abridgment of English History* (1757).

[9] W. Folkierski, 'Montesquieu et Vico', *Actes du Congrès Montesquieu*, Bordeaux, 1956, pp. 127–40; R. Shackleton, 'Montesquieu et Doria', *Revue de littérature comparée*, 29 (1955), pp. 173–83. Giannone, *The Civil History of the Kingdom of Naples . . . by Pietro Giannone . . . translated by James Ogilvie*, 2 vols., 1729–31.

in the eighteenth century.[1] It is more important to note that English
writers would have found nearer home ideas which were in some
ways similar to those of Montesquieu. In an age of science, and in
the country of Newton, it was not unnatural to find writers attempting to apply to history the method which had been so successful in
the field of the natural sciences. This was, however, attempted
only very sporadically.[2] Perhaps the best example of this is in the
writings of Sir William Temple, who showed an unusual awareness
of the continuity of historical experience, comparing it to a river to
whose source the historian must ascend.[3] He also understands the
importance of physical factors like climate, and its effect on the
character of the people.[4] But Temple is incapable of welding these
ideas into a coherent historical method, and his historical writings
are usually written to illustrate his political beliefs.[5] Again, in many
legal historians and antiquarians we find a similar sporadic understanding of the genetic method in history;[6] but it is only in Montesquieu that English writers of the early and mid-eighteenth century
would have found the method fully developed and in a form available for historians, and not subordinated to some other branch of
study. The importance of this will become clear when we examine
Burke's *Abridgment of English History*, where he reveals himself as
the first British historian to copy the historical method of Montesquieu.

It is in the *Esprit des lois* that we find the culmination of Montesquieu's thought. It is, in a sense, the whole of Montesquieu:
most of the problems touched on in the *Lettres persanes* and other
early works are here re-examined with maturer wisdom; and the
historical method developed in the *Romains* is given a wider field of
application, being applied, indeed, to the whole range of laws and
institutions. Here too we find his famous classification of governments according to their nature and principle; his theory of climate;
the theory of the separation of powers; the doctrine of the *esprit
général*; and his studies of feudal law in the early French monarchy.
It is mainly in terms of these theories that his influence in England
can be traced.

---

[1] Giannone was obviously better known in England, through Ogilvie's translation, than
Vico and Doria.
[2] Sir George Clark, *The Later Stuarts*, 1660–1714, Oxford, 1934, pp. 363–4.
[3] *Works*, 4 vols., 1757, i, p. 64.   [4] Ibid., i, 161.
[5] His *Introduction to the History of England* (*Works*, iii, pp. 67–194) is political propaganda in
disguise; Cf. H. E. Woodbridge, *Sir Willaim Temple*, New York, 1940, chap. 19.
[6] J. G. A. Pocock, *The Ancient Constitution and the Feudal Law*, Cambridge, 1957, chap. i,
and *passim*.

In the preface to the *Esprit des lois* Montesquieu takes some trouble to explain the purpose and method of the work as a whole. He explains that, confronted with the bewildering variety of laws and customs, he believes that it is possible to discover their underlying principles:

> J'ai d'abord examiné les hommes, et j'ai cru que, dans cette infinie diversité de lois et de mœurs, ils n'étaient pas uniquement conduits par leurs fantaisies.

He applies the method of the physical sciences to laws and institutions, advancing hypotheses which, if they are consistent with the data observed, have then the status of inductive laws: 'J'ai posé les principes, et j'ai vu les cas particuliers s'y plier comme d'eux mêmes'.[1] It is his rigorous application of this method that constitutes the main originality of Montesquieu. His method is, however, by modern standards, not sufficiently rigorous, and leaves too large a place for vague general hypotheses; but this was a general fault of the science of his time.

Montesquieu defines laws as 'les rapports nécessaires qui dérivent de la nature des choses',[2] and this definition is intended to include the laws of the natural scientist as well as those of the jurist. The laws of science refer to the uniformity of the behaviour of physical bodies; but Montesquieu believes that there is a uniform pattern of behaviour relevant to intelligent and moral beings. No doubt men make certain laws; but there exist other laws which bind them as moral beings, and which are not man-made: these are the laws of eternal justice:

> Dire qu'il n'y a rien de juste ni d'injuste que ce qu'ordonnent ou défendent les lois positives, c'est dire qu'avant qu'on eût tracé de cercle, tous les rayons n'étaient pas égaux.[3]

Montesquieu, refuting the notion, attributed to Hobbes, that positive laws are the only laws, thus believes that there is a higher moral order.[4] He understands, however, that though the physical world normally presents a pattern of uniform behaviour, this is not so with the intelligent world, which obeys its law—the higher moral law or Natural Law—very erratically. This is so because intelligent beings are imperfect, and thus subject to error; and because they are free, in a way that physical bodies are not, to disobey their laws. Man is

---

[1] E.L., *préface.*   [2] E.L., i, 1.   [3] *Idem.*
[4] Cf. *Traité des devoirs* (*Œuvres*, Pléiade, i, p. 109), where, in an earlier draft of this passage, Montesquieu makes explicit reference to Hobbes.

part physical and part intelligence: as a physical being he is 'gouverné par des lois invariables'; but as an intelligent being, 'il viole sans cesse les lois que Dieu a établies, et change celles qu'il établit lui-même'.[1] Thus man, like all finite creatures, is subject to error, and, besides, he is liable to be misled by his passions: these faults require correction by religious, moral and political instruction.[2]

By his references to the higher moral law, which he sees as the law of God and of a 'raison primitive' Montesquieu is in the great tradition of Natural Law thinkers which stretches from the Stoics and Aristotle through Aquinas to Grotius, Pufendorf and Gravina. These thinkers saw the Natural Law as a higher ethical standard, the emanation of God's reason and will; and they taught that the Natural Law was self-evident to man thanks to his 'right reason' which enabled him intuitively to distinguish right from wrong. Positive laws might differ according to time and place, but they were to be judged ultimately by the light of the higher Natural Law. This doctrine, which was normally conservative, by laying great stress on man's duties, had in it the seeds of a much more radical theory: the theory of natural rights. The latter theory, assuming that man has, under the Natural Law, certain self-evident rights, deduces from these a complete *a priori* system of rights. Such a system, being purely abstract, has no reference to time and place or to circumstances. To demand an immediate realization of these rights would, in fact, amount to making a clean sweep of existing laws and institutions. Such theories usually avoid this practical difficulty by describing a hypothetical pre-social man living in a 'state of nature', where he is in full possession of all his natural rights. These theories, by setting up an ideal of this kind, imply criticism of all existing civil societies. We find such ideas in certain aspects of the thought of Hobbes and in Locke; and the theory of the rights of man, in its crudest form, was exploited by English radicals throughout the eighteenth century. It was given its most powerful expression by Jean-Jacques Rousseau, and in the works of his disciples during the French Revolution.[3]

Montesquieu has little sympathy for the theory of natural rights, and, as we have seen, in the *Lettres persanes* he ridicules speculations about the state of nature. In the *Esprit des lois* he writes, it is true, a

---

[1] E.L., i, 1.   [2] *Idem.*

[3] On Natural Law and natural rights see: Leo Strauss, *Natural Right and History*, Chicago, 1953; Sir Ernest Barker, *Natural Law and the Theory of Society, 1500 to 1800, by Otto Gierke*, 2 vols., Cambridge, 1934; A.P. d'Entrèves, *Natural Law*, 1951.

C

chapter entitled 'Des lois de la nature';[1] but the laws that he mentions—peace, desire for food, sexual attraction, desire to live in
society, religion—are not laws in the moral sense: they are empirical
generalizations about man's behaviour; and Montesquieu is thus
using the word 'law' in this context not as moral command but as
scientific law or inductive generalization.[2] He does not attempt to
erect an *a priori* theory of law on a number of self-evident moral
commands: he simply makes certain generalizations about matter-
of-fact, and proceeds to base his theory on the inductive laws thus
discovered by observation.

Whereas for Montesquieu the Natural Law is the law of God, of a
'raison primitive', positive laws are the product of 'la raison humaine,
en tant qu'elle gouverne tous les peuples de la terre'. Positive laws
are relative, the laws of each nation being 'les cas particuliers où
s'applique cette raison humaine'. It follows that 'c'est un très
grand hasard si celles d'une nation peuvent convenir à une autre'.[3]
He then outlines the essential programme of the *Esprit des lois* in
words which it will be well to quote in full. First, speaking of
laws, he says,

> Il faut qu'elles se rapportent à la nature et au principe du gouvernement qui est
> établi, ou qu'on veut établir; soit qu'elles le forment, comme font les lois politiques;
> soit qu'elles le maintiennent, comme font les lois civiles.

This programme he fulfils in the twelve books that follow. The
second part of his task is outlined thus:

> Elles doivent être relatives au *physique* du pays; au climat glacé, brûlant ou tem-
> péré; à la qualité du terrain, à sa situation, à sa grandeur; au genre de vie des peuples,
> laboureurs, chasseurs ou pasteurs; elles doivent se rapporter au degré de liberté que
> la constitution peut souffrir; à la religion des habitants, à leurs inclinations, à
> leurs richesses, à leur nombre, à leur commerce, à leurs mœurs, à leurs manières.
> Enfin elles ont des rapports entre elles; elles en ont avec leur origine, avec l'objet
> du législateur, avec l'ordre des choses sur lesquelles elles sont établies. C'est dans
> toutes ces vues qu'il faut les considérer.[4]

It is by exploring all these relationships, this network of physical
and moral causes that Montesquieu will lay bare what he understands by the 'esprit des lois'.

It is unnecessary to insist at this point on the originality of Montesquieu: his method of seeking the 'esprit des lois' is a development
of the historical method he had already used in the *Romains*; and we

---

[1] E.L., i, 2.
[2] Cf. R. Shackleton, 'Montesquieu in 1948', FS, 3 (1949), pp. 299–323.
[3] E.L., i, 3.   [4] *Idem.*

have seen that in this he was anticipated mainly by a few Italian writers, who do not appear to have been well known or influential in England. It is certain that neither in Italian nor in French was there at this time another such comprehensive and ambitious project for applying the method of the physical sciences to the study of laws and institutions. Burke refers to Montesquieu as 'the greatest genius' of the age: in his own particular field Montesquieu had no rival.

In the section of the *Esprit des lois* devoted to the relations of laws to different types of government[1] it is of particular interest to note what he says about monarchy. Types of government he classifies according to their 'nature' and 'principle' and he explains,

Il y a cette différence entre la nature du gouvernement et son principe, que sa nature est ce qui le fait être tel, et son principe ce qui le fait agir. L'une est sa structure particulière et l'autre les passions humaines qui le font mouvoir.[2]

He first classifies governments according to their 'nature', and finds three types: republic (democracy and aristocracy), monarchy, and despotism. He thus does not follow the more usual classification, common since Aristotle, of democracy, aristocracy, and monarchy. He probably felt that his new classification was more in touch with reality: he wants us to consider his three types not as mere logical classifications, but as empirical generalizations: 'Je suppose trois définitions, ou plutôt trois faits'.[3] Indeed, behind his rather abstract descriptions there lie the wisdom and the information gathered during his travels and researches.[4]

Montesquieu's description of monarchy was of the greatest interest to his French and English readers in the eighteenth century. He describes the nature of monarchy:

Les pouvoirs intermédiaires, subordonnés et dépendants, constituent la nature du gouvernement monarchique, c'est-à-dire de celui où un seul gouverne par des lois fondamentales.[5]

These intermediary powers are 'des canaux moyens par où coule la puissance',[6] and their purpose is to weaken the power of the monarch:

Comme la mer, qui semble vouloir couvrir toute la terre, est arrêtée par les herbes et les moindres graviers qui se trouvent sur le rivage; ainsi les monarques, dont le pouvoir paraît sans bornes, s'arrêtent par les plus petits obstacles, et soumettent leur fierté naturelle à la plainte et à la prière.[7]

---

[1] E.L., ii–xiii.   [2] E.L., iii, 1.   [3] E.L., ii, 1.
[4] There is no proof that, as is often assumed, these books were written before 1728: the evidence is rather the other way. See the *Mémoire pour servir à l'éloge historique de M. de Montesquieu*, Vian, op. cit., pp. 396–407.
[5] E.L., ii, 4.   [6] *Idem.*   [7] *Idem.*

The most natural of these intermediary powers is the nobility, which is, indeed, essential in a monarchy: 'point de monarque point de noblesse; point de noblesse point de monarque'.[1] The clergy and the bourgeoisie are other intermediary powers, Montesquieu mentioning the 'prérogatives des seigneurs, du clergé, de la noblesse et des villes'.[2] Besides these intermediary powers, it is essential that a monarchy have a 'dépôt de lois',[3] by which he means the parlements, with their right of remonstrance and appeal to the fundamental law of the constitution. In all this Montesquieu is, in fact, making a plea for a return to what he regards as the true nature of the French constitution, which he considers distorted under the *Ancien régime* It is an appeal for the restoration of the political powers which he thinks should belong to the nobility, clergy, bourgeoisie and parlements.[4]

Considering the 'principle' of each of the different types of government, Montesquieu finds that in republics it is virtue,[5] in despotic governments fear, and in monarchies honour. By honour he means 'le préjugé de chaque personne et de chaque condition', and he adds that 'la nature de l'honneur est de demander des préférences et des distinctions', thus it is a cohesive force in a hierarchical society.[6] An important aspect of this principle is that it places limitations on the power of the monarch:

cet honneur nous dicte que le prince ne doit jamais nous prescrire une action qui nous déshonore, parce qu'elle nous rendrait incapables de le servir.[7]

At the same time Montesquieu indicates that he regards the honour of monarchies as an 'honneur faux' that has little or nothing to do with moral values.[8] His preferences for the idea of the republic are very strongly marked in the first eight books of the *Esprit des lois*; and he considers monarchy as a form of government liable to degenerate almost fatally into despotism.[9]

The question of the corruption of the different types of government is dealt with by Montesquieu in some detail. His main theme is: 'La corruption de chaque gouvernement commence presque toujours par celle des principes'.[10] This corruption sets in in democracy, 'non seulement lorsqu'on perd l'esprit d'égalité, mais encore

---

[1] E.L., ii, 4.   [2] *Idem.*   [3] *Idem.*
[4] Cf. A. Lemaire, *Les lois fondamentales selon les parlementaires*, 1907, pp. 211–14; E. H. Price, 'Montesquieu's historical conception of the fundamental law', *Romanic Review*, 38 (1947), pp. 234–42.
[5] In the *Avertissement de l'auteur* to the 1757 edition of E.L. Montesquieu explains that by virtue he means only 'political virtue', i.e. love of laws, equality, frugality.
[6] E.L., iii, 7.   [7] E.L., iv ,2.   [8] E.L., iii, 7.   [9] E.L., iv, 2.   [10] E.L., viii, 1.

quand on prend l'esprit d'égalité extrême'.[1] Monarchy becomes corrupt when the intermediary powers become ineffectual, thus allowing the monarch to wield uncontrolled despotic power. The principle of monarchy will also decay:

Le principe de la monarchie se corrompt lorsque les premières dignités sont les marques de la première servitude, lorsqu'on ôte aux grands le respect des peuples, et qu'on les rend de vils instruments du pouvoir arbitraire.[2]

Montesquieu's ideas on the 'nature' and 'principle' of types of government, and his theory of corruption of each type being the corruption of its 'principle', probably owe much to Plato and Aristotle, and much more to Machiavelli and Doria. But the synthesis he makes of these ideas, and the additional ideas which he owes to his own observation, especially of the French monarchy, result in a theory which is quite distinctive.[3]

Much as Montesquieu's theory of monarchy and other forms of government was of interest to the English, these doctrines had a more obvious application to the continent than to England, which had a form of government peculiar to itself. Montesquieu realized this, and devoted two chapters of the *Esprit des lois* specially to England. This was certainly the most read and most imitated part of the whole work, as far as England was concerned.

In the first eight books Montesquieu describes unitary states, in which sovereignty is lodged with the many, the few or the one; but when he describes the British form of government he deals with a state in which he finds no one indivisible sovereign power.[4] In England power is divided functionally into executive, legislative and judicial, and Montesquieu finds in this division the secret of the liberty of the English:

La démocratie et l'aristocratie ne sont point des états libres par leur nature. La liberté politique ne se trouve que dans les gouvernements modérés. Mais elle n'est pas toujours dans les états modérés; elle n'y est que lorsqu'on n'abuse pas du pouvoir; mais c'est une expérience éternelle que tout homme qui a du pouvoir est porté à en abuser; il va jusqu'à ce qu'il trouve des limites. Qui le dirait! la vertu même a besoin de limites.[5]

The essential point is,

Pour qu'on ne puisse abuser du pouvoir, il faut que, par la disposition des choses, le pouvoir arrête le pouvoir.[6]

[1] E.L., viii, 2.   [2] E.L., viii, 7.
[3] Cf. J. Dedieu, *Montesquieu*, 1913; L. M. Levin, *The Political Doctrine of Montesquieu's Esprit des lois : its Classical Background*, New York, 1936; E. Levi-Malvano, *Montesquieu e Machiavelli*, Paris, 1912; R. Shackleton, 'Montesquieu et Doria', loc. cit.
[4] Cf. R. Shackleton, 'Montesquieu, Bolingbroke, and the separation of powers', FS, 3 (1949), pp. 25–38.   [5] E.L., xi, 4.   [6] *Idem.*

It is in these terms that Montesquieu understands the British constitution, and his theory is best given in his own words:

> Lorsque dans la même personne ou dans le même corps de magistrature, la puissance législative est réunie à la puissance exécutrice, il n'y a point de liberté; parce qu'on peut craindre que le même monarque ou le même sénat ne fasse des lois tyranniques pour les exécuter tyranniquement.
> Il n'y a point encore de liberté si la puissance de juger n'est pas séparée de la puissance législative et de l'exécutrice...

He summarizes the theory thus:

> Tout serait perdu si le même homme, ou le même corps des principaux, ou des nobles, ou du peuple, exerçaient ces trois pouvoirs : celui de faire des lois, celui d'exécuter les résolutions publiques, et celui de juger les crimes ou les différends des particuliers.[1]

Of these three powers the judicial is different from the other two, according to Montesquieu, in that it is not lodged in a permanent body, but in juries which, once they have performed the immediate task before them are again dissolved into the body of the people from whence they were drawn. The legislative power is delegated by the people to their representatives; but by 'people' Montesquieu does not mean all the people, many of the lowest orders having no vote. The higher orders, by which he means those 'distingués par la naissance, les richesses ou les honneurs' have their own representatives in the House of Lords. This means that the legislative power is lodged in Lords and Commons, the former serving as a 'puissance réglante' between the Commons and the King, who is vested with the executive power. Montesquieu is here combining his theory of separation of powers with the theory of the mixed state: he sees the British constitution as a mixture of monarchy, aristocracy and democracy. He sees in this combination of mixture and separation the 'constitution fondamentale' of the British constitution:

> Le corps législatif y étant composé de deux parties, l'une enchaînera l'autre par sa faculté mutuelle d'empêcher. Toutes les deux seront liées par la puissance exécutrice, qui le sera elle-même par la législative.
> Ces trois puissances devraient former un repos ou une inaction.[2]

Montesquieu makes it quite clear that he does not suppose that the separation of the three powers is absolute. He mentions that the King has legislative powers (he can veto bills sent up from Parliament); and he understands that the process of impeachment

---

[1] E.L., xi, 6.   [2] *Idem.*

involves the legislative power (Lords and Commons) assuming judicial functions. These exceptions, however, he does not feel to be of sufficient weight to invalidate his theory of the separation of powers. Such is, in bare outline, the most famous of Montesquieu's theories.[1] It was enormously popular in England, and was copied slavishly by Blackstone in his *Commentaries*.[2] It was also developed in more detail by J.-L. de Lolme in his *Constitution de l'Angleterre*.[3] We shall have the opportunity of studying how it was quoted in parliamentary debates.

Montesquieu was interested not only in the working of the constitution, but also in its origin. He believed that it originated among the primitive Germanic tribes described by Tacitus,

> Si l'on veut lire l'admirable ouvrage de Tacite, *sur les mœurs des Germains*, on verra que c'est d'eux que les Anglais ont tiré l'idée de leur gouvernement politique. Ce beau système a été trouvé dans les bois.[4]

This short passage had a great fortune in England, and though Montesquieu was by no means the first to put forward the idea of a Germanic origin of the British constitution,[5] it was he who in England, after 1748, received most of the credit for it.[6]

Also extremely important for the question of Montesquieu's influence in England is his theory of the *esprit général*, which forms the core of what we might consider the second main division of the *Esprit des lois*.[7] In this second part he examines the relations between laws and various physical and moral factors: climate, situation, customs, manners, commerce, population and religion. The most famous of these chapters are those dealing with climate, and it is worth noting that though the influence of climate on the laws and institutions and character of nations had been a commonplace since classical antiquity, it was with the help of an English source that Montesquieu developed his theory of climate.[8] It is, however, in the theory of the *esprit général* that Montesquieu gives the essence of what he has to say about the relation of laws to physical and moral factors.[9]

Montesquieu explains what he means by the *esprit général*:

---

[1] For a more detailed account see below, chap. iv.

[2] T. Régnault, *Tableaux analytiques de l'Esprit des lois suivis de la comparaison de plusieurs passages de Montesquieu et de Blackstone*, 1824.

[3] Geneva, 1771; translated as *The Constitution of England*, 1775.

[4] E.L., xi, 6.   [5] Pocock, op. cit., p. 56 seq.   [6] Fletcher, op. cit., pp. 83–9.

[7] E.L., xiv–xxvii.

[8] For Montesquieu's debt to Arbuthnot see: J. Dedieu, *Montesquieu et la tradition politique anglaise en France*, 1909.

[9] E.L., xix.

Plusieurs choses gouvernent les hommes : le climat, la religion, les lois, les maximes du gouvernement, les exemples des choses passées, les mœurs, les manières; d'où il se forme un esprit général qui en résulte.[1]

He had said that positive laws were the product of 'la raison humaine'. Here he shows that the legislator must devise laws in accordance with the *esprit général* which is itself the product of various physical and moral factors. The rôle of the legislator is, indeed, the main theme of this book:

Il y a deux sortes de tyrannie : une réelle, qui consiste dans la violence du gouvernement; et une d'opinion, qui se fait sentir lorsque ceux qui gouvernent établissent des choses qui choquent la manière de penser d'une nation.[2]

C'est au législateur à suivre l'esprit de la nation, lorsqu'il n'est pas contraire aux principes du gouvernement; car nous ne faisons rien de mieux que ce que nous faisons librement, et en suivant notre génie naturel.[3]

Montesquieu realizes that this is not a counsel of perfection: if laws are determined by the *esprit général* one must not look for the immediate projection into society of the abstract principles of any higher moral system. But he takes an optimistic view of the result of following the *esprit général*:

Qu'on nous laisse comme nous sommes...La nature répare tout.[4]

He believes that 'les hommes, fripons en détail, sont en gros de très honnêtes gens'.[5] At the same time he makes it clear that it is the duty of the legislator to conform as closely as possible to the precepts of the Natural Law, correcting, when necessary, the *esprit général*. He does not allow his determinism to obscure his higher moral standards:

Je n'ai point dit ceci pour diminuer rien de la distance qu'il y a entre les vices et les vertus : à Dieu ne plaise![6]

He understands, however, that the *esprit général* is not to be changed overnight by mere legislation, that a more subtle technique is required:

Nous avons dit que les lois étaient des institutions particulières et précises du législateur; et les mœurs et les manières, des institutions de la nation en général. De là il suit que lorsqu'on veut changer les mœurs et les manières, il ne faut pas les changer par les lois : cela paraîtrait trop tyrannique : il vaut mieux les changer par d'autres mœurs et d'autres manières.[7]

Thus the legislator, while not forgetting that there is a higher moral

---

[1] E.L., xix, 4.   [2] E.L., xix, 3.   [3] E.L., xix, 5.   [4] E.L., xix, 6.
[5] E.L., xxv, 2.   [6] E.L., xix, 11.   [7] E.L., xix, 14.

standard, must work with, and not against, the *esprit général*. Montesquieu's ideal legislator is Solon, who, when asked whether the laws he had given to the Athenians were the best, replied: 'Je leur ai donné ... les meilleures de celles qu'ils pouvaient souffrir.'[1]

The problem of how Montesquieu reconciles his historical determinism with his moral idealism has been discussed frequently by scholars.[2] The key to this problem is to be found in the section of the *Esprit des lois* where Montesquieu points out that, among the factors which make up the *esprit général*, in primitive societies the purely physical factors predominate:

> La nature et le climat dominent presque seuls sur les sauvages : les manières gouvernent les Chinois; les lois tyrannisent le Japon; les mœurs donnaient autrefois le ton dans Lacédémone; les maximes du gouvernement et les mœurs anciennes le donnaient dans Rome.[3]

It is in this sense that Montesquieu sees climate, the basic physical factor, as 'le premier de tous les empires'.[4] It is thus conceivable that there was a time when the only factor that shaped the *esprit général* was the purely physical factor of climate. The legislator cannot alter physical factors, but Montesquieu explains that it is his duty to resist any bad effects that such factors have on the *esprit général*; and this is to be done by moving the emphasis to other, and non-physical factors.[5] Thus Montesquieu, without denying the force of purely physical factors or sacrificing his determinism shows that this is not incompatible with moral idealism.

Montesquieu thus has a vision of mankind progressing from a primitive state where purely physical factors are the main forces that govern, to a more advanced state where moral factors predominate. But his idea of progress does not alter the fact that his tendency, in the doctrine of the *esprit général*, is conservative. Nowhere better in Montesquieu do we see the conception of human institutions as a slow growth, not the product of an hour's legislation, but the result of the mind of the legislator working in co-operation with a complex network of physical and moral factors. Montesquieu never underestimates the part played by the legislator: to him the state is not a mere organic growth, the product of blind forces; it is,

---

[1] E.L., xix, 21.
[2] The most recent study, on which I draw for this paragraph, is, R. Shackleton, 'Montesquieu in 1948', FS, 3 (1949), pp. 299–323. Cf. the following: G. Davy, 'Sur la méthode de Montesquieu', RMM, 46 (1939), pp. 571–86; C. J. Beyer, 'Le problème du déterminisme social dans l'*Esprit des lois*', *Romanic Review*, 39 (1948), pp. 102–6. One of the most valuable articles on this problem is that of G. Lanson, 'Le déterminisme historique et l'idéalisme social dans l'*Esprit des lois*', RMM, 23 (1916), pp. 177–202.
[3] E.L., xix, 4.   [4] E.L., xix, 14.   [5] Cf. E.L., xiv, 5.

to a great extent, what men make it. It was this concession to human factors that displeased the positivists of the nineteenth century, who refused to see in Montesquieu a wholehearted sociologist.[1] It is, however, Montesquieu's refusal to disregard the human factor which is most admired to-day, and it is one of the signs of his profound understanding of the complexity of political problems.[2] He never forgets that man is a moral as well as a physical being. He was in his early days interested actively in natural science, but he does not make the mistake of applying to society a method which was made for the purely physical: he always seeks moral as well as physical causes.

The remainder of the *Esprit des lois* was not of great interest to England, or at least not as obviously so as the parts we have analysed. It is worth noting, however, that in the books on religion Montesquieu has receded from the open scepticism of the *Lettres persanes*, and though there is nothing to show that in the *Esprit des lois* he accepts the dogmas of the Christian religion, he at least speaks highly of the moral teaching of Christianity, stating, in opposition to Bayle:

> Les principes du christianisme, bien gravés dans le cœur, seraient infiniment plus forts que ce faux honneur des monarchies, ces vertus humaines des républiques, et cette crainte servile des états despotiques.[3]

There follow a number of books on feudal law and the origin of the French constitution,[4] which were probably of little interest to English readers unless they had some special antiquarian interest in this field. However, these books are of great importance for the understanding of the nature of Montesquieu's thought. In the earlier books of the *Esprit des lois* he had defined the French constitution as consisting of a system of intermediary powers, and this could be taken as an oblique criticism of the *Ancien régime*, which to Montesquieu's mind was despotism. In the books on feudal law Montesquieu is entering the controversial field of the problem of the origin of the French constitution.[5] Boulainvilliers, Dubos, and others had already written on this subject, their object being not so much disinterested antiquarianism as political propaganda. Boulainvilliers had written his accounts of early institutions to show that the French system of government was by right an aristocracy; and

---

[1] A. Comte, *Cours de philosophie positive*, 4 vols, 1835–52, iv. pp. 243–63; E. Durkheim, *Quid Secundatus politicae scientiae instituendae contulerit*, Bordeaux, 1892.
[2] Sir Isaiah Berlin, 'Montesquieu', *Proceedings of the British Academy*, 41 (1955).
[3] E.L., xxiv, 6.   [4] E.L., xxviii, xxx, xxxi.
[5] Cf. E. Carcassonne, *Montesquieu et le problème de la constitution française au XVIIIe siècle*, n.d. [1927].

against this Dubos maintained that from its origins it was an absolute monarchy.[1] Montesquieu, covering the same field, maintains the rights of the intermediary orders—and especially the parlements—mentioned earlier in the *Esprit des lois*.

It was possibly not of much interest to Englishmen to know the history of the origin of the French constitution; but it is important to note that here Montesquieu reveals clearly that he is in a tradition which had a close parallel in England, and to which, indeed, Burke belongs. Montesquieu belongs to that tradition of thinkers who, when confronted with the problem of the constitution, appeal not to theories of rights or the social contract, but to history. In the seventeenth century English opponents of the Stuarts had fought against the idea of absolutism by appealing to the ancient constitution and the Common Law, which, they maintained, were beyond the power of the monarch to alter.[2] This tradition finds expression especially in Coke and Hale, and, as we shall see, is continued in Burke. In Montesquieu we find assumptions similar to those of the Common Law, that the ancient constitution cannot be altered by the will of the king, and that ancient rights must be respected. Montesquieu does not attach any value to abstract claims of right, and, indeed, the French revolutionaries were to hold this against him, and to regard him as the defender of an outworn creed.[3]

Montesquieu, with his dislike of radical reform and his respect for established tradition was a moderate and conservative thinker. He thus sums up the general lesson of the *Esprit des lois*:

> Je le dis, et il me semble que je n'ai fait cet ouvrage que pour le prouver : l'esprit de modération doit être celui du législateur; le bien politique, comme le bien moral, se trouve toujours entre deux limites.[4]

Above all he respects the value of the individual, and dislikes sweeping plans of reform which would force the individual into conformity with some general abstract idea:

> Il y a certaines idées d'uniformité qui saisissent quelquefois les grands esprits ... mais qui frappent infailliblement les petits.[5]

The best policy, in his mind, is for men to respect the laws and institutions of their own country, while at the same time never losing sight of their duties:

---

[1] Comte H. de Boulainvilliers, *Essais sur la noblesse de France*, 1732; *Histoire de l'ancien gouvernement de la France*, 3 vols., 1727; J. B. Dubos, *Histoire critique de l'établissement de la monarchie française dans les Gaules*, 3 vols., 1734.
[2] Cf. Pocock, op. cit., *passim*. [3] See below, chap. viii. [4] E.L., xxix, 1.
[5] E.L., xxix, 18.

Si je pouvais faire en sorte que tout le monde eût de nouvelles raisons pour aimer ses devoirs, son prince, sa patrie, ses lois; qu'on pût mieux sentir son bonheur dans chaque pays, dans chaque gouvernement, dans chaque poste où l'on se trouve, je me croirais le plus heureux des mortels.[1]

This is a view which was to bring him close in spirit to English empirical and conservative thought; and the greatest spokesman of this English tradition is Edmund Burke.

[1] E.L., *préface*.

CHAPTER II

BURKE AND FRANCE

EDMUND BURKE was born in Dublin on 1st January 1729 (O.S.), the year in which Montesquieu first visited England. In spite of Montesquieu's interest in Ireland and Irishmen, there is nothing to show that he ever crossed the Irish Sea. As Burke cannot be shown to have visited France before the date of Montesquieu's death, it must be assumed that the two thinkers who are the object of this study never met. It is certain, however, that Burke met many people who had a personal acquaintance with Montesquieu, and that he was interested in France and the French long before he became involved in the controversy that raged around the French Revolution. As a young man he had some knowledge of French language and literature, and he went on at least one occasion to France. As an eminent politician and man of letters he made, in 1773, a much more famous visit, and, while there, formed impressions important for his later thought. Again, when his writings on the Revolution brought him European fame, his personal contacts with French people increased. These are aspects of Burke's career worth considering in some detail before proceeding to a direct examination of the influence of Montesquieu on his thought.

In the eighteenth century Burke's native city, as the second city of the Empire, was an important intellectual and cultural centre.[1] There were important links between Ireland and France, and especially between France and Irish Roman Catholics. Since the sixteenth century there had been much emigration from Ireland to the continent, and this increased during the period of proscription and confiscation which characterized the English rule of Ireland in the seventeenth century. Many Irish Catholics followed James II into exile after his defeat at the Battle of the Boyne. The Penal Laws which were enacted against Catholics forbade them from having proper educational establishments, and debarred them from many careers, notably from the army. The consequence of this was a closer relationship between Ireland and the Catholic countries on the continent, and especially with France. A number of Irish colleges, designed mainly to educate young Irishmen willing to become priests, were founded on the continent, supported by wealthy Irish

[1] Cf. C. Maxwell, *Dublin under the Georges*, 1714–1830, 1936.

families.[1] Also many Irishmen entered foreign armies, and especially the Irish Brigade, in the service of the King of France.[2] At the same time there had always existed close trading links between Ireland and France, and Montesquieu, as an exporter of wine, played his part in this.[3] The outcome of the close relationship of the two countries was that,

> There was scarcely a Popish family in Ireland which had not some relative a priest or enlisted in a foreign army or engaged in trade in France or Spain.[4]

These remarks are particularly relevant when we remember that Burke's mother was a Catholic, and that Burke spent much of his childhood with his Catholic relations, the Nagles of county Cork, some of whom were educated abroad.[5] Burke's father-in-law, Dr. Nugent, was also educated abroad.[6] It is interesting to note that the links between county Cork and the Irish college at Bordeaux were extremely intimate,[7] and county Cork families sent their sons to receive their education at this college near the home of Montesquieu. It is possible that during his childhood and youth spent in Ireland Burke may have been acquainted with a fellow-countryman educated at Bordeaux and who knew Montesquieu. However, the only link between Burke and Montesquieu we can establish by this line of enquiry is the indirect one whereby Burke's friend Charles O'Conor received from his brother in the Irish Brigade a copy of the abbé Routh's letter describing Montesquieu's death.[8]

Ireland was also closely related to France by the immigration of large numbers of Huguenot refugees at the end of the seventeenth century.[9] They were an extremely important cultural influence in Dublin and other parts of Ireland. Burke met some Huguenot boys at school, but showed an intense dislike of them.[10] However, there was yet another link between Ireland and the continent, important for the study of Burke and Montesquieu. This link was formed by the tradition whereby wealthy Protestant gentlemen rounded off their education by a grand tour. One of the best examples of this

---

[1] Cf. P. Boyle, *The Irish College in Paris*, 1901.

[2] Cf. R. Hayes, *Ireland and Irishmen in the French Revolution*, 1932; *Irish Swordsmen of France*, Dublin, 1934; *Old Irish Links with France*, Dublin, 1940.

[3] *Œuvres* (Nagel), iii, p. 970.

[4] R. Hayes, *Ireland and Irishmen in the French Revolution*, 1932, p. 3.

[5] There are two Dr. Nagles mentioned in Burke's correspondence; one a doctor of Divinity, the other a doctor of Medicine: these degrees must have been obtained abroad.

[6] See *Dictionary of National Biography*.

[7] T. J. Walsh, 'The Irish College at Bordeaux: some Cork associations with the Gironde', *Journal of the Cork Historical and Archaeological Society*, 52 (1947).

[8] See above, chap. i, pp. 6–7.   [9] Cf. G. Lee, *Huguenot Settlements in Ireland*, 1936.

[10] Samuels, op. cit., p. 39, p. 55.

type of Irishman was Burke's intimate friend Lord Charlemont.[1] We have seen that Charlemont met Montesquieu in 1754 and 1755. While he was in Rome in 1754 Charlemont had also met Nivernais, who was carrying out negotiations in connection with the proscription of the *Esprit des lois*.[2] From Charlemont Burke must surely have heard at first hand the racy account that Hardy, Charlemont's biographer, was later to give to posterity, of Montesquieu at La Brède. We are told by the same biographer that Charlemont had many distinguished French friends, and that he frequently entertained foreign visitors at his home near Dublin.[3] A friend of Charlemont's, and another example of the cultured Irish gentleman of the time, was Edward Wingfield, Viscount Powerscourt, who was known as 'the French Lord Powerscourt', which, we are told, 'was an epithet not of frivolity, but acquired merely by his long residence in France'.[4]

It is not easy to say to what extent the awareness of French culture, so common in Ireland, impinged upon Burke. He received his early education at his mother's knee, and then at a dame school in Dublin, after which he was sent for some five years to live with the Nagles in county Cork, where he was taught by the village pedagogue O'Halloran, who held a hedge school in the ruined castle of Monanimy, and was later to boast that he was the first to put a Latin grammar into the hands of Edmund Burke. After this Burke went to school in Dublin for a year, and then, in 1741, was enrolled in the Quaker school of Abraham Shackleton at Ballitore. There is nothing to show that he learned French at any of these schools; and during his student days at Trinity College Dublin (1744–48) modern languages were not taught.[5] There is some evidence, however, to show that he was learning French towards the end of 1747.[6] His early correspondence contains a few references to French authors, notably Pascal, Bayle and Voiture, but it is not clear whether he is referring to translations or to the original French.[7] It is often noted by scholars that in his early correspondence he makes allusion to the *Lettres persanes*; but on examination of the text in question it proves

[1] Burke knew Charlemont in 1759, and possibly before: see Sir James Prior, *Life of Edmund Burke*, 5th ed., 1891, p. 67.

[2] F. Hardy, op. cit., i, pp. 56–7.   [3] Ibid., ii, p. 167.

[4] Ibid., i, p. 212. For Burke's acquaintance with Powerscourt see, *Correspondence*, ed. T. W. Copeland, Cambridge, 1958, vol. i, p. 221, n. 5.

[5] J. W. Stubbs, *The History of the University of Dublin*, Dublin, 1889, pp. 260–61.

[6] Burke's friend Dennis in a letter of August 1747 (Samuels, op. cit., p. 148) alludes to Burke's desire to learn French, and in letters written immediately after this (Samuels, pp. 151–3) Burke uses French phrases.

[7] Samuels, op. cit., pp. 83, 105–6.

to be Lyttelton's *Letters from a Persian* to which Burke is alluding.[1] There is nothing to show that during his youth Burke had a very profound knowledge of French literature, though he knew enough to admire 'French bienséance and exactness'.[2] On the whole, he did not think highly of the French, whom he characterized as 'a nation of fops'.[3] Thus, from what we know of Burke during the early years of his life spent in Ireland, it appears that French thought and culture had very little effect on him, though he was obviously an avid reader, and had ambitions to become a writer. Among his activities during these years were the founding of the college debating club and the editing of a periodical called *The Reformer*. But his preferences are all for classical and English literature, and not for French. We must not imagine the young Burke nourishing his thought on the writings of Montesquieu: it would seem that his discovery of Montesquieu came later.

In 1750 Burke went to London to keep terms at the Middle Temple; and the next ten years of his life were spent mainly in literary activity. He does not appear to have taken his law studies very seriously, and was never called to the bar. It may, however, have been as a law student that he became acquainted with the *Esprit des lois*. The first reference we have in Burke to Montesquieu is in a notebook which he kept jointly with his kinsman (his 'cousin') William Burke, with whom he became associated about this time. In the notebook, which contains original literary compositions by the two Burkes we read,

> Montesquieu is of opinion that the climate affects, or rather causes, the dispositions, of the mind.[4]

This passage was written in 1754, and is in William Burke's hand. It is just three years later that Burke makes his reference to Montesquieu as 'the greatest genius which has enlightened this age',[5] and at the same time shows that he has a detailed knowledge of the text of the *Esprit des lois*, quoting from it, in French, a long and not very well known passage on a problem of feudal law.[6] It is at this

---

[1] Samuels, op. cit., p. 60, is the first to make this error: Burke refers to Zelim and Mirza, a clear allusion to the Selim and Mirza of Lyttelton; there is no Zelim in Montesquieu.
[2] Samuels, op. cit., p. 163.
[3] *Reformer*, no. 3 (11 Feb., 1747–8), Samuels, op. cit., p. 304.
[4] The notebook is in Fitzwilliam MSS. (Sheffield) collection. Recently published as *A Note-Book of Edmund Burke*, ed. H. V. F. Somerset, Cambridge, 1957: see p. 32.
[5] *Works*, vi, p. 297.   [6] *Idem.*

point that the influence of Montesquieu on Burke may be said to begin.[1]

The years 1750–60 are the most obscure and difficult of Burke's career. Apart from keeping law terms and writing essays with his cousin, Burke spent a great deal of time, for health reasons, travelling about the country. At Bath, before 1752, he became acquainted with Dr. Christopher Nugent, and in 1757 married his daughter. We have noted that Nugent was a friend and probably a relation of the translator of the *Esprit des lois*. In 1756 Burke published the *Vindication of Natural Society*, and in 1757 the *Sublime and Beautiful*, both of which reveal some knowledge of French writers.[2] It would also appear that before August 1757 he made a journey to France; but nothing is known of what he did there, or where exactly he went.[3]

In 1758 Burke became editor of the *Annual Register*, and this work meant that he kept abreast of contemporary writing both in England and France. He was principal editor of the *Annual Register* until about 1766,[4] and it can be assumed that the book reviews are from his pen, and that the choice of French literature that was translated in it depended on him. He reviewed some of Rousseau's works, and included a translation of Montesquieu's *Essai sur le goût*.[5] Also, in the first volume of the *Annual Register* there is a translation of part of the *Eloge* written on Montesquieu by D'Alembert.[6]

It was in 1759 that Burke became secretary to W. G. Hamilton, and, when the latter became Chief Secretary in Ireland, Burke went there with him for the parliamentary sessions 1761–2 and 1763–64. It was probably at this time that he became acquainted with Charles O'Conor, John Curry, and others who were interested in the repeal of the Penal Laws.[7] He spent much time in the

---

[1] In the *Catalogue of the Library of the Late Right Hon. Edmund Burke*, 1833, there is listed (p. 14, lot 307), 'Montesquieu: Œuvres, 7 volumes, 1757'. This would show that the date 1757 is of some importance for our study, though the catalogue is wrong in stating that there is a seven-volume edition of Montesquieu's works in 1757. Would it mean that Burke possessed the 1757 ed. of the E.L. (4 vols., London) along with the *Romains* and *Lettres persanes*, making seven volumes in all? On the other hand the Bodleian Library, Oxford, has a copy of E.L., 3 vols., London, 1751, with 'Edmund Burke Beaconsfield' stamped in ink on the first of the two title pages of each volume.

[2] The *Vindication* was probably written partly to refute Rousseau (see below, chap. iii, pp. 41–2); and the *Sublime* as well as containing a reference to Montesquieu's theory of despotism (see below, p. 44) shows knowledge of the abbé Dubos' *Réflexions critiques sur la poésie et sur la peinture*, 2 vols., 1719 (*Works*, i, p. 91).

[3] The only evidence is in *Corr.*, i, 32, where, writing in August 1757 he says he has been 'sometimes in London, sometimes in remote parts of the country, sometimes in France . . .'

[4] See above, p. x n.3.   [5] See below, chap. iii.

[6] 'Anecdotes of the Life of Baron Montesquieu', *Annual Register*, 1758, pp. 239–45.

[7] Cf. *Corr.*, ii, p. 237. That Burke helped O'Conor in his history of Ireland is acknowledged in the latter's *Dissertations on the History of Ireland*, 2nd edition, Dublin, 1766.

D

company of his old friend Thomas Leland, a Fellow of Trinity College, whom Burke persuaded to write a history of Ireland.[1] At the same time Burke may have known Francis Stoughton Sullivan, Fellow of the college, and professor of law. Sullivan's *Historical Treatise on the Feudal Law and the Constitution and Laws of England* (1772) is interesting in that it is largely inspired by Montesquieu, and was originally delivered as lectures at Trinity College.[2]

When in 1765 Burke took up politics as a full-time career he probably met many eminent politicians who had had some personal contacts with Montesquieu. Among these were Charles and Philip Yorke, friends of Lord Rockingham. David Hume he already knew.[3] However, there is no sign, during these years, of Burke having any higher opinion of the French nation than during his college days, when he thought them a nation of fops. He was critical of the influence of French life on Hume:

> Mr. Burke was accustomed to tell his friends, speaking of Hume in familiar conversation, that in manners he was an easy unaffected man, previous to going to Paris as secretary to Lord Hertford, the British ambassador; but that the adulation and caresses of the female wits of that capital had been too powerful even for a *philosopher*. The result was, he returned a literary coxcomb.[4]

More serious was the case of Burke's protégé James Barry, the artist, who returned from abroad with atheistical ideas. Burke 'assailed this opinion with the most powerful arguments and a few good books, particularly Bishop Butler's *Analogy*',[5] and succeeded in demolishing Barry's recently acquired notions. Burke was to encounter such ideas, at their source, during his visit to France in 1773.

Burke's visit to France in 1773 is important in that it left a permanent impression on his mind, and furnished him with some first-hand information about that country, which he was to use later in his writings on the French Revolution. The immediate purpose of his visit to France was to establish his son Richard there for a year to learn the language.[6] Burke and his son were accompanied by Thomas King, who acted as tutor to Richard Burke. They arrived in Paris on January 16, and spent some days sightseeing.[7] On January 21 Burke dined with the Duc de Nivernais, and on the

---

[1] Prior, op. cit., p. 97.
[2] On Sullivan see Fletcher, op. cit., 85–89; for Burke's acquaintance with Sullivan see *Corr.*, i, p. 96.
[3] Prior, op. cit., p. 60; Hume, *Letters*, ed. J. Y. T. Greig, i, p. 312.
[4] Prior, op. cit., p. 61.   [5] Ibid., p. 128.   [6] *Corr.*, i, pp. 418–9.
[7] For the details of Burke's visit to France I draw on Fitzwilliam MSS. (N.R.S. and Sheffield): letters of E. Burke, R. Burke and T. King for January, February and March 1773.

previous day he had dined with Jean Drumgold. The latter was a writer, diplomat and soldier of some distinction, and head of the Ecole Militaire. In 1762 he had been in England with Nivernais who at that time was negotiating with England for peace, and Burke certainly knew Drumgold before 1773.[1] Drumgold was of Irish origin,[2] and it was he who introduced Burke to Jean-Baptiste-Marie Champion de Cicé, bishop of Auxerre. The bishop was in Paris, but arranged for Richard Burke and Thomas King to stay in Auxerre with the family of a M. Jean-Baptiste Parisot, who was an écuyer secrétaire du roi.[3] Burke accompanied his son and King to Auxerre, and spent three days there before returning to Paris alone. During his short stay in Auxerre he spent much time conversing with the clergy of the bishop's household, especially with the abbé Vaultier and the abbé Morangis; and he had personal contact with the noble Sparre family, who lived in a nearby château.[4] The impression which he formed of the French nobility and clergy was extremely favourable, and in his *Reflections* he later alludes to these pleasant days he spent in Auxerre.[5]

By February 2 Burke was back in Paris, and remained there for the rest of the month. During this time he was introduced into the fashionable salons and lionized as a great literary and political figure. On February 10 he was in the salon of Mme du Deffand, which had, twenty years earlier, been frequented by Montesquieu. There Burke met the comte de Broglie, who was head of the ministère secret, the bishop of Mirepoix, Caraccioli, ambassador of Naples, and many others.[6] On February 18 he went to Versailles and was presented to the King. It was presumably at this time that he saw Marie Antoinette and received the impression of her beauty which was many years later to inspire the most famous passage of the *Reflections*. He returned several times to the salon of Mme du Deffand, who on one occasion made the following interesting comment:

[1] In a letter to James Barry of July 24, 1772 (Burke MSS. National Library of Ireland), Burke mentions Drumgold.
[2] R. Hayes, *Biographical Dictionary of Irishmen in France*, Dublin, 1949, pp. 73–4.
[3] There is some material on the Parisot family in the Archives départementales de l'Yonne, Auxerre (see Bibliography below).
[4] The editors of *Corr.* transcribe 'abbé Vaullier' and 'comte d'Esper' (*Corr.*, i, pp. 426–7). This is in fact what Burke writes; but in the Archives départementales de l'Yonne, Auxerre, frequent mention is made of the abbé Vaultier, a vicaire-général of the bishop; and the comtes de Sparre are mentioned in several legal documents in connection with the Parisot family. T. King writes 'De Spar' in one of his letters.
[5] *Works*, ii, 416–7.
[6] H. Walpole, *Correspondence*, ed. W. S. Lewis, New Haven, 1937 seq., v, pp. 329–32.

Je donne ce soir à souper à votre M. Burke; il y a des gens ici qui l'appellent *Junius*; il me paraît avoir infiniment d'esprit. Il parle très difficilement notre langue.[1]

In another letter she congratulates herself on the favourable impression she has managed to give Burke of her country: 'il partira content de notre nation'.[2] But in her next letter she is more cautious:

il va tous les jours au Palais écouter nos avocats : je ne sais s'il dit ce qu'il pense, mais il prétend en être content.[3]

On February 28 Burke was at a supper given by the duchesse de Luxembourg, where he heard a reading of the *Barmécides* of La Harpe.[4] He appears to have left Paris on March 1,[5] and was certainly back in England by March 10, when he spoke in Parliament.[6]

It has been supposed that during Burke's visit to Paris he was seen not only in the salon of Mme du Deffand, but also in that of her rival, Julie de Lespinasse. If this is so it means that Burke could have met Diderot; but the evidence for this is not very reliable. In a letter of March 18 Mme du Deffand writes to Horace Walpole: 'Il est extraordinaire que M. Burke, vous ayant parlé du *Connétable*, ne vous ait dit un mot du *Barmécide*'.[7] It has been supposed that Burke must have heard *Le Connétable* by Guibert, Julie de Lespinasse's lover, in the salon of the latter,[8] but it appears that this play was read, previous to its performance, in a number of salons.[9] It is certain, however, that Burke did visit salons where he met *philosophes* of a type he did not find in the rather reserved salon of Mme du Deffand. He met men of whose religious opinions he disapproved, and we can see a reflection of the kind of discussion he had with them in a letter written from Morellet to Lord Shelburne at this time:

Je veux vous parler un peu de M. Burke : il est très aimable et plein d'espoir et de chaleur; mais milord, j'ai cru lui voir une philosophie incertaine encore des principes, qui ne sont ni bien fixes, ni bien liés les uns aux autres. Si vous me permettez de vous l'avouer ici, il m'a semblé que cette incertitude est fort commune chez vous et parmi vos meilleurs esprits. Il se peut que nous autres, philosophes français, nous tombions dans un défaut opposé, d'être trop décidés, trop sûrs, de nos opinions; mais au moins nous avons le repos de l'esprit : bonheur qui me paraît rare parmi vous.[10]

---

[1] H. Walpole, *Correspondence*, ed. Lewis, v, pp. 331–2. 　　　　　[2] Ibid., v, p. 334.
[3] *Correspondance complète*, ed. le marquis de Ste Aulaire, 1866, ii, p. 357.
[4] H. Walpole, *Correspondence*, ed. Lewis, v, p. 338. 　　　　　[5] Ibid., v, p. 339.
[6] P.H., xvii, pp. 764–5. 　　　　　　　　　[7] H. Walpole, *Correspondence*, v, p. 343.
[8] For discussion of this see S. Skalweit, *E. Burke und Frankreich*, Cologne and Opladen, 1956, p. 22.
[9] Grimm, *Correspondance littéraire*, ed. M. Tourneux, 16 vols., 1877–82, x, p. 170.
[10] *Lettres de l'abbé Morellet à Lord Shelburne*, ed. Lord Fitzmaurice, 1898, pp. 21–24.

It is also from Morellet that we learn how full Burke's days were at Paris: he regrets he has been unable to introduce Burke to Trudaine: 'Je n'ai pu lui mener M. Burke, dont tous les jours ont été pris, et qui n'a pas pu répondre à tout l'empressement qu'on lui a montré de l'avoir'.[1]

In Parliament, on his return to England, Burke spoke on the second reading of a bill for the relief of Dissenters, and in it launched an attack on atheism, which is probably a reflection of his conversations with the *philosophes*.[2] His speech did not please Morellet, who wrote to his friend David Garrick,

> Notre ami Mr. Burke nous a quittés trop tôt. Nous lui aurions peut-être fait adopter des maximes de tolérance un peu plus étendues que celles qu'il établit à la chambre des communes.[3]

Again, we see another reflection of these discussions in Horace Walpole's ironical remark that Burke, 'happening to dispute with the philosophers it grew the fashion to be Christians', and he adds that 'Saint Patrick himself did not make more converts'.[4]

Burke had the impression that during his stay in France he saw a fairly representative cross-section of French life: 'I looked at everything and lived with every kind of people, as well as my time admitted'.[5] He was impressed by the French nobility and clergy, but never changed his dislike for the *philosophes*, who simply confirmed his early distrust of French ideas on religion. He was to hold the *philosophes* responsible for the Revolution, and, indeed, in the speech on March 17, referred to above, he said of atheists:

> Under the systematic attacks of these people I see some of the props of good government already begin to fail.[6]

Here in 1773 we have the essentials of his later great works on the French Revolution. In these later works he defends the *Ancien régime* against those who want to make a clean sweep of all the old institutions. Burke's opinion of the value of the French monarchy, with its clergy and nobility, comes largely from his experiences in France at this time; and, as we shall see, this combined with theory, partly derived from Montesquieu, who by 1789 was considered old-fashioned and an apologist of the old order. As is usual in Burke we find a blend of the theoretical and the practical.[7]

[1] Ibid., p. 25.   [2] P.H., xvii, 764 seq., *Works*, vi, 112 seq.
[3] D. Garrick, *Correspondence*, 2 vols., 1832, ii, p. 604.
[4] H. Walpole, *Letters*, ed. Paget Toynbee, 16 vols., Oxford, 1903-5, viii, p. 252.
[5] *Works*, iii, p. 288.   [6] *Works*, vi, p. 112; Cf. P.H., xvii, 770-83.
[7] Cf. below, chap. viii.

After 1773 Burke never returned to France, and does not seem to
have maintained many personal contacts with that country. Between
1773 and 1789 he did not receive many letters from French people,
though among these few correspondents are well known figures
like Necker, Mme de Genlis, and the comte de Sarsfield. He also
received letters from Mme du Deffand and the Parisots.[1] He met a
number of French people in England, among whom were the
abbé Raynal, Suard, Mme de Genlis, and Mirabeau.[2] The account
of Burke's conversation with Mirabeau, some time before he was
known as the great orator of the Constituent Assembly, is of
interest:

> It was very singular to see Mirabeau and Burke in controversy. Mirabeau
> could speak little English, Burke French imperfectly. Yet these celebrated men
> argued with as much earnestness and continuation as if they had been speaking a
> language common to both. Mirabeau was astonished at the eloquence and force
> with which Burke expressed his meaning, though he could only do it by uniting
> words of different languages.[3]

Later, during the period of the Revolution, Burke felt obliged to
apologize for the fact that he had had Mirabeau in his house.[4]

It was in 1785 that Burke met Charles-François de Pont, the 'very
young gentleman' to whom the *Reflections* were later addressed.
But at this time the meeting did not leave much impression on
Burke, and when De Pont wrote to him in 1789, he felt obliged to
remind Burke of the time and place of their original meeting.[5]

Burke does not seem to have been intimately acquainted with
French people during these years between his visit to France and the
Revolution. In 1786 he writes to Philip Francis:

> I scarce know anybody in France. Dick [i.e. Richard Burke, his son] is better
> acquainted there. . . . The only persons I know are the Bishop of Auxerre and his
> family and the Parisots of Auxerre.[6]

On reflection he adds that he knows the abbé Dillon and his brother
the chevalier Dillon, who were of Irish origin.[7]

We have seen that there was an increase in the volume of Montesquieu's correspondence with Englishmen after the publication of

---

[1] See T. W. Copeland and M. S. Smith, *A Checklist of the Correspondence of E. Burke*,
Cambridge, 1955.
[2] Cf. D. C. Bryant, *E. Burke and His Literary Friends*, Washington, 1939, pp. 304–6.
[3] J. Greig (ed.), *The Farington Diary*, 8 vols., 1923–8, i, p. 5.
[4] *Corr.*, iii, pp. 197–209.
[5] These letters are in Fitzwilliam MSS. (N.R.S.). On De Pont see H. V. F. Somerset, 'A
Burke Discovery', *English*, 8 (1951), pp. 171–8.
[6] J. Parkes and H. Merivale, *Memoirs of Sir Philip Francis*, 2 vols., 1867, ii, pp, 247–8.
[7] Ibid., p. 248.

his great work in 1748. We find a similar phenomenon in the case of Burke: after the publication of his *Reflections* in 1790 he became of interest to all the French who disapproved of the Revolution, and there was an increase in his correspondence and friendship with French people. Most of his correspondence at this time is, however, of a purely formal nature, often from admirers, or from *émigrés* asking for help. Burke made a large number of contacts with *émigrés*, though it is doubtful whether such contacts added much to his thought, which by this time was fully mature. His most important pronouncement on the French Revolution is the *Reflections*, and the majority of his friendships with *émigrés* are after, not before, the publication of this work.

To examine Burke's relations with French *émigrés* would be beyond the scope of the present study.[1] It is of interest to note, however, that among those he met were distinguished figures like Calonne and Cazalès.[2] He also renewed his connection with the Champion de Cicé family: the bishop of Bordeaux (brother of the bishop of Auxerre) was an *émigré* in England, as were his nephews, the abbé and chevalier de La Bintinnaye.[3] To all of them Burke offered hospitality. One of the *émigrés* who came to England, and who was known to Burke was Charles-Louis de Secondat, grandson of Montesquieu. He came to England shortly before 1795, having married in the same year the daughter of an Irish gentleman named Geoghegan.[4] On June 20, 1796, Burke writes to Geoghegan, who had offered to visit him at Beaconsfield, regretting that he will be unable just then to see him and his son-in-law.[5] Two days later Burke writes again:

> When I mentioned Mons. de Montesquieu, it was not as a man I wished to see on account of his own distinguished merit or the fame of his family, which the world is so full of, and to whose labours the world owes so much. It is as part of an old friend that I, who refuse all new acquaintance, took the liberty of desiring him to accompany you.[6]

We do not know what kind of discussion passed between Burke and Secondat. The latter, we know, was devoted to his grand-

---

[1] There is much useful material on this in: Skalweit, op. cit.; *Correspondence of Edmund Burke and William Windham*, ed. J. P. Gilson, Cambridge, 1910.

[2] Letters in *Corr.*, in Fitzwilliam MSS. (N.R.S. and Sheffield); Cf. T. W. Copeland and M. S. Smith, op. cit.

[3] Letters in *Corr.*; Sheffield and N.R.S.; Cf. Copeland and Smith, op. cit. The editors of *Corr.* and subsequent biographers have stated incorrectly that the bishop of Auxerre was an *émigré* in England, confusing him with his brother. For the correct view see L. Lévy-Schneider, *L'Application du Concordat par un prélat d'ancien régime, Mgr Champion de Cicé*, 1921, p. 72.

[4] *Corr.*, iv, p. 347 and notes; J. Delpit, *Le Fils de Montesquieu*, Bordeaux, 1888, p. 156.

[5] *Corr.*, iv, p. 347.   [6] Ibid., iv, p. 349.

father's memory. In his writings on the Revolution Burke had given great praise to Montesquieu[1] and in a letter had said that if Montesquieu had been alive in 1789 he would have been among the first of the *émigrés*.[2] The presence of Charles-Louis de Secondat in England must have seemed to Burke to confirm this prediction.

It emerges from this brief survey that Burke, though spending the first twenty years of his life in a country which had close ties with France, did not, during these years, appear to have a very profound knowledge of French culture, or a very high opinion of the French. During his years as a law student and literary man in England he showed a greater knowledge of French literature, went once to France, and—most interesting for our purpose—wrote a work on English history which bears the stamp of Montesquieu, and refers to the latter as 'the greatest genius' of the age. But Burke did not have a general admiration for contemporary French writers, and he disliked intensely certain French ideas on religion. His visit to France in 1773 enabled him to form at first hand his opinion about certain aspects of French life. That visit confirmed his dislike of the attitude of the *philosophes* to religion, and at the same time he formed a high opinion of the French royal family, the nobility and the clergy. These opinions were to re-emerge in his writings on the Revolution seventeen years later, when his dislike of the *philosophes* had become more intense, and when time had made him idealize the different orders of the French constitution.

The only contemporary French thinker whom Burke speaks of with genuine admiration is Montesquieu. He presumably discovered Montesquieu's writings sometime after 1750, possibly in 1754; but thereafter his admiration for Montesquieu is constant. It is unfortunate that, so far as is known, Burke did not meet Montesquieu, but at least he knew others who were friendly with the President, especially Lord Charlemont, David Hume and the Yorkes; and he knew Montesquieu's grandson. Such indirect contacts are not without interest: they no doubt furnished Burke with information about Montesquieu which enhanced his interest in the great French thinker. It was in such an indirect way that Burke learned that Montesquieu died a Christian. In Montesquieu Burke saw a kindred spirit, a thinker who defended the same values as himself in religion and politics.

[1] *Works*, iii, p. 113.   [2] Prior, op. cit. (2nd ed.), ii, p. 50.

CHAPTER III

BURKE'S EARLY LITERARY WORKS

THE purpose of this chapter is to examine the influence of Montesquieu on the works which Burke wrote up to 1765, that is, before he abandoned a literary for a political career. Enough has been said in the previous chapter to show Burke's opinion of French thought and literature during this part of his life; we shall now give a more detailed account of the relation that some of these early works bear to Montesquieu. The juvenilia and early note-books we shall not examine further, since there we find only one rather casual reference to Montesquieu and no trace of his influence on Burke's thought.[1] The *Vindication of Natural Society* (1756) is important for an understanding of Burke's dislike of *a priori* philosophy, and the *Sublime and Beautiful* (1757) is, among other things, interesting for its pronouncements on methodology. The *Annual Register*, edited by Burke from 1758 to about 1766, is interesting for its book reviews and for certain translations, while the *Tracts on the Popery Laws* show Burke interested in Natural Law and an enemy of Hobbes. But of all the early works the most important for our purpose is the *Abridgment of English History*, where Burke first reveals himself as a disciple of Montesquieu.

The *Vindication of Natural Society*

This work was first published anonymously in 1756 and was intended as a parody of the style and philosophy of Lord Bolingbroke, who had died in 1751, and whose works had been published in 1754. The parody was at first not entirely successful—or perhaps too successful—in that its irony was so well concealed that many eminent judges of literature, such as Lord Chesterfield and Warburton, thought it a serious work really from the pen of Bolingbroke.[2] However, in the second edition, published in 1757,[3] Burke added a preface to explain the ironical intention of the work. He explains that it is meant to ridicule the destructive rationalism 'which this noble writer and several others have been pleased to dignify with the name of philosophy'.[4] He explains,

---

[1] See above, chap. ii, p. 30.   [2] Prior, op. cit. (5th ed.), p. 45.
[3] T. W. Copeland, 'Burke's *Vindication of Natural Society*', Library, 4th series, 18 (1937–8), pp. 461–2.   [4] *Works*, i, p. 3.

The design was, to show that, without the exertion of any considerable forces, the same engines which were employed for the destruction of religion, might be employed with equal success for the subversion of government; and that specious arguments might be used against those things which they, who doubt of everything else, will never permit to be questioned.[1]

Thus Burke wishes to out-Bolingbroke Bolingbroke: the latter did not go far enough in his rationalistic attacks, since he only directed them against religion and morals, and not against civil society. Burke wants to demonstrate the consequences of such an 'abuse of reason':[2]

a mind, which has no restraint from a sense of its own weakness, of its subordinate rank in the creation, and of the extreme danger of letting the imagination loose upon some subjects, may very plausibly attack everything the most excellent and venerable.[3]

Such attacks can easily be directed against 'the creation itself'.[4] Burke thus puts strict limitations on the power of reason, which is powerless when it attempts to examine 'the result of a reason which is not our own'.[5] Within a certain limited sphere our reason is, no doubt, competent, but,

Even in matters which are, as it were, just within our reach, what would become of the world, if the practice of all moral duties, and the foundations of society, rested upon having their reasons made clear and demonstrative to every individual.[6]

Turning from the preface to the work itself, we find that Burke begins (ironically) with the praise of reason and the rationalistic method of examining institutions: his object, he tells us, is truth, which is to be found by means of definitions and logical deductions; and he sweeps aside with contempt any practical considerations which might be opposed to this method:

There is a most absurd and audacious method of reasoning avowed by some bigots and enthusiasts, and through fear assented to by some wiser and better men; it is this: they argue against a fair discussion of popular prejudices, because, say they, though they would be found without any reasonable support, yet the discovery might be productive of the most dangerous consequences.[7]

Burke, in his later works, often defends prejudices and established institutions; but here the pseudo-Bolingbroke decries such ideas as 'absurd and blasphemous',[1] for the philosopher should be interested

---

[1] *Works*, i, p.3.
[2] Ibid., p. 5. On the irony of the *Vindication* see J. C. Weston, 'The ironic purpose of Burke's *Vindication* vindicated', *Journal of the History of Ideas*, 19 (1958), pp. 435–41.
[3] *Works*, i, p. 4.   [4] *Idem.*   [5] *Idem.*
[6] *Idem.*   [7] Ibid., p. 8.   [8] *Idem.*

not in facts, but only in the kind of truth discoverable by logical processes: he rejoices that superstition is disappearing and that 'we begin to think and to act from reason and from nature alone'.[1]

In his parody of Bolingbroke's *a priori* method Burke says he will appeal to history and experience, and consider civil society both from an 'external' and 'internal' point of view. He begins by considering them 'externally', i.e. in their relations with each other. In this his appeal to history and experience consists of juggling with facts and figures to estimate the number of people killed in wars throughout the course of human history; and this slaughter he ascribes to the existence of human society. He uses facts and figures not as a basis for inductive generalizations; he employs them arbitrarily and selectively to confirm what the writer has already assumed *a priori*: that civil society is an evil. He then considers states 'internally', i.e. the relationship of governors and governed. Burke considers in turn despotism, aristocracy and democracy, and by ingenious and specious logic shows that each is worse than its predecessor. He then considers the mixed state—traditionally supposed to combine the virtues of the other three—and by perverse logic he shows that it combines the faults of the three types of simple government. He supports his demonstration with an arbitrary selection of historical facts. This condemnation of civil society is followed by a condemnation of law and lawyers, his method being to enumerate some abuses associated with the legal profession and then to take these abuses as sufficient reason for total condemnation. He then considers the class divisions of society: the poor are miserable because they are exploited by the rich; but then he demonstrates that the rich are even more miserable than the poor. His conclusion is that,

> We are indebted for all our miseries to our distrust of that guide, which Providence thought sufficient for our condition, our own natural reason, which rejecting both in human and divine things, we have given our necks to the yoke of political and theological slavery.[2]

The remedy is to return to a state of nature, casting off the restrictions of civil society.

Although Burke's main object in writing the *Vindication* was to ridicule the *a priori* method of Bolingbroke, it is fairly certain that, by his attack on the notion of the superiority of natural to civil society, he was aiming also at Rousseau's *Discours sur l'inégalité*,

[1] Ibid., p. 9.   [2] Ibid., p. 47.

which had been published in 1755.[1] Thus in his early work Burke is anticipating his later attack on Rousseau and the rationalistic philosophy of the Revolution. It is instructive to look at the *Annual Register* for these early years, where some of Rousseau's works are reviewed, presumably by Burke. In a review of the *Lettre à d'Alembert* we read words reminiscent of the preface of the *Vindication*:

> None of the present writers have a greater share of talents and learning than Rousseau; yet it has been his misfortune and that of the world, that those of his works which have made the greatest noise, and acquired to their author the highest reputation, have been of little real use or emolument to mankind.[2]

He complains that he finds in Rousseau 'a tendency to paradox', 'a splenetic disposition carried to misanthropy', an 'austere virtue pursued to an unsociable fierceness', and adds, once again in the spirit of the *Vindication*,

> A satire upon civilized society, a satire upon learning, may make a tolerable sport for an ingenious fancy; but if carried farther it can do no more, (and that in such a way surely is too much) than to unsettle our notions of right and wrong, and lead by degrees to universal scepticism.[3]

Again, in a review of *Emile*, he writes, 'To know what the received notions are upon any subject, is to know with certainty what those of Rousseau are not',[4] and after referring to Rousseau's system of education as being largely impracticable, chimerical, and 'dangerous both to piety and morals', Burke, again anticipating his later attack on Rousseau during the Revolution, writes:

> He seldom can discover that precise point in which excellence consists, where to exceed is almost as bad as to fall short, and which every step you go beyond you grow worse and worse.[5]

Burke thus pleads for moderation and avoidance of extremes. He seeks a sort of mean between extremes; and Montesquieu is, likewise, an admirer of the mean in politics.[6]

The *Vindication*, by its rejection of the *a priori* method, and its dislike of speculations regarding the state of nature, is, in fact, a plea for the empirical method in political philosophy. In developing his own empirical method Burke will, as we shall see, take Montesquieu as his model, and this appears clearly in the *Abridgment of English History*. It is worth noting that Montesquieu disliked the philosophy of Bolingbroke, and that when Warburton sent him the posthumous

---

[1] See R. B. Sewall, 'Rousseau's second Discourse in England from 1755 to 1762', *Philological Quarterly*, 17 (1938), pp. 97–114.
[2] *Annual Register*, 1759, p. 479.   [3] *Idem.*   [4] Ibid., 1762, p. 225.
[5] *Idem.*   [6] Cf. below, chap. viii, p. 158.

works in 1754 the President wrote a reply, part of which was published in translation in the *Annual Register* for 1760:

> I have dipped into some of my lord Bolingbroke's discourses, and, if I may be allowed to say in what manner they affected me, I must own that he writes with a good deal of warmth: but methinks he generally employs it against things, whereas it ought to be employed only in painting them.[1]

He objects to Bolingbroke's attack against religion.[2] Thus at the same time we see Burke as anti-Rousseau and anti-Bolingbroke, and we note that Montesquieu is on his side in the disagreement. It has, indeed, been suggested[3] that part of Burke's inspiration in the *Vindication* may have come from a passage of the *Esprit des lois*:

> C'est mal raisonner contre la religion, de rassembler dans un grand ouvrage une longue énumération des maux qu'elle a produits, si l'on ne fait de même celle des biens qu'elle a faits. Si je voulais raconter tous les maux qu'ont produits dans le monde les lois civiles, la monarchie, le gouvernement républicain, je dirais des choses effroyables.[4]

Whether or not Burke had this passage in mind, it certainly shows that there was a remarkable affinity between his mind and that of Montesquieu. Montesquieu in the *Lettres persanes* had ridiculed speculations about the state of nature, and, like Burke, he preferred empirical facts to *a priori* notions. However, the full significance of the *Vindication* does not become clear until we examine the more positive side of Burke's thought at this time. In the *Vindication* he has condemned the method of Rousseau and Bolingbroke; in his next work, the *Sublime and Beautiful*, he shows himself an exponent of the method of empirical investigation.

The *Sublime and Beautiful*[5]

This work was first published in April, 1757; a second edition, enlarged, and with the *Essay on Taste*, appeared in January, 1759.[6] The *Sublime and Beautiful* was, indeed, begun during Burke's undergraduate years in Dublin, and shows influence of writers like Locke, Dubos and Hutcheson, who had shown or implied that the method

---

[1] 'A Letter from Montesquieu to the Author of the View of Bolingbroke's Philosophy', *Annual Register*, 1760, p. 189.
[2] *Idem.* Cf. for the original of this letter, *Œuvres* (Nagel), iii, 1508–10, and on its authenticity see R. Shackleton, 'Montesquieu's correspondence: additions and corrections, FS, 12 (1958), pp. 324–45.
[3] Fletcher, op. cit., p. 109.   [4] E.L., xxiv, 2.
[5] The full title is *A Philosophical Enquiry into the Origin of Our Ideas of the Sublime and Beautiful*.
[6] R. Straus, *Robert Dodsley*, 1910, p. 255, p. 367.

of empirical investigation was best suited to studies of this nature.[1] There is no question of the influence of Montesquieu on the central argument of *Sublime*;[2] but it will be worth considering briefly the method Burke employs. Montesquieu's contribution to aesthetics, the *Essai sur le goût*, did not appear until 1757, when it formed part of the article GOUT in the *Encyclopédie*. We can be certain that Burke knew this article, for the *Annual Register* for 1758 contains an abridged translation of it.[3] The *Essai sur le goût* was thus too late to influence the *Sublime*, but Burke may have read it before composing the *Essay on Taste*. However, the enormous output of literature on this subject at this time makes the question of influence very difficult. It would seem that Burke was replying to Hume, who in 1757 had published his *Four Dissertations*, containing *Of the Standard of Taste*.[4]

In the preface to the second edition Burke outlines the method he employs in the work:

> In considering any complex matter, we ought to examine every distinct ingredient in the composition, one by one; and reduce everything to the utmost simplicity; since the condition of our nature binds us to a strict law and very narrow limits. We ought afterwards to re-examine the principles by the effect of the composition, as well as the composition by that of the principles.[5]

He stresses the 'weakness of our own understandings' and insists that his method is experimental; and he understands that 'a theory founded on experiment, and not assumed, is always good for so much as it explains'.[6] He considers himself as conducting an experiment in psychology to discover the origin of our ideas of the sublime and beautiful. In the *Essay on Taste* he stresses the limitations of the *a priori* method which works in terms of definitions and deduction:

> when we define, we seem in danger of circumscribing nature within the bounds of our own notions, which we often take up by hazard, or embrace on trust, or form out of a limited and partial consideration of the object before us; instead of extending our ideas to take in all that nature comprehends, according to her manner of combining.[7]

He is convinced that 'the method of teaching which approaches most nearly to the method of investigation is incomparably the

---

[1] Cf. J. T. Boulton (ed.), *The Sublime and Beautiful*, 1958, p. xxvii seq.
[2] There is, however, an allusion to Montesquieu (E.L., iii, 9) when Burke refers to 'despotic governments, which are founded on the passions of men, and principally upon the passion of fear' (*Works*, p. 89).
[3] *Annual Register*, 1758, pp. 311–18.   [4] Boulton, op. cit., pp. xxix–xxx.
[5] *Works*, i, p. 50.   [6] Ibid., p. 51.   [7] Ibid., p. 53.

best'.[1] Burke is, like many of his contemporaries, reacting against the neo-classical aesthetic with its faith in abstract reason; and in place of *a priori* systems he wishes to ground his principles on direct empirical observation of human nature.

Burke, in the *Essay on Taste*, follows the tradition of sensationism, well established since Locke, and assumes that all our ideas and all our pleasures are grounded in the senses. Since all men are alike in their organs of perception, it follows that there will be a uniformity of response to the objects of taste, and therefore it will be possible to fix a standard of judgement: 'the standard both of reason and taste is the same in all human creatures'.[2] Burke, however, does not believe that taste and judgement are separate faculties of the mind: he resists Hutcheson's theory of 'internal sense'. In Burke's opinion the aesthetic response involves the senses, imagination and judgement, and all three depend on sense experience. He thus gives his fullest definition of taste:

> Taste, in its most general acceptation, is not a simple idea, but is partly made up of a perception of the primary pleasures of sense, of the secondary pleasures of the imagination, and of the conclusions of the reasoning faculty, concerning the various relations of these, and concerning the human passions, manners, and actions.[3]

Montesquieu, in the *Essai sur le goût*, shares the belief that there is a standard of taste, which he relates to the uniformity of sensory organs in men. However, unlike Burke, Montesquieu believes that there are pleasures which concern only the mind completely independent of the senses.[4] This does not prevent him from defining taste as 'ce qui nous attache à une chose par le sentiment',[5] and even going far as to describe it in physiological terms:

> L'esprit est le genre qui a sous lui plusieurs espèces : le génie, le bon sens, le discernement, la justesse, le talent et le goût.
> L'esprit consiste à avoir les organes bien constitués, relativement aux choses où il s'applique.[6]

But he is unwilling to see taste simply as irrational pleasure of the senses, and he writes,

> J'ai dit souvent que ce qui nous fait plaisir doit être fondé sur la raison; et ce qui ne l'est pas à certains égards, mais parvient à nous plaire par d'autres, doit s'en écarter le moins qu'il est possible.[7]

Thus, like Burke, he believes that the aesthetic evaluation concerns

---

[1] Ibid., p. 54.   [2] Ibid., p. 52   [3] Ibid., pp. 63–64.
[4] *Œuvres* (Pléiade), ii, p. 1241.   [5] Ibid., ii, p. 1243.   [6] *Idem.*
[7] Ibid., ii, p. 1260.

both the senses and reason, though his ideas on the relations of these faculties to each other seem to be rather vague. Montesquieu's *Essai sur le goût* is one of his weakest works, and obviously had very little to offer Burke. It is sufficient to note that both authors have some ideas in common, that both believe that there is a standard of taste, and that this involves both the senses and the judgement. Both are in the same mid-eighteenth century tradition, turning away from neo-classicism to something which is not yet romantic, but which is a kind of compromise, or harmony, between reason and emotion.

The *Abridgment of English History*

This is Burke's only formal contribution to English historical writing. As it was never completed it was published posthumously, first appearing in 1812.[1] The work, as it stands, was written in 1757, and in 1760 a few sheets of it were printed by Dodsley.[2] It is not certain why it was never completed, but Prior says this was so 'probably from hearing that Hume was engaged in treating of the same period, and perhaps from being unable to satisfy his own taste which, on an historical subject, was fastidious'.[3] There is, however, no good reason for accepting Prior's conjectures, for Hume's *History* had begun to appear in 1754, and it is hardly conceivable that Burke would have begun his work after that date if he had feared competition from Hume. In any case, as we shall see, Burke's work has a different conception of historical writing from Hume's.

Since the *Abridgment* remains a fragment, and was not published in Burke's lifetime it is not surprising that it has received little attention from scholars.[4] It is, however, of great value to the student of Burke's ideas, especially during the pre-political part of his career. Besides, the work is not without its intrinsic merits, though one recent critic has written of it:

> Of this work I need only observe: first that it is very dull; second that it is written in very bad English, that it is demonstrably a translation from the French.[5]

The first two judgements are subjective; but the statement that the *Abridgment* is a translation requires some proof to support it. The *Abridgment* is certainly an original work by Burke, and he was paid £300 for it by Dodsley, who would not have offered so much for

---

[1] As vol. v of *The Works of the Right Honourable Edmund Burke*, 1792–1827.
[2] There are copies of this in the British Museum and the Bodleian library. Cf. *Correspondence*, ed. T. W. Copeland, Cambridge, 1958, vol. i, p. 164 n.1.
[3] Prior, op. cit. (5thed.), p. 54.
[4] The fullest treatment is in F. Meinecke, *Die Entstehung des Historismus*, Munich and Berlin, 1936, i, pp. 288–304. [5] G. M. Young, 'Burke', *Proceedings of the British Academy*, 1943.

a mere translation.[1] As for the literary value of the work, it is interesting to read the following evaluation from Lord Acton's writings:

Lappenberg, speaking of Burke's most remarkable literary production, *The Abridgment of English History*, says, that if Burke had devoted himself continuously to historical pursuits, England might have possessed a history worthy to rank with the masterpieces of the Attic and Tuscan historians. If we may believe the story that Burke desisted from the undertaking because Hume had taken up the same subject, it must ever be regretted that the reverse did not occur, and that the philosopher did not give way to the politician. We should certainly have had a much better history of England; for there is very little doubt that as Burke was our greatest statesman, so he would have been the first of our historians.[2]

This judgement is probably over-generous to the qualities of the work; but at least it understands the potentialities of Burke as historian.

At the time when Burke was writing the *Abridgment* historiography was at a low ebb in England, and was just beginning to show signs of a brighter promise for the future with the publication of the first volumes of Hume's *History*. Up to this time the standard histories of England were those of Laurence Echard and the Huguenot refugee Rapin-Thoyras.[3] These authors wrote in the tradition of seventeenth-century historiography, in which histories were massive compilations of events, but with none of the qualities we noticed in the works of Voltaire, Hume or Montesquieu. That Burke shared the very common despair of his compatriots with regard to the sterility of English historiography is certain: in a review of Hume's *History* which he wrote for the *Annual Register* he says:

Our writers had commonly so ill succeeded in history, the Italians and even the French had so long continued our acknowledged superiors, that it was almost feared that the British genius, which had so happily displayed itself in every other kind of writing, and had gained the prize in most, yet could not enter the lists in this. The historical work of Mr. Hume first published, discharged our country from this opprobium.[4]

The references to French and Italian historians are interesting. It

---

[1] For discussion of this see *The Correspondence of Edmund Burke*, ed. T. W. Copeland, Cambridge, 1958, i, p. 164n.
[2] Quoted by H. Butterfield, *Man on His Past*, Cambridge, 1955, p. 69. Cf. Lord Acton, *Essays on Church and State*, ed. D. Woodruff, 1952, p. 455.
[3] L. Echard, *The History of England*, 3 vols., 1707–18; Paul de Rapin-Thoyras, *Histoire de l'Angleterre*, 13 vols., The Hague, 1724–36; translated as *The History of England, done into English by N. Tindal*, 15 vols., 1725–31.
[4] *Annual Register*, 1761, p. 301.

E

is not quite clear to what Italian historians Burke is referring;[1] but the French historians he had in mind can hardly be other than Voltaire and Montesquieu, and in the *Abridgment* his greatest admiration is reserved for the latter. The achievement of Hume was great when compared with writers like Echard and Rapin-Thoyras, and Burke pays tribute to his greatness. In the *Abridgment*, however, it is Montesquieu and not Hume that he takes as his model. In his review of Hume's *History* Burke praises Hume for depicting 'the idea of the growth, as I may call it, of our present constitution'.[2] However, as already noted, in such parts of his *History* Hume draws on Montesquieu.[3] The *Abridgment* was written when Hume had published only two volumes of the *History of England*,[4] in which there was, in fact, no question of the growth of the constitution.

The most striking feature which we find in the *Abridgment* is the author's constant preoccupation with tracing events to a network of inter-related physical and moral causes, among which climate, geographical situation, and the general spirit of the people, are prominent. He attempts to establish an unbroken causal chain to explain events, and has a remarkable awareness of the continuity of historical experience. He is particularly interested in the origin of laws and institutions, and especially in the origin of the British constitution. In all this he is a disciple of Montesquieu.

One of the best illustrations of Burke's historical method is the first chapter of the work, entitled 'Causes of the Connection between the Romans and Britons—Caesar's two Invasions of Britain'. Burke's predecessors usually attributed this great event simply to the ambition of Caesar. Echard subscribes to this view, and sees behind the ambition of Caesar the hand of God at work.[5] Rapin-Thoyras says that Caesar's pretext for invading Britain was that the Britons had proved dangerous to Rome by assisting the Gauls; but that the true reason was Caesar's thirst for glory and desire of enlarging the bounds of empire.[6] These historians thus attribute the invasion of Britain to the ambition of one man. When we consider Burke's

---

[1] Possibly to Machiavelli, Giannone, and Guicciardini. Of the works of the first the eighteenth century were provided with several translations, notably, *The Works of the famous Nicolas Machiavel*, 3rd ed., 1720; *The Works of Nicolas Machiavel newly translated by E. Farneworth*, 2 vols., 1762; for Giannone see above, p. 12; in 1753 there appeared Guicciardini's *History of Italy, translated by Austin Parke Goddard*. In the last Burke would have found no 'historical method'; for the contribution of Machiavelli to Montesquieu's method see Levi-Malvano, op. cit.

[2] *Annual Register*, loc. cit.   [3] See above, p. 12.

[4] Vols. v-vi were the first to appear, in 1754.

[5] Echard, op. cit., i, pp. 9–13.

[6] Rapin-Thoyras, op. cit. (English translation), i, pp. 30–1.

treatment of the same episode we cannot but be astonished at the originality of his approach. He does not neglect the importance of Caesar's ambition; but he traces the invasion back to causes which he thinks more fundamental: the basic physical factors of climate and situation. His analysis is, indeed, rather laboured, but, in order to understand his method, it is worth following him.

He begins by observing that in Europe there are, geographically, two main divisions: first, a vast northern plain which stretches from the Atlantic to the Tartary Sea and is bounded on its southern side by ranges of mountains; and, secondly, the more or less self-contained peninsulas of Iberia, Italy and Greece. Burke develops the consequences of these geographical features. The great northern plain, not being interrupted by any sea, and being inhabited by one sort of people, the warlike Scythians, the result was that throughout the whole of that immense region there was for many ages a perpetual flux and reflux of barbarous nations. This explains why northern Europe remained in a barbarous state until partly conquered by Rome. As for the south, on account of the nature of the country, broken up by seas, the inhabitants 'were restrained from wandering into a pastoral and unsettled life'.[1] Also, they were open to invasion only from one side by land, and,

Whoever made an attempt on any other part must necessarily have arrived in ships of some magnitude; and must therefore have, in a degree, been cultivated if not by the liberal, at least by the mechanic arts.[2]

Burke is, of course, simply rationalizing what happened: the southern part of Europe was invaded and colonized by peoples from Phoenicia, Asia Minor and Egypt. Considering especially the Greeks and Romans, Burke accounts for their superiority over the rest of the world at this time in terms of climate and situation:

they profited so much by their guarded situation, by the mildness of their climate favourable to humanity, and by the foreign infusions, that they came greatly to excel the northern nations in every respect, and particularly in art and discipline of war. For not being so strong in their bodies, partly from the temperature of their climate, partly from a degree of softness induced by more cultivated life, they applied themselves to remove the few inconveniences of a settled society by the advantages which it affords in art, disposition, and obedience. And as they consisted of many small states, their people were well exercised in arms and sharpened against each other by continual war.[3]

Thus the superiority of the Greeks and Romans over the rest of the ancient world is, for Burke, accountable to physical factors of

[1] *Works*, vi, p. 185.   [2] Ibid., p. 185.   [3] Ibid., pp. 185–6.

climate and geographical situation. Of this superiority, he tells us, the northern tribes were jealous and contemptuous, and this led to incursions of hostile barbarians to the south. It was when these barbarians had suffered defeat at the hands of the Romans that Britain became involved. The barbarians appealed for help to British tribes, and it was this alliance that brought Britain to the notice of Rome. Caesar's object in invading Britain was to suppress this alliance which was dangerous to Rome. Burke has thus gone back a long way to discover the causes of the Roman invasion of Britain, which other historians had simply accounted for by mentioning the ambition of Caesar. However, Burke does not underestimate the importance of the character of Caesar: he, likewise, says that the ambition of Caesar was a cause of the invasion. But he does not stop at this point: he believes that if one man's ambition could have such an important effect at a certain time, this must be accounted for in terms of the political background in Rome:

That Republic had receded from many of those maxims, by which her freedom had been hitherto preserved under the weight of so vast an empire. Rome now contained many citizens of immense wealth, eloquence, and ability. Particular men were more considered than the Republic, and the fortune and genius of the Roman people, which formerly had been thought equal to everything, came now to be less relied upon than the abilities of a few popular men.[1]

Thus, even when conceding the importance of the part played by individuals in history, Burke's determinism leads him to look behind the individual, to examine the milieu that has given the individual the power to produce certain effects.

It would be easy to multiply examples from the *Abridgment* to illustrate Burke's historical method. He applies the same method with great care to the phenomenon of the migration of peoples, the rebellion under Boadicea, the formation of the Holy Roman Empire, the Norman invasion of England, and the quarrel between Henry II and Thomas à Beckett. Of particular interest is his treatment of the last, which is the episode in Hume's *History* he singled out for quotation in the *Annual Register* in 1761. Some historians saw in the quarrel between Henry II and Beckett simply the result of the clash of two individuals of incompatible temper.[2] Hume is more subtle and sees it as the culmination of a long-standing quarrel between Church and State.[3] But it is to Burke that we must turn—though

[1] *Works*, vi, p. 187. Cf. *Romains*, chaps. 17–18.
[2] Echard, op. cit., ii, pp. 194–202; Rapin-Thoyras, op. cit. (English translation), iii, pp. 18–51.
[3] *History of England*, i, pp. 271–96.

his history is a short one—if we want to see the origin of this episode carefully analysed. He makes a plea for a patient historical approach, and outlines a rather massive programme:

It will not be unpleasing to pause a moment at this remarkable period, in order to view in what consisted that greatness of the clergy, which enabled them to bear so very considerable a sway in all public affairs; what foundations supported the weight of so vast a power; whence it had its origin; what was the nature, and what the ground, of the immunities they claimed; that we may the more fully enter into this important controversy, and may not judge, as some have inconsiderately done, of the affairs of those times by ideas taken from the present manners and opinions.[1]

Burke sets about explaining the causes of this incident along these lines, and he discovers them in the custom of the early Christians of trying civil cases before the bishop rather than in secular courts. This custom persisted into the Roman Empire; but with the expansion and decay of the Empire and the growth of feudalism this custom no longer operated smoothly. The clergy, now an order in the state, were eager to extend their powers, and this, along with the ignorance of laymen, led to the extension of the jurisdiction of the clergy into almost every aspect of the life of the state. At the same time the clergy claimed immunity from the secular courts. Burke describes how this arrangement existed in England at least as early as the period of the laws of Ethelred, and how the situation gradually deteriorated, culminating in the dispute between Henry II and Thomas à Beckett. Burke's method of writing history is patient and detailed, showing a genuine desire to discover causes and to trace developments as far back into the past as possible.

The passage we have just analysed embodies the belief that customs and laws cannot simply be transplanted from one type of government into another, that when the form of the state changes the old laws will not survive without change. Montesquieu had taught that laws were relative to the form of government,[2] and a similar idea is contained in the theory of the *esprit général*. We find a clear example of Burke's application of Montesquieu's doctrine of the *esprit général* in the part of the *Abridgment* where he describes Agricola. Agricola, he tells us, was a legislator who understood the importance of governing according to the character of the people, and that where a new form of government is to be instituted this is not to be done merely by legislating, but by gradually changing the character of the people:

---

[1] *Works*, vi, pp. 356–7.   [2] E.L., i, 3.

Agricola reconciled the Britons to the Roman government by reconciling them to the Roman manners. He moulded that fierce nation by degrees to soft and social customs; leading them imperceptibly into a fondness for baths, for gardens, for grand houses, and all the commodious elegancies of a cultivated life.[1]

Very different was William of Normandy, who had no respect for the character and natural tendencies of the people, and whom Burke condemns on this account.[2]

This emphasis on the importance of the rôle of the legislator, and his duties, would suggest that in history Burke is not a strict determinist: he never underestimates the part played by the individual. But this does not prevent him from establishing a rigid chain of cause and effect to explain historical events. For example, in analysing the causes which led to the revolution under King John, he traces the growth of the power of the people in such a way that when he writes the terse sentence, 'Then came John to the Crown,'[3] we feel that the king's fate is sealed. But even here Burke shows that the disasters of John's reign were largely the fault of the king himself: his arbitrary power, his quarrels, blunders, weakness of character; and we are left with the impression that a wiser king might have saved the situation.

Burke's debt to Montesquieu in the *Abridgment*, which is so far fairly obvious, becomes quite explicit in the account which he gives of the origin of the British constitution. We have seen that Montesquieu had put forward the view that the British constitution originated in the woods of Germany and that the sources for the study of its origins were Tacitus and Caesar.[4] Montesquieu's hints were not neglected by British historians, especially Gilbert Stuart and Francis Stoughton Sullivan, but their works were not published at the time Burke was working on the *Abridgment*.[5] Burke therefore seems to be the first British historian to base a theory of the origin of the constitution on Montesquieu.[6]

Burke's account of the origin of the constitution need not be summarized here. His footnotes, full of Latin quotations, make it clear that he has consulted the sources—Tacitus and Caesar— recommended by Montesquieu. It is in his conclusion that Burke mentions Montesquieu:

[1] *Works*, vi, p. 215. [2] Ibid., p. 311 seq. [3] Ibid., p. 411.
[4] E.L., xi, 6; xxx, 2–4.
[5] Stuart's *An Historical Dissertation Concerning the Antiquity of the English Constitution* was pub. in 1768; Sullivan's *Treatise* (see above, p. 32) in 1772. On Stuart and Sullivan see Fletcher, op. cit., pp. 86–88.
[6] J. Dalrymple's *An Essay towards a General History of Feudal Property* was pub. in 1757 (Cf. Fletcher, op. cit., pp. 84, 89); but this is not a general theory of the constitution.

Thus were delineated the faint and incorrect outlines of our constitution, which has since been so nobly fashioned and so highly finished. This fine system, says Montesquieu, was invented in the woods; but whilst it remained in the woods, and for a long time after, it was far from being a fine one; nor more indeed than a very imperfect attempt at government, a system for a rude and barbarous people. . . .[1]

Burke and Montesquieu are both in agreement that at this early stage the constitution is imperfect: Montesquieu writes:

Il avait cet inconvénient que le bas peuple y était esclave. C'etait un bon gouvernement qui avait en soi la capacité de devenir meilleur.[2]

This is exactly Burke's view: it is the fully mature constitution of the eighteenth century that he and Montesquieu admire, not the primitive constitution that existed in the woods.

Though Burke follows Montesquieu in his theory of the origin of the constitution, for its later development in Anglo-Saxon times Montesquieu offered no guidance, and here Burke draws, with acknowledgement, on antiquarians like Madox, Brady, Spelman and Lambarde. There was, however, one question of feudal law where Montesquieu's opinion interested Burke: the problem of the origin and significance of ordeal by fire. It is worth giving the passage in full, as it is the only time Burke quotes Montesquieu in French, and is of particular interest on account of the opinion of Montesquieu he there expresses:

The greatest genius which has enlightened this age, seems in this affair to have been carried by the sharpness of his wit into a subtlety hardly to be justified by the way of thinking of that unpolished period. Speaking of the reasons for introducing this method of trial, 'Qui ne voit,' says he, 'que chez un peuple exercé à manier des armes la peau rude et calleuse ne devait pas recevoir assez l'impression du fer chaud pour qu'il y paraissait trois jours après; et s'il y paraissait c'est une marque que celui qui faisait l'épreuve, était un efféminé'. And this mark of effeminacy, he observes, in these warlike times, supposed that the man has resisted the principles of his education, that he is insensible to honour, and regardless of the opinion of his country.[3]

Burke is, however, not prepared to accept Montesquieu's opinion, and he points out various defects in Montesquieu's theory, especially that it does not explain how the same test was used against women. Rejecting Montesquieu's theory, he suggests one of his own: amongst the primitive Germans the administration of law was in

---

[1] *Works*, vi, p. 281.   [2] E.L., xi, 8.
[3] *Works*, vi, p. 297; the quotation (somewhat garbled) is from E.L., xviii, 17.

the hands of the Druids, to whom the elements of fire and water were sacred, and,

> it was very natural that they, who abounded with so many conjurations for the discovery of doubtful facts, or future events, should make use of these elements in their divination.[1]

Burke rejects Montesquieu's theory, but in the same breath calls him the greatest genius of the age. Burke rejects Montesquieu's authority on one particular question of feudal law, but he retains Montesquieu's historical method, which enables him to advance a theory of his own, tracing the trial by fire to the customs of the primitive Germans.

One aspect of Montesquieu's historical method, in its relation to Burke, requires special mention. It was one of Montesquieu's achievements to reject providential interpretations of history and to seek only naturalistic causes.[2] In Burke, however, we find a tendency to see, in great historical events, the hand of God. Thus, for example, after giving a purely naturalistic account of the phenomenon of the migration of peoples, he says:

> And thus, by a wonderful disposition of the Divine Providence, a life of hunting which does not contribute to increase, and war, which is the great instrument in the destruction of men, were the two principal causes of their being spread so early and so universally over the whole earth.[3]

However, Burke does not mean that God intervenes directly in human affairs, but only that behind the naturalistic causes discoverable by the historian can be felt a Divine purpose:

> It is not wholly unworthy of observation, that Providence, which strongly appears to have intended the continual intermixture of mankind, never leaves the human mind destitute of a principle to effect it.[4]

He disapproves of the type of history which sees the intervention of God in every event, though he understands that it is tempting for the historian, in the face of extraordinary events, to explain things in this way. In his account of the invasion of Britain by the Saxons he mentions that historians who lived at that time 'saw nothing but the arm of God stretched out for the punishment of a sinful and disobedient people'. He then comments that, when we consider all that happened at that time,

---

[1] *Works*, vi, p. 298.
[2] There are parts of Montesquieu, not published in Burke's lifetime, with a tendency to providentialism. Cf. *Œuvres* (Pléiade), i, p. 39.
[3] *Works*, vi, p. 193.   [4] Ibid., p. 248.

we are almost driven out of the circle of political enquiry: we are in a manner compelled to acknowledge the hand of God in those immense revolutions by which at certain periods He so signally asserts his supreme dominion and brings about that great system of change, which is, perhaps, as necessary to the moral as it is found to be in the natural world.[1]

It is, however, only exceptionally that Burke allows himself to be 'driven out of the circle of political enquiry'; otherwise he applies with great care the naturalistic method of Montesquieu.

The most striking feature of the *Abridgment* is the consistency with which Burke uses the historical method of Montesquieu, and exploits all its refinements. He seeks physical and moral causes, never confuses occasion with cause, understands the continuity of historical experience, and the importance of the *esprit général*. We have noted that Montesquieu was anticipated, in a fragmentary way, by various English writers, especially seventeenth-century historians like Sir William Temple, and legal historians.[2] Burke was acquainted with the works of Temple and legal historians, and appended to the *Abridgment* is an attempt by Burke to write a history of English law.[3] From native writers Burke would have learned something of the genetic method of tracing institutions to their origin, and of seeking historical causes. He may also have known certain Italian writers, who anticipated to some extent Montesquieu's historical method. From all these sources Burke may have learned much, but it is in Montesquieu that he found the historical method fully developed in theory and practice, and his explicit references to Montesquieu make it certain that the main inspiration of the method applied in the *Abridgment* is not to be found in English or Italian sources, but in the *Romains* and the *Esprit des lois*. Burke would therefore be one of the earliest British disciples of Montesquieu. He accepts Montesquieu's method, but does not follow his master slavishly, and does not hesitate to disagree with him. The application of Montesquieu's method to British history by Burke is, however, rather clumsy, and one often feels that his attempts to trace everything to physical or moral causes result in rather vague and unlikely hypotheses, but the work is one of great promise. If Burke had remained a purely literary man he might have perfected the technique he learned from Montesquieu. But he abandons literature for politics, and henceforth his application of Montesquieu's method is not to the past, but to the present, which requires a different technique from that of the *Abridgment*.

---

[1] Ibid., p. 236; Cf. pp. 241–2.   [2] See above, p. 13.   [3] *Works*, vi, pp. 412–22.

Tracts on the Popery Laws

This is the most neglected of Burke's early works, and yet it is extremely valuable as a record of his ideas just before 1765.[1] Like the *Abridgment* it is an unfinished work. It is interesting principally for what it says on the subject of Natural Law, and the light it throws upon Burke's ideas on the duty of the legislator. Although in the *Abridgment* Burke had put great stress on the importance of the empirical approach to politics, and condemned the *a priori*, this is not incompatible with a belief in Natural Law. In the *Tracts* he first makes it clear that he rejects the theory attributed to Hobbes that positive laws are the only laws, and that there is no higher moral law:

> It would be hard to point out any error more truly subversive of all the order and beauty, of all the peace and happiness, of human society, than the position that any body of men have a right to make what laws they please; or that laws can derive any authority from their institution merely and independent of the quality of the subject-matter.[2]

Thus, like Montesquieu,[3] Burke refutes Hobbes, and gives a clear statement of his faith in Natural Law. Like Montesquieu, Burke is an admirer of Cicero, and it is Cicero that Burke quotes against Hobbes.[4] For Burke,

> All human laws are, properly speaking, only declaratory; they may alter the mode and application, but have no power over the substance of original justice.[5]

Burke also says that one of the foundations of law is utility; but this is not to be understood in any sense that contradicts Natural Law. Burke's utility must be understood,

> not of partial or limited, but of general and public, utility, connected in the same manner with, and derived directly from, our rational nature.[6]

Again, he says that laws are based on consent, and that 'the people is the true legislator', but he hedges this around with qualifications to make it clear he does not mean law to be simply the expression of the will of the people, but rather of their rational nature:

> The people, indeed, are presumed to consent to whatever the legislature ordains for their benefit; and they are to acquiesce in it, though they do not clearly see into the propriety of the means by which they are conducted to that desirable end. This they owe as an act of homage and just deference to a reason which the necessity of government has made superior to their own.[7]

[1] The *Tracts* were presumably written when Burke was in Ireland with Hamilton in 1761–2, or 1763–4.
[2] *Works*, vi, p. 21.   [3] See above, pp. 14–15.   [4] *Works*, vi, p. 21 and notes.
[5] Ibid., p. 22.   [6] *Idem*.   [7] Ibid., pp. 20–21.

But he does not seem to mean that this consent is always passive, for there are some things in which the judgement of the people must be respected:

> no one is so gross and stupid as not to distinguish between a benefit and an injury.[1]

The similarity of Burke's opinions here to Montesquieu's needs no stressing: the same faith in Natural Law and dislike of Hobbes; the same idea that justice is always the same, though particular laws may vary; the same attitude to the people, who, though not fitted to take an active part in governing, have the basic rational faculty of distinguishing right from wrong. In all this there is no question of influence of Montesquieu, but rather both writers are drawing on their classical and eighteenth-century background.

Our examination of Burke's early literary works has shown his dislike of *a priori* systems of philosophy, and particularly those of Bolingbroke and Rousseau. Burke's *Sublime and Beautiful* is an attempt to place aesthetics on an empirical basis. It is in the *Abridgment of English History* that we find the first positive influence of Montesquieu on Burke. Burke's empirical cast of mind, and his interest in history would have been enough to make Montesquieu attractive to him. In the *Tracts on the Popery Laws* we do not find any direct influence of Montesquieu, but we learn much about Burke's views on general political theory, and these general views, derived largely from Burke's reading of the classics, reveal him as being interested in the same things as Montesquieu, and sharing some of the same ideas, particularly on Natural Law.

Some of the works we have been considering in this chapter are fragments: it is not surprising, therefore, that our picture of Burke's thought at this time should be fragmentary. His ideas on some questions are fairly clear; but he gives no complete synthesis. It is obvious enough, however, that before taking up a political career he was an admirer of Montesquieu, and in one work had attempted to apply the historical method of Montesquieu to fresh material. We shall find that Burke's debt to Montesquieu usually consists of applying ideas from Montesquieu to something new.

---

[1] Ibid., p. 21. Cf. Montesquieu's views on 'le peuple' in E.L., ii, 2.

CHAPTER IV

THE BRITISH CONSTITUTION: FROM THE FIRST ROCKINGHAM ADMINISTRATION TO THE *PRESENT DISCONTENTS* (1765–1770)

IN July 1765 Burke became private secretary to the Marquis of Rockingham, and in December of the same year he was returned to Parliament for Wendover. These two events mark a turning-point in his career, and he now becomes a politician confronted with practical problems, no longer primarily a man of letters. The problem of the influence of Montesquieu on Burke is therefore no longer merely a literary problem, though Burke is, of course, still interested in writing, and puts his literary talents at the disposal of his colleagues. The practical problems which occupied him most during the first Rockingham administration and in the years immediately following, were especially constitutional problems. On such questions Montesquieu was considered an authority; and in this chapter we shall be largely concerned with examining to what extent Montesquieu's views on the British constitution are accepted by Burke. Burke's views on the constitution are expressed in his speeches and political pamphlets; but such speeches and writings are unintelligible unless we approach our subject historically, and relate Burke's opinions to those of his political colleagues and patrons. His most important work of these years is the *Thoughts on the Cause of the Present Discontents*, published in 1770. The ideas expressed in this work are, as we shall see, largely a rationalization of the behaviour of Lord Rockingham and his friends during their period of office from 1765 to 1766. It cannot be considered as merely an academic work of political theory, though in it Burke does not hesitate to borrow ideas from political philosophers, and not least from Montesquieu.

We have already seen that Montesquieu defines the British constitution in terms of functionally divided powers, and as a mixed state, combining the features of monarchy, aristocracy and democracy.[1] Before attempting to examine the influence of this theory on Burke it is important to know to what extent it is original, and —since we are dealing with practical issues—to what degree it corresponds to the real constitution of the eighteenth century.

[1] See above, pp. 19–20.

The first question, that of sources, is an old one, and is familiar to students of Montesquieu. Such ideas are found in one form or another in Aristotle, Polybius, Cicero, Machiavelli, Sidney, Swift, and Bolingbroke.[1] However, none of the sources proposed is entirely convincing, and, indeed, it has always been assumed by Montesquieu scholars that his sources must be literary sources: it does not seem to have been understood that the real sources of the theory may have been Montesquieu's actual observation of the working of the British form of government during his stay in England. It can hardly be doubted that he learned a great deal from what he saw, and from discussions with British politicians. To this we must add his study of political theorists and, possibly, of constitutional enactments after 1688. That all these factors added something to Montesquieu's ideas on the British constitution is fairly obvious from the *Notes sur l'Angleterre*, the *Pensées*, *Spicilège*, and from what we know of his stay in England. From these works we know that he attended debates at Westminster, that he had many British friends who were politicians, and that he was interested in the struggle between Walpole and Bolingbroke in the years 1729–31.[2]

Those who seek Montesquieu's sources in earlier political theorists are usually literary scholars who make no serious attempt to relate Montesquieu's theory to the real constitution as it existed in the eighteenth century. Such scholars are perhaps too apt to assume that Montesquieu's theory is wildly incorrect, and feel that it is therefore pointless in looking for sources in the constitution itself. It is true, of course, that Montesquieu's theory has some grave shortcomings, but these should not blind us to the amount of truth that it contains. It is not altogether surprising that those who are readiest to condemn Montesquieu's theory are often themselves incompetent judges of the eighteenth-century constitution.[3] It must be remembered that competent judges like David Hume, Charles Yorke, Lord Chesterfield and others were unanimous in applauding the accuracy of Montesquieu's theory, and that it was generally accepted throughout the eighteenth century. This was because the British constitution was, to a large extent, as Montesquieu had described it.

The shortcomings of Montesquieu's theory can be dealt with

---

[1] The most important studies of Montesquieu's sources are: J. Dedieu, *Montesquieu et la tradition politique anglaise en France*, 1909; W. Struck, 'Montesquieu als Politiker', *Historische Studien*, 228, Berlin, 1933; R. Shackleton, 'Montesquieu, Bolingbroke, and the separation of powers, FS, 3 (1949), pp. 25–38.

[2] See above, pp. 3–4.

[3] Montesquieu scholars seem to be unacquainted with the work of constitutional historians such as Sir Lewis Namier.

fairly rapidly.[1] The most serious shortcoming to the theory of separation of powers, as applied to the eighteenth-century constitution, is that in local government such separation did not exist. This can be seen from the rôle of the Justices of the Peace, in whose hands most of the functions of local government lay. It would seem that Montesquieu did not understand local government in England. It is, perhaps, fairer to assume that the principle of separation is meant to apply only to some of the more obvious features of the central government, the King, Lords, Commons, courts and juries. But here again his theory has certain shortcomings, especially in that the King had a legislative function in his power to reject bills, and the Lords and Commons had certain judicial functions which enabled them to impeach servants of the Crown. However, Montesquieu himself mentions these exceptions, but does not seem to think them of sufficient importance to invalidate his theory of separation. It can also be pointed out that the office of Lord Chancellor combined judicial and legislative functions, and included executive functions as well. However, no English writer or politician of the eighteenth century appears to have objected to Montesquieu's theory on these grounds, not even Charles Yorke, who was son of a Lord Chancellor, and later Chancellor himself. It is sometimes objected to Montesquieu's theory that he did not understand the importance of the cabinet or political parties. But at the time the *Esprit des lois* was published the cabinet did not have the constitutional importance it was to have in the nineteenth century: the head of the executive was, as Montesquieu said, the King, who had not yet been replaced by a prime minister and cabinet. He does not mention Whigs and Tories; but in the reign of George II there were no highly organized political parties as there are to-day, and the old Whig and Tory parties of the seventeenth century had split into small factions grouped around individuals and often held together loosely by family loyalties.

If we turn from the inadequacies of Montesquieu's theory to its more valuable side, it can best be understood by looking at the constitution historically. Part of his theory is that the British constitution is a mixed one, consisting of King, Lords and Commons. This was commonplace, and, as far as it goes, correct. The theory of the mixed state first became important in English constitutional history in the seventeenth century, during the prolonged

[1] Cf. Sir William Holdsworth, *A History of English Law*, 6th ed., 13 vols., 1938–52, x, pp. 718–24.

struggle for power between the Stuart monarchs and their parliaments.[1] Against the exponents of absolute monarchy and the Divine Right of Kings, the theory of the mixed state was a useful propaganda weapon, which was first used during the Civil War.[2] The theorists of Divine Right maintained that the sovereign power in the state was lodged in the King; against this it was said that the sovereign power was held jointly by King, Lords and Commons. The theory of the mixed state was given great popularity in *His Majesties Answer to the XIX Propositions* drawn up in 1642, and this was thereafter reproduced in innumerable pamphlets.[3] It is in the theory of the mixed state as put forward at this time that we can see the origins of the doctrine of the separation of powers. Thus in the *Answer to the XIX Propositions* we read that the legislative power is held jointly by King, Lords and Commons; but at the same time it is made clear that the executive power is held by the King alone.

The men who opposed absolutism in the name of mixed government saw the triumph of their cause in the Revolution of 1688 and in the enactments which made up the Revolution Settlement.[4] In the Bill of Rights it is made clear that the King can no longer rule without Parliament: it prunes away his suspending and dispensing power, his power to raise taxes or keep an army without the consent of Parliament. It is indeed difficult to see what legislative powers remain to him apart from the right to veto bills. On the other hand, his executive power is left intact, though the Lords and Commons can impeach his servants. As for the judicial power, judges had long considered Common Law beyond the competence of Parliament to alter,[5] and after 1701 judges were appointed *quamdiu se bene gesserint*, which meant that though the King could appoint them they could no longer be dismissed at pleasure. This made for a greater degree of separation between the judicial and executive powers.

To anyone basing his knowledge of the British constitution on the Bill of Rights it must appear that there is a very high degree of separation of powers, especially between executive and legislative, the King and Parliament being supreme in their respective spheres.

---

[1] Holdsworth, op. cit., vi, p. 61 seq.

[2] Clarendon says he had never heard of the theory until the Civil War: see S. Pargellis, 'The theory of balanced government', in *The Constitution Reconsidered*, ed. Conyers Read, New York, 1938, p. 40.   [3] Pargellis, op. cit.

[4] On the Revolution Settlement see Holdsworth, op. cit., vi, 163 seq.

[5] This belief was rather old-fashioned by the eighteenth century. It had been expressed by Coke in Bonham's Case (see Holdsworth, op. cit., v, p. 475). Chatham is one of the last to challenge the omnicompetence of Parliament, see below, chap. v, p. 87 seq.

Indeed, this separation was so real that there was a danger that there would be a deadlock between King and Parliament that would stultify all government. The main problem of the eighteenth-century constitution was the problem of bridging the gap left by the Revolution Settlement between the King and Parliament. In modern cabinet government the executive emerges naturally from the party that has a majority in Parliament; but in the eighteenth century, when there were no organized parties, and when the King was still active head of government, the modern system did not exist and another had to be evolved.

It has been one of the great achievements of modern scholarship to discover how the eighteenth-century constitution in practice avoided the deadlock which the Bill of Rights seemed to prescribe.[1] The main problem which confronted the King was to secure the consent of Parliament to measures which he thought necessary. His first task was to find a group of ministers capable of carrying these measures through Parliament, and to reward with patronage those members who normally gave their support to government. It was principally by this patronage, which his enemies called 'corruption' or 'influence', that the King was able to bind together the executive and legislative powers. It was also extremely important that the King's ministers should be acceptable to Parliament, otherwise the system would not work smoothly. The 'interest' which the King thus established in Parliament was composed of two main sections: the more or less permanent placemen, forerunners of the Civil Service, who generally supported the government; and the ministers, who would be subject to change. Any ministry would be a coalition of small groups, each group consisting of some prominent political figure around whom would gather a few friends, relations and dependants. In opposition there would be similar small groups, all eager for office; but in opposition there would also be a large number of country gentlemen with no ambitions for office. If the placemen were permanent 'ins', then the country gentlemen must be considered permanent 'outs'.[2] As the combined strength of ministers and placemen rarely exceeded one third of the total membership of the House of Commons, it is obvious that the opinions of the country gentlemen were not unimportant. However, the lack of any

[1] Sir Lewis Namier, *The Structure of Politics at the Accession of George III*, 2nd ed., 1957; *England in the Age of the American Revolution*, 1930; *Monarchy and the Party System*, Oxford, 1952. Cf. R. Pares, *King George III and the Politicians*, Oxford, 1954; J. B. Owen, *The Rise of the Pelhams*, 1957; J. H. Plumb, *Sir Robert Walpole*, vol. i, 1956.
[2] Namier, *Monarchy and the Party System*, p. 12.

properly organized opposition, along with the feeling that it was disloyal to go into formed opposition, meant that the power and prestige of the Crown were sufficient, in normal times, to enable the King to have his measures carried through Parliament without difficulty. It was only some national crisis, such as a war which was being waged inefficiently, that could interrupt this pattern.

It is natural that opposition politicians should have felt that the power of the Crown was such that the work of the Revolution of 1688 was being undone, and that the practice of having a Crown 'interest' in Parliament was contrary to the constitution. The main object of opposition wrath was the body of placemen who usually voted for the government, and in the 1690s a number of place bills were introduced, thus setting the pattern for the eighteenth century's means of expressing displeasure with the practice of the Crown in bridging the gap between executive and legislature. The greatest achievement of those who urged place bills was the Act of Settlement (1701), passed by a government composed of politicians who for some time had been in opposition. It will be well to quote the following clauses of the Act in full, as they stress not only the separation of executive and legislative, but also the separation of the judicial power from the other two:

> That no person who has an office or place of profit under the King, or receives a pension from the Crown shall be capable of serving as a member of the House of Commons.
>
> That after the said limitation shall take effect as aforesaid judges' commissions be made *quamdiu se bene gesserint* . . .
>
> That no pardon under the Great Seal of England be pleadable to an impeachment by the Commons in Parliament.[1]

Fortunately for the working of Parliament the place clause of the Act of Settlement never came into effect in this rigid form, and it was modified to make placemen observe certain conditions, usually amounting to their seeking re-election after their appointment.[2] But the opposition, throughout the century, continued to agitate for place bills, which was the same thing as demanding a greater separation of executive and legislative powers. During Montesquieu's stay in England Bolingbroke made himself the spokesman of this line of attack on the government, and in the *Craftsman*—read by Montesquieu[3]—called for separation of executive and legislative powers:

---

[1] C. Grant Robertson, *Select Statutes, Cases and Documents to illustrate English Constitutional History*, 1660–1832, 1904, p. 91.   [2] Ibid., p. 91 and notes.
[3] R. Shackleton, 'Montesquieu, Bolingbroke, and the separation of Powers', FS, 3 (1949), pp. 25–38.

F

The dependence of the legislative on the executive power hath been contended for by the same persons, under the same direction; and yet nothing surely can be more evident than this; that in a constitution like ours the safety of the whole depends on the balance of the parts, and the balance of the parts on their mutual independency on one another.[1]

Bolingbroke is here animated by the same spirit as that which produced the place clause in the Act of Settlement, and he is, in fact, urging a return to the deadlock of 1688.[2] One of his opponents very rightly accused him of ignorance and folly in suggesting a 'Utopian scheme' of 'maintaining government by powers absolutely distinct'.[3] David Hume, some years later, is likewise opposed to Bolingbroke: Hume sees that some kind of link is required between King and Parliament if the constitution is to function, and he puts forward the following moderate view which, while acknowledging the need for a link, sees that there is always the danger that this will result in Parliament becoming subservient to the Crown:

Instead, then, of asserting absolutely, that the dependence of Parliament in every degree, is an infringement of British liberty, the country party should have made some concessions to their adversaries, and have only examined what was the proper degree of this dependence, beyond which it became dangerous to liberty.[4]

We shall see that Montesquieu's ideas on the working of the constitution are the same as Hume's, and opposed to Bolingbroke; it was not for nothing that Hume admired Montesquieu's theory of the constitution. Montesquieu's theory of the constitution in *Esprit des lois*, xi, 6, is the constitution as it existed in theory, which is, as we have seen, an unworkable system of deadlock between powers which are functionally divided. If we wish to find what Montesquieu knew about the actual practice of the constitution we must turn to the last chapter of the *Esprit des lois*, xix. This chapter is usually ignored by scholars who comment on Montesquieu's theory of the British constitution. A careful reading of it will show that he understood the British constitution better than is usually realized.

In the *Esprit des lois*, xix, 27, Montesquieu shows that he understands the importance of Crown patronage in the working of the

---

[1] Bolingbroke, *Works*, 5 vols., 1754, i, p. 296 (originally in *The Craftsman* no. 208, June, 1730).

[2] Cf. H. N. Fieldhouse, 'Bolingbroke and the idea of non-party government', *History*, 23 (1938–9), pp. 41–56.

[3] Quoted by Shackleton, loc. cit., p. 34.

[4] *Of the Independency of Parliament* (first pub. 1742), in *Essays Moral, Political and Literary*, ed. T. H. Green and T. H. Grose, 2 vols., 1875, i, p. 121.

constitution, and that he understands how the executive power has its supporters among those eager to enjoy its patronage:

> Comme il y aurait dans cet état deux pouvoirs visibles : la puissance législative et l'exécutrice, et que tout citoyen y aurait sa volonté propre, et ferait valoir à son gré son indépendance, la plupart des gens auraient plus d'affection pour une de ces puissances que pour l'autre, le grand nombre n'ayant pas ordinairement assez d'équité ni de sens pour les affectionner également toutes les deux.
>
> Et, comme la puissance exécutrice, disposant de tous les emplois, pourrait donner de grandes espérances et jamais de craintes, tous ceux qui obtiendraient d'elle seraient portés à se tourner de son côté, et elle pourrait être attaquée par tous ceux qui n'en espéreraient rien.

Montesquieu therefore understands that the executive power is normally attacked by malcontent politicians in opposition, and he stresses the importance of maintaining both the executive and legislative powers. Unlike Bolingbroke he does not urge a return to the purity of the letter of the constitution in which there is a complete separation of powers: he sees in the struggle between court and the opposition a healthy sign:

> Toutes les passions y étant libres, la haine, l'envie, la jalousie, l'ardeur de s'enrichir et de se distinguer, paraîtraient dans toute leur étendue : et si cela était autrement, l'état serait comme un homme abattu par la maladie, qui n'a point de passions parce qu'il n'a point de forces.

Montesquieu sees that this struggle between court and opposition takes place among 'hommes libres' who are not irrevocably tied to either side, and this ultimately assures a balance between them:

> Ces partis étant composés d'hommes libres, si l'un prenait trop le dessus, l'effet de la liberté ferait que celui-ci serait abaissé, tandis que les citoyens, comme les mains qui secourent le corps, viendraient relever l'autre.

He therefore believes that both 'partis' must be maintained if the constitution is to survive, which means that, unlike Bolingbroke, but like Hume, he did not want to abolish the 'influence' of the Crown in Parliament. He is aware, of course, of the danger of Parliament becoming the mere servant of the Crown, and had already said that the constitution would perish 'lorsque la puissance législative sera plus corrompue que l'exécutrice'.[1]

In this same chapter of the *Esprit des lois* we find a number of shrewd remarks on the constitution. Montesquieu does not mention Whigs and Tories, and understands that 'partis' are 'composés d'hommes libres'. Modern constitutional historians have likewise

[1] E.L., xi, 6.

found that it is more accurate to explain the eighteenth-century constitution in terms of government and opposition, of small fluctuating groups, rather than in terms of Whig and Tory.[1] Montesquieu also understands that, though the King is theoretical head of the executive, he may have to yield to pressure from Parliament and delegate his executive power to ministers he dislikes, being 'obligé de donner sa confiance à ceux qui l'auraient le plus choqué, et de disgracier ceux qui l'auraient le mieux servi'. This, in fact, amounts to an encroachment of the legislative on the executive power, and shows how Montesquieu understood that in practice the principles of separation were subject to many modifications.

It is clear, then, that Montesquieu understood the more important features of the working of the constitution, and especially the way in which the theoretical gap between the executive and legislative powers was bridged. If there seems to be a contradiction between the two chapters which he devotes to the British constitution the contradiction should be sought, perhaps, in the constitution itself, where the convention of the Crown's placing an 'interest' in Parliament was thought by many to be contrary to the principles of the Revolution Settlement.

Thus, though Montesquieu's theory of the separation of powers, as applied to the British constitution, has grave faults, especially when it is applied to local government, it has at least the virtue of describing some of the main features of the central government. The chapter in the eleventh book of the *Esprit des lois* is a fairly accurate description of the theory of the constitution, as the authors of the Revolution Settlement presumably wished it to be; but in the *Esprit des lois*, xix, 27, Montesquieu shows that he understands that the practice of the constitution permits a certain amount of mingling of powers which in theory are separate. It is easy to see why this theory of the constitution should have been popular in the eighteenth century: it was the culmination of a long tradition to which politicians, lawyers and political thinkers had all contributed something. Since the seventeenth century many Englishmen had been urging greater separation of powers, though they had not said it like that. They had been speaking prose all their lives without knowing it, and it was Montesquieu who formulated their vague ideas into a coherent theory. His theory was immediately popular because the public were ready for it. It remained the accepted theory until the

---

[1] This is not to deny that the terms Whig and Tory had some meaning in the eighteenth century. Cf. J. B. Owen, op. cit., p. 66 seq.

constitution itself was to change. It was eventually replaced by the theory of Bagehot, who did for the nineteenth-century constituton what Montesquieu did for that of the eighteenth.[1] However, a constitution is never something rigidly fixed, and in the eighteenth century itself we can see the constitution slowly developing and changing from the version described by Montesquieu. It is ironical that this change can be best observed in Montesquieu's greatest disciple, and it is in Burke that we can see the growth of new ideas which eventually are absorbed into the system of cabinet government in the next century. However, to understand Burke's ideas on the constitution we must turn to his political career, which began in 1765.

The formation of the Rockingham administration in July 1765 was an example, to use Montesquieu's words, of a King being 'obligé de donner sa confiance à ceux qui l'auraient le plus choqué'. It is true that the majority of the new ministers were 'all young and inexperienced men, unknown to the nation and great by nothing but their rank and fortune',[2] but their leader, and the Duke of Newcastle, who was of their number, had opposed the King in 1762 when the Duke of Devonshire had been dismissed from office.[3] The new ministry was formed mainly because the King wanted to rid himself of George Grenville, which he would have preferred to do by forming a ministry under Pitt, but Pitt would not accept office. The Duke of Cumberland was therefore authorized to negotiate with Lord Rockingham, and after a certain amount of preliminary bargaining the new ministry was formed.[4] Rockingham had stipulated that a few placemen who were appointed by Lord Bute should be dismissed, and that Bute should not be allowed to take any part in government, it being thought at this time that the King was too much under the influence of his 'Favourite', whose brief ministry had lasted from 1761 to 1763. The new ministry was formed by filling the important posts, vacated by Grenville and his colleagues, with friends of Rockingham and Newcastle, and by leaving the minor places occupied by men who had been appointed mostly under Lord Bute. Burke, though not of much importance

[1] *The English Constitution . . . Reprinted from the 'Fortnightly Review'* appeared in 1867.

[2] Horace Walpole, *Memoirs of the Reign of George III*, ed. G. F. R. Barker, 4 vols., 1894, ii, p. 135.

[3] Cf. Sir Lewis Namier, *England in the Age of the American Revolution*, 1930, p. 331 seq.

[4] M. Bateson, *A Narrative of the Changes in the Ministry, 1765–67, told by the Duke of Newcastle*, 1898, p. 25 seq.; Earl of Albemarle, *Memoirs of the Marquis of Rockingham*, 2 vols., 1852, i, p. 191 seq.

at this time, approved of this plan of not turning out men who were not considered avowed enemies.[1]

The events of the short Rockingham administration need not be related here.[2] Weak from the first, under inexperienced leadership, weakened further by the death of the Duke of Cumberland, faced with a major crisis in the American colonies, and opposed by Pitt and Grenville, it was not destined to last. In July 1766 it was replaced by the administration of Pitt, who then became Earl of Chatham. Burke played an active part in the Rockingham administration, both as debater and organizer, distinguishing himself particularly in his speeches on America.[3] He also wrote a pamphlet shortly after the fall of the ministry, the *Short Account of a Late Short Administration*, in which he relates the achievements of Lord Rockingham and his colleagues. He mentions especially the repeal of the Stamp Act and the passing of the Declaratory Act. He also makes some remarks of constitutional significance. He says that 'they treated their sovereign with decency, with reverence', and, speaking of the fall of the ministers, he writes,

In the prosecution of their measures they were traversed by an opposition of a new and singular character; an opposition of placemen and pensioners. They were supported by the confidence of the nation.[4]

It is important to understand what Burke means here. The Rockinghams thought that the King had not exerted his patronage and prestige enough in their favour in order to secure the support of the placemen who had been appointed originally under Lord Bute. They thought that the King secretly favoured Bute at their expense, and that they had proof of this, for during the debates on the repeal of the Stamp Act some placemen had voted against the ministers, and when Newcastle took their names to the King with the request that they should be removed or disciplined, the King declared himself unable to force men to vote against their conscience.[5] There was also some unfortunate misunderstanding between Lord Rockingham and the King as to whether the latter was or was not in favour of the repeal of the Stamp Act, and when Lord Strange, who had no connection with the ministry, declared himself authorized

---

[1] Burke to Charles O'Hara, June 6, 1765: R. J. S. Hoffman, *E. Burke, New York Agent*, Philadelphia, 1956, p. 315.

[2] See D. A. Winstanley, *Personal and Party Government*, 1760–1766, Cambridge, 1910, chap. vi.

[3] *Corr.*, i, pp. 97–98.   [4] *Works*, i, pp. 183–4.

[5] Bateson, op. cit., p. 50; Albemarle, op. cit., i, p. 321.

to say that the King was in favour only of modification and not of repeal, the ministers felt that they had been betrayed.[1] Again, in June 1766 the King refused Rockingham's request to dismiss Jeremiah Dyson, a placeman and friend of Bute's who had moved a motion against the ministry; and the King also refused Rockingham's request to grant new peerages.[2] Most of these incidents were in themselves insignificant. There is nothing to show that the King did not give his confidence to his ministers, and certainly he was not planning with Lord Bute. There was probably some genuine misunderstanding over the repeal of the Stamp Act; and his refusal to do what Rockingham asked in June 1766 was certainly because at this time the Rockingham administration was practically defunct, and about to be replaced by that of Pitt. However, the Rockinghams, all too conscious of their weakness and inferiority, were apt to magnify the significance of small incidents of this nature, and by 1766 Burke was convinced that the King was playing a sinister game of encouraging placemen to vote against the ministers, while the real control of affairs was put in the hands of Lord Bute.

The *Short Account* shows a certain amount of solidarity among the friends of Lord Rockingham, but this must not be exaggerated, for, after the formation of the Chatham ministry, those of Rockingham's friends who did not have to vacate their places to accommodate Chatham's supporters, remained in the new ministry. Among those who remained was Henry Seymour Conway, who led the ministry in the Commons, and to whom William Burke was secretary. Rockingham encouraged his friends to remain in office if they could, for they were too few to attempt an effective opposition, and the presence of Conway in the ministry was taken to mean that Chatham would pay special deference to the Rockinghams.[3] Burke approved of this plan, and did not see any point in going into formed opposition. He even hoped that, through the influence of Conway, he would be offered a place.[4] However, it soon became obvious that Chatham had no intention of giving any kind of special attention to the friends of Rockingham, and we find Burke complaining that 'If an house had changed its master, more attention would have been paid to the footmen of the former family'.[5] To make matters worse, Burke and Rockingham thought they saw favours being heaped on the friends of Lord Bute, especially when Bute's brother, Stuart

---

[1] Albemarle, op. cit., i, pp. 300–2; Sir John Fortescue, *The Correspondence of King George the Third*, 6 vols., 1927–8, nos. 242, 247, 248.

[2] Albemarle, op. cit., i, pp. 346–7.   [3] Ibid., ii, pp. 12–13.

[4] Hoffman, op. cit., p. 357.   [5] *Idem.*

Mackenzie, whom Grenville had forced the King to dismiss, was restored to his former place.[1] Chatham's conduct probably helped to consolidate the *esprit de corps* of Rockingham's friends, and some interesting light is shed on this in an interview Burke had with Conway, when the latter sounded him on the possibility of taking employment with the government. Burke explained,

> that I had begun with this party, that it was now divided in situation, though I hoped not in opinions or inclinations; that the point of honour lay with that division which was out of power,

and he added that he could accept a place only on condition that he would be understood to belong not to the ministry, but to Lord Rockingham.[2] It is not surprising that Conway did not accept such terms, which formulated unheard-of constitutional ideas, in which Burke is already putting King Rockingham before King George.

The culmination of the insults which the Rockinghams felt were being directed against them came on November 17, when one of their number, Lord Edgcumbe, was dismissed by Chatham from his post of Treasurer of the Household. Burke relates how 'the party took fire, and General Conway seemed to be mortally offended'.[3] He feared that 'Lord Chatham had resolved the ruin of the party',[4] and it would seem that Burke was one of the foremost in encouraging Rockingham to go into formed opposition and to call for his friends in office to resign.[5] Rockingham called for resignations, but this move was not particularly successful, for only seven resignations were secured, and, worst of all for the Rockinghams, Conway remained in office, leaving the ministry with its essential leadership in the Commons.

The Rockinghams liked to believe that they were going into opposition on principle, and not simply because of personal resentment to Chatham. Thus on November 20 we find Rockingham writing to Lord Scarborough that 'the corps must keep together, or . . . all our struggles for the last four or five years, would be thrown away in regard to the material object of being the check to Lord Bute'.[6] Rockingham is of course merely rationalizing the situation: four or five years earlier the Rockinghams had not existed as a 'corps' to resist Lord Bute or anyone else. But this was an excellent propaganda theme, and it gave the Rockinghams a respectable ancestry, looking back to the Pelhams and their followers who

---

[1] Hoffman, op. cit., p. 357.   [2] Ibid., p. 369.   [3] Ibid., p. 375.
[4] *Idem.*   [5] Albemarle, op. cit., ii, p. 19 seq.   [6] Ibid., ii, p. 21

had been dismissed in 1762.[1] The Rockinghams could thus think of themselves as having since 1762 tried to rescue the King and the constitution from the evil and misleading influence of Lord Bute. It is this propaganda theme, which we have seen developing in response to circumstances, that Burke is to use in the *Present Discontents*.

Although the Rockinghams could now feel that they had a set of principles to guide them, and a certain amount of solidarity, there was not much they could do in practice, as their numbers were small. Rockingham admitted that they must appear a forlorn hope, but,

> we are not in an uncomfortable situation, because every dictate of honour and principle encouraged us to persevere in acting on the same plan as we had done for years.[2]

They thus consoled themselves with the belief that they were virtuous. In practice, however, they could do little but oppose more or less everything that was government policy, and even went so far as to move for a reduction of the land tax, which was little more than an easy bid for popularity and an attempt to embarrass the government.[3]

The opposition to the Chatham ministry was composed mainly of the groups of followers of Rockingham, Grenville and the Duke of Bedford, and by the summer of 1767 it was becoming clear that the ministry would have to win over some part of this opposition if it were to survive. Negotiations were begun in July, and the story of this has been told more than once.[4] The King was willing to receive Rockingham and some of his friends into the ministry; but Rockingham, thinking, wrongly as it turned out, that at this time he had the full support of Grenville and Bedford, was unwilling to come to terms with the King unless Chatham's ministry was considered at an end. Rockingham planned to form a new ministry, a 'comprehensive administration', filling all the places with his own friends or allies, thus avoiding what he regarded as the danger of opposition within the ranks of the ministry from placemen who claimed they owed allegiance to the King alone, or, in Lord

---

[1] There was, in fact, a certain amount of continuity in that Rockingham had in 1765 reinstated a number of Pelham placemen dismissed in 1762; see W. J. Smith, *The Grenville Papers*, 4 vols., 1852-3, iii, p. 74, p. 86.

[2] Albemarle, op. cit., ii, p. 32.

[3] Burke and some others did not take part in this debate, see Horace Walpole, *Memoirs of the Reign of George III*, ii, p. 298.

[4] The most recent account is J. Brooke, *The Chatham Administration*, 1956; Cf. D. A. Winstanley, *Lord Chatham and the Whig Opposition*, Cambridge, 1912.

Rockingham's terminology, to Lord Bute.[1] In his interview with
the King, Rockingham said,

> that when I had the honour of being in his Majesty's service, the measures of
> administration were thwarted and obstructed by men in office, acting like a corps;
> that I flattered myself that it was not entirely with his Majesty's inclination, and I
> would assure him it was very detrimental to his service.[2]

But the King rejected Rockingham's plan for a comprehensive
administration as 'most indecent',[3] and Horace Walpole said that the
King was not desirous of giving himself a minister who would be
master both of him and parliament.[4] The King did not yield to
pressure from Rockingham, and managed to patch up the ministry
with a number of the Duke of Bedford's supporters. The Rockinghams thus remained in opposition with less hope than ever of returning to office, their attempt to storm the closet having been a
complete failure.

Burke was in absolute agreement with Rockingham's policy at
this time.[5] After the failure of the negotiations of July 1767 the
Rockinghams continued to console themselves with the thought
that their conduct was virtuous, and that it had been consistent with
their previous policy.[6] Their 'consistency' did not permit them,
immediately after 1767, to form an alliance with the Grenvilles,
who had opposed them in 1765–66, and thus there was no strong
united opposition to the Chatham ministry, in spite of the fact that
Chatham himself, after the summer of 1767, was prevented by illness
from playing any active part in its direction, leaving the Duke of
Grafton in control. However, the divided opposition were soon to
be united in a cause which gave them the support of public opinion
and brought the ministry into disrepute. This took place when
controversy arose over the Middlesex election. John Wilkes, who
since 1764 had been under the charge of outlawry, returned to
England in 1768 and was elected for the county of Middlesex, but
was expelled from the House of Commons. His subsequent re-
elections and expulsions, culminating in his being declared incapable
of being elected, and the seating of his rival Luttrell, who had received
a minority vote, created a wave of popular discontent that released a
great deal of latent radical feeling in the people. The opposition
were ready to exploit this discontent against the ministry.

---

[1] The persistence of the Bute legend is examined in the 'Introduction' to R. Sedgwick,
Letters from George III to Lord Bute, 1939.
[2] Albemarle, op. cit., ii, p. 53.   [3] *Correspondence of George the Third*, i, p. 58.
[4] *Memoirs of the Reign of George III*, ii, p. 240.   [5] *Corr.*, i, pp. 132–7.
[6] Albemarle, op. cit., i, pp. 57–58.

Burke was among the foremost of the opposition against the government's action in expelling Wilkes.[1] The opposition could not deny the right of the House to expel one of its members, but the question of declaring that Wilkes was incapable of being elected was a more serious matter, and was a sign for a general attack by the opposition. In this the Rockinghams and Grenvilles were at one, and on May 9 a dinner was arranged at the Thatched House Tavern, more than seventy opposition members attending.[2] At this time the country was petitioning, the ministry was under the weak leadership of Grafton, Junius had begun his attacks on the ministers, and when Chatham reappeared, in the summer of 1769, he denounced the administration he had formerly led. There were thus great hopes for the opposition, who spent most of the summer and autumn working with the petitioners, Burke playing an important part in this.[3] The general theme of the petitions was that Parliament was servile to the designs of the King's ministers.[4] This is, of course, only the old opposition cry embodied in place bills, and which we find in Montesquieu when he predicts that the British constitution will perish when the legislative power is more corrupt than the executive. Indeed, this passage from Montesquieu was quoted at this time with reference to the ministry.[5] Although the Rockinghams took part in the petitioning movement, they were not entirely at ease in doing so, for they were an aristocratic group with no liking for radicalism.[6] They were eager to exploit the petitioning movement against the ministry, but were unwilling to go all the way with the petitioners, whose demands were often for more frequent parliaments, extension of the franchise, and a general place bill.[7] Rockingham and his friends insisted that petitions should be restricted to demanding the dissolution of the present Parliament.[8]

There were certain difficulties which, however, prevented the opposition from becoming properly united. The Rockinghams distrusted Chatham since 1766, and at the same time they felt that a close alliance with the Grenvilles would make them lose their identity and betray their principles.[9] The Grenvilles, in any case,

---

[1] J. Wright, *Sir Henry Cavendish's Debates of the House of Commons*, 2 vols., 1841–3, i, pp. 348–50.   [2] *Corr.*, i, pp. 163–7.
[3] Burke wrote the Buckinghamshire petition, see Dowdeswell MSS. quoted in *Cavendish's Debates*, i, p. 585; Cf. *Corr.*, i, pp. 186–94.
[4] On the petitions see S. MacCoby, *English Radicalism*, 5 vols., 1935–55, vol. i, chaps. v–vi.
[5] *The Whisperer*, March 31, 1770.
[6] *Corr.*, i, p. 186 seq.; Albemarle, op. cit., ii, p. 1 seq.
[7] Albemarle, op. cit., ii, pp. 104–6; 132–42.   [8] Ibid., ii, pp. 104–5.
[9] *Corr.*, i, p. 203.

did not share the Rockingham view that every administration should be 'comprehensive', and so composed that placemen were strictly under the control of the head of the ministry. Burke had an interesting discussion on this point with Grenville's brother, Lord Temple:

> We talked of the court system, and their scheme of having dependent administrations. I spoke of this as the reigning evil; and particularly mentioned the favourite idea of a King's making a separate party for himself. He said this latter did not seem so bad a thing, if Lord Bute had not spoiled it. I said I thought it was mischievous, whether Lord Bute had a hand in it or not, and equally so.[1]

Thus the principles evolved by the Rockinghams were peculiar to themselves: they alone wanted to deprive the King of his constitutional right to be real head of the executive and to appoint his own servants who would look to him and not to ministers.

At the opening of the parliamentary session in January 1770 the opposition, united in their views on Wilkes and the Middlesex elections, launched an attack on the government. The attacks succeeded in forcing Grafton to resign, but he was replaced by Lord North, whose adroitness did much to save the situation for the King. After this the case of Wilkes wore thin, the opposition weakened, and North remained impregnable until 1782, when the Rockinghams had their second period of office.

It was in the course of these years that Burke formed ideas on the constitution that are the basis of the pamphlets which he was writing at this time. He learned ideas of solidarity, and of the importance of a ministry making quite sure that it would be supported by placemen. He learned a profound distrust of the King, and, finding it impossible to govern with him, the Rockinghams adopted tactics which would enable them to govern without him. Burke also believed that the King was under the influence of Lord Bute, or at least he gives the impression that he believes this. These essential ideas of the Rockinghams are given literary expression by Burke mainly in his two important pamphlets, the *Observations on a Late Publication, intituled, 'The Present State of the Nation'*, and the *Thoughts on the Cause of the Present Discontents*. The first of these works is sometimes mentioned because it shows that Burke had a sound grasp of fiscal details; but we shall be interested in it mainly for its ideas. The other work is of especial interest in that it was handed around the members of the Rockingham group inviting criticism, and it was intended to represent their policy.[2]

[1] *Corr.*, i, p. 209.   [2] Ibid., pp. 197–8.

In the *Observations,* written in reply to a pamphlet by William Knox, one of Grenville's supporters, Burke is particularly concerned to justify the principles of party solidarity which the Rockinghams had been developing. The way in which he does this is interesting: he rejects any attempt to vindicate party *a priori*, and prefers to base his argument on experience and tradition, appealing not to metaphysics but to history:

> Party divisions, whether on the whole operating for good or evil, are things inseparable from free government. This is a truth which, I believe, admits little dispute, having been established by the uniform experience of all ages.[1]

As for the part to be played by a citizen belonging to a party division, Burke refuses to give any abstract rule: this question, 'like most of the others which regard our duties in life, is to be determined by our station in it'.[2] With his eye on the events that followed 1765 he says that it is necessary for a minister to be backed by a body of supporters, held together by party spirit, and he contrasts this with what usually happens:

> This will give to such a person, in such a body, an authority and respect that no minister ever enjoyed among his venal dependents, in the highest plenitude of his power; such as servility never can give, such as ambition never can receive or relish.[3]

This is accompanied with a description that reads like a caricature of the events of 1765–66, describing how the ministers are made the victims of placemen, who 'are put about them in appearance to serve, in reality to govern them', and who eventually 'abandon and destroy them in order to set up some new dupe of ambition, who in his turn is to be abandoned and destroyed'.[4]

Burke objects that his opponent Knox has dealt too much in vague *a priori* arguments and neglected facts. In his attack on Knox's ideas on revenue in Ireland, India and America, he makes this same complaint. In conclusion Burke makes a plea for an empirical approach to political problems, which will not neglect the individual for the sake of general plans, and which will respect tradition. He stresses the fact that institutions grow slowly, and that sudden change is undesirable. He ends with an admirable allusion:

> Among all the great men of antiquity, Procrustes shall never be my hero of legislation: with his iron bed, the allegory of his government, and the type of some modern policy, by which the long limb was to be cut short, and the short tortured into length. Such was the state-bed of uniformity![5]

---

[1] *Works,* i, p. 185.   [2] Ibid., p. 185.   [3] Ibid., p. 294.
[4] Ibid., p. 298.   [5] Ibid., p. 258.

In the *Observations* Burke is not demonstrably writing under the influence of Montesquieu, but his empiricism, his respect for tradition, and his dislike of procrustean planning are all very much in the spirit of Montesquieu. He is very close indeed to Montesquieu in some of the speeches he made at this time, as for example when on May 13, 1768, he said,

> Evils . . . cannot be put an end to by the common execution of the laws. The disposition of men's minds must be changed first.[1]

The *Present Discontents* is a much more important work, a complete rationalization of the activities of the Rockinghams since 1765. It is here that we find the legend, since destroyed by modern scholarship,[2] that George III was a monarch who tried to subvert the constitution and introduce personal government. Those who were misled by Burke's propaganda theme were unfamiliar with the eighteenth-century constitution, thinking in terms of modern cabinet government, and thus, by a 'double distortion', George III has been 'represented as having endeavoured to imitate the Stuarts when he ought to have anticipated Queen Victoria'.[3] However, Burke was simply reviving an old literary device which, instead of attacking the King directly, attacked his advisers.[4] It is difficult to say to what extent Burke and his colleagues believed the Bute legend; however Burke is attacking not only Bute, but also the system of patronage which placed servants of the Crown directly under the control of the King:

> This system has not arisen solely from the ambition of Lord Bute, but from the circumstances which favoured it, and from an indifference to the constitution which had been for some time growing among our gentry.[5]

Burke's aim is not to make personal attacks, but to concentrate on the diagnosis of the malady which he thinks has seized the constitution.[6] He intends to show that only the Rockinghams have true constitutional principles; and to do this he discusses the nature of the constitution in the traditional terminology of the balance of powers in the mixed state, and separation of powers. In such a discussion it is inevitable that he should invite comparison with Montesquieu.

The *Present Discontents* is a work of great literary ability, and Burke obviously takes a great deal of care in the presentation of his

---

[1] *Cavendish's Debates*, i, p. 14. Cf. E.L., xix, 14.
[2] By Sir Lewis Namier, Cf. above, p. 62.   [3] R. Sedgwick, op. cit., p. viii.
[4] Ibid., p. xvii, seq.   [5] *Works*, i, p. 330.
[6] In an earlier form the *Discontents* did make personal attacks, e.g. on Chatham: *Corr.*, i, p. 200.

argument. He does not come at once to the essential point, but begins by elaborating some general maxims of political wisdom. He says that a people should be governed according to their general temper and character; that every age is different, and will therefore have its own particular problems; and he develops other such maxims, which are similar in spirit to some of Montesquieu's ideas on the *esprit général*. It is possible that Burke may have Montesquieu in mind, especially when he writes,

> Yet as all times have *not* been alike, true political sagacity manifests itself in distinguishing that complaint which only characterizes the general infirmity of human nature, from those which are symptoms of the particular distemperature of our own air and season.[1]

Here the words 'air and season' are highly suggestive of Montesquieu's theory of climate. Also, it would be difficult to find a more urgent appeal for the legislator to follow the general character of the people, as Montesquieu had recommended it, than when Burke says,

> We have no other materials to work upon, but those out of which God has been pleased to form the inhabitants of this island. If these be radically and essentially vicious, all that can be said is that those men are very unhappy, to whose fortune or duty it falls to administer the affairs of this untoward people.[2]

This is an extreme statement of the empiricist creed, and, if Burke were writing only on the elevated plane of political philosophy it would require further development. But Burke is writing propaganda, and what he really means is that the King and his ministers should grant the petitioners and opposition what they wanted.

Burke, still before coming to the essential point of his analysis, devotes some pages to an account of monarchy and despotism in terms unmistakably taken from Montesquieu. We have seen that Montesquieu analysed monarchy into intermediary powers, which distinguished it from despotism. It is with this theory in mind that Burke writes,

> It is the nature of despotism to abhor power held by any means but its own momentary pleasure; and to annihilate all intermediate situations between boundless strength on its own part, and total debility on the part of the people.[3]

He complains that the policy of George III was to abolish these intermediary powers. It is important to note that it was extremely unusual to analyse the British constitution in such terms, Montesquieu

---

[1] *Works*, i, p. 307.   [2] Ibid., p. 309.   [3] Ibid., p. 314.

himself having found it better to employ the analysis of mixed state
and separation of powers. Burke is here making use of Montesquieu's doctrines for the purposes of propaganda, and is slightly
distorting Montesquieu's theory to make it fit. He also uses Montesquieu's theory of the principles of different types of state. He
follows this theory in seeing honour as the principle of monarchy,
and the corruption of this honour as a sign of the general corruption
of monarchy:

> Those high and haughty sentiments, which are the great support of independence,
> were to be let down gradually. Points of honour and precedence were no more to
> be regarded in parliamentary decorum, than in a Turkish army.[1]

It is after these introductory passages, largely inspired by Montesquieu, that Burke comes to grips with the essential problem of the
Present Discontents, which is to show that the constitution is being
perverted by the policy of King and court. A great deal of what
Burke says is rather sententious repetition of the commonplace that
the constitution was a mixed one, consisting of King, Lords, and
Commons, and that the purpose of this arrangement is that 'the
Prince shall not be able to violate the laws'.[2] However, Burke does
not get much help from the theory of the constitution, for the King
had the constitutional right to choose his own servants. Burke is
forced to shift his ground, and he directs his attack against 'a system,
which without directly violating the letter of any law, operates
against the spirit of the whole constitution'.[3] Thus, while granting
that the King has the theoretical right to choose his own ministers,
Burke insists that in practice this is limited. On this Burke is on
firm ground, and, as we have seen, Montesquieu had noted this
point.[4] But Burke, seizing on this fairly obvious truth, pushes it to
an extreme form, enumerates the conditions that ministers should
fulfil to win the confidence of Parliament, and puts his conclusion in
a particularly aggressive manner:

> These are considerations which in my opinion enforce the necessity of having
> some better reason, in a free country, and a free parliament, for supporting the
> ministers of the Crown, than that short one, *That the King has thought proper to
> appoint them*.[5]

He regrets that both Houses of Parliament are subservient to the
executive power. The Lords,

---

[1] *Works*, i, p. 316.   [2] Ibid., p. 331.   [3] Ibid., p. 331.
[4] See above, p. 66.   [5] *Works*, i, p. 335.

far from supporting themselves in a state of independent greatness, are but too apt to fall into an oblivion of their proper dignity, and to run headlong into an abject servitude.[1]

As for the Commons,

In Parliament the whole is executed from the beginning to the end. In Parliament the power of obtaining their object is absolute.[2]

It is then, according to Burke, as though the prophecy of Montesquieu has been fulfilled, and the legislative is more corrupt than the executive power. However, Burke does not mention Montesquieu here, and his analysis is based simply on what he saw—or thought he saw—and commonplaces of constitutional theory.

Burke finds a further example of corruption in the case of the incapacitation of Wilkes, and it is possible that here Burke owes something to Montesquieu, who had been quoted at least once in the debates on the Middlesex elections by George Grenville, who said,

Let us remember the well-known observation of the learned and sensible author of *L'Esprit des lois*, who states it as one of the excellencies of the English constitution . . . that 'the judicial power is separated from the legislative' . . .[3]

Burke's argument is that the House of Commons, acting in its judicial capacity, has arrogated to itself the power of making laws, a power which belongs to the three branches of the legislature together, and not to one alone. As there was no law according to which the Commons were competent to declare Wilkes incapable of being elected, they had, in declaring his incapacitation, confused their legislative and judicial powers. Since Burke was maintaining that the legislative power was already completely dominated by the executive, it follows that he thinks he sees in the Wilkes case a complete mingling of the executive, legislative and judicial powers.

A further example of the corruption of the legislature Burke finds in the practice of paying the Civil List without previously seeing the account: such a practice taken together with that of declaring incapacities,

must establish such a fund of rewards and terrors as will make Parliament the best appendage and support of arbitrary power that ever was invented by the wit of man.[4]

The whole implication of Burke's analysis is that liberty depends on the separation of powers, though he arrives at this conclusion

[1] Ibid., p. 323.   [2] Ibid., p. 350.   [3] P.H., xvi, 565-6.
[4] *Works*, i, p. 365.

G

not from the study of Montesquieu so much as from his experience in politics.

Burke considers certain remedies which had been suggested to restore the power of Parliament. The first remedy, that of shortenng the duration of Parliaments, he rejects as being a means of achieving nothing more than more frequent occasions for corruption at elections. The second proposed remedy was to introduce a general place-bill—the time-honoured remedy for such alleged cases of corruption. Burke's rejection of this remedy might at first seem surprising, since his main complaint is that placemen are obeying 'secret influence' from the King and Lord Bute. Burke says he refuses to believe that a place-bill will remedy the situation because, though, 'it were better undoubtedly, that no influence at all could affect the mind of a member of Parliament', he sees such a measure as impracticable, and fears that if there were fewer places there would be more secret influence. Burke's reasoning is not very convincing here. The truth is that Burke and his friends had no objection to patronage or places so long as they were placed at their, and nobody else's disposal. Their quarrel with the King in 1766 was that he would not discipline the placemen who had voted against them. Their concept of solidarity really demanded that there should be places for their own supporters to fill.[1]

The remedy which Burke proposes is what he vaguely calls 'the interposition of the body of the people itself'.[2] He means that Parliament should be more closely under the eye of the electors, and that correct lists of how members voted should be made available. Burke is not at his best here, and his proposal was not very realistic in a Parliament elected on such a narrow franchise. In the *Short Account* he had said that the Rockingham administration 'were supported by the confidence of the nation',[3] and his contention throughout the years 1766–70 is that only Lord Rockingham and his supporters have this confidence of the nation. This was untrue, for Chatham was a far more popular figure. In any case Burke is sophistical in his use of the terms 'nation' and 'people', by which he means,

The great peers, the leading landed gentlemen, the opulent merchants and manufacturers, the substantial yeomanry,[4]

and he looks back wistfully to the 'great Whig families' who were in

---

[1] *Works*, i, pp. 367–8.   [2] Ibid., p. 369.   [3] Ibid., p. 184.
[4] Ibid., p. 337.

office under George II, qualified for government by such qualities as,

> Long possession of government; vast property; obligations of favours given and received; connection of office; ties of blood, of alliance, of friendship . . . the name of Whig, dear to the majority of the people; the zeal early begun and steadily continued to the royal family.[1]

Burke is thus defending the aristocratic character of the Rockingham connection, and he concludes with a defence of party, which he conceives to be the only means of ending the 'system' of George III.

The 'system' which Burke was attacking was the normal constitution of the eighteenth century as worked by George III, who was a constitutional monarch. One might say that it was the constitution as described by Montesquieu that Burke was attacking. The action of Parliament in incapacitating Wilkes was of doubtful legality, but Burke's other charges against George III are unfounded. Burke's ideas on the constitution have their origin in the resentment of the Rockinghams to the events of 1765–66 when they thought the King was conspiring against them. They developed a certain amount of solidarity in the years that followed, and convinced themselves that they stood for certain principles. They had a feeling of party solidarity before the age of parties, and consequently their attempts to place limitations on the prerogative of the King freely to choose his own servants were resented as unconstitutional. If they had succeeded in storming the closet in 1767 the King would have found the executive power taken out of his hands and given to Lord Rockingham. Nor would this have meant that Lord Rockingham would have assumed the rôle of a modern prime minister at the head of a modern cabinet, for the modern cabinet is formed from the party in Parliament which has a majority, and there were no such parties in the eighteenth century. The Rockinghams were a small aristocratic clique who, even if they had been again in power at this time, would have experienced great difficulty in finding a majority in Parliament. Thus, when they eventually returned to office in 1782, they had to form a coalition with Lord Shelburne. It follows that Burke's plan for government by an aristocratic clique is unrealistic. His ideas are only superficially modern, for though he urges party he does not mean a party elected on a wide electoral franchise, or having the discipline of modern political parties. He understands party in the eighteenth-century sense of connection of

---

[1] Ibid., pp. 318–19.

friends and colleagues around a great man or number of great men. The system recommended by Burke places limitations on the King which amounts to depriving him of his executive power and lodging it with the legislative power. This is contrary to Montesquieu's ideas on both the theory and practice of the constitution, and we shall see that at a later date Burke's ideas are attacked in the name of the true constitution as expounded by Montesquieu.[1]

We have seen that in the *Present Discontents* Burke embellishes his political propaganda with ideas from Montesquieu. His use of Montesquieu's ideas here is not scholarly or disinterested as in the *Abridgment of English History*: Burke uses Montesquieu for propaganda purposes, and is not over-careful about distorting Montesquieu's ideas. There is, indeed, a sort of tension between Burke the writer and admirer of Montesquieu, and Burke the politician whose ideas on the constitution are essentially different from those of Montesquieu. Burke's first attempt to use Montesquieu's ideas for political purposes is not perhaps successful, but in his next great political campaign he has learned better how theory can be wedded to practice, and this we shall see in his works on America.

[1] See below, pp. 119–20.

CHAPTER V

BURKE AND THE AMERICAN REVOLUTION

IN 1757 William Burke, assisted by Edmund, published *An Account of the European Settlements in America*.[1] This is an historical and descriptive work, containing few political ideas, and interesting only in that it shows that at this time Burke had some interest in the American colonies, and some knowledge of their history. It was as Lord Rockingham's secretary in 1765 that Burke first became involved in the complexities of American politics, for at this time the colonies were in revolt against the Stamp Act and other restrictive measures that had been passed under the Grenville administration. Thus American affairs loomed large during Rockingham's short administration, and it was on the American problem that Burke first distinguished himself as a rising orator and 'man of business'.[2] After the fall of the Rockinghams, American affairs were again of urgent importance, especially following the Townshend duties of 1767, and the government's mishandling of the colonies was an obvious target for the opposition. However, the lack of union among the opposition, as well as the Rockinghams' dislike of the strong radical element that was becoming more pronounced in American demands, prevented Burke and his friends from identifying themselves fully with the American cause for some time. It was not until 1774, when Lord North introduced his Coercive Acts, and when the government seemed determined to stiffen their attitude to the colonies, that the Rockinghams began to make a serious attempt to formulate an American policy. It was in 1774 and 1775 that Burke delivered his great speeches on America, which embody the policy of the Rockinghams on this question. In the *Letter to the Sheriffs of Bristol*, written in 1777, he is still expressing the same policy. Burke always insisted that this had not changed since 1765, when the Rockinghams were in office, and what this policy amounted to was the recognition of the theoretical sovereignty of Great Britain, combined with, in practice, readiness to grant the colonies more or less whatever they desired, short of independence. But after the defeat of the British army at Saratoga the Rockinghams began to

---

[1] Evidence for the participation of E. Burke in this is summarized in C. B. Cone, *Burke and the Nature of Politics*, Lexington, Kentucky, 1957, pp. 29–30.

[2] Cf. above, p. 68.

press for recognition of American independence, convinced that any other solution, such as imperial connection through the Crown alone, would be subversive of the constitution, and increase the influence of the Crown. After 1777 it becomes difficult to distinguish their American policy from their attack on the influence of the Crown, and they continue the latter in the same terms as in 1769 and 1770, thus continuing the policy expounded by Burke in the *Present Discontents*. After Saratoga the opposition saw that they had some hope of dislodging Lord North from office, and it was on the failure of its American policy that the North administration eventually collapsed in March 1782, allowing the Rockinghams to return to power.

American affairs are thus inseparably connected with Burke's parliamentary career; so much, indeed, that it has been supposed that for him and the Rockinghams the American problem was merely a useful stick with which to beat the government and to force themselves back into power. The fact that since 1770 Burke was the paid agent of the New York assembly gives the impression that his efforts on behalf of America were not wholly disinterested.[1] We are not concerned here with the question of whether Burke's original motives were of the purest; but it is important to understand that his approach to the problem of America is not primarily that of a political philosopher, but of a politician dealing with urgent practical problems. The problem of America involved important constitutional principles, the fundamental question being that of imperial relationship. It is within the framework of the imperial relationship that we shall consider the connection between the thought of Montesquieu and Burke. We shall see, at the same time, that Burke becomes more skilled in wedding political propaganda and political theory, in adapting ideas from Montesquieu for his political speeches and writings.

It was after the Peace of Paris, in 1763, that the problem of the imperial connection between Britain and the American colonies assumed great importance. At this time the connection between colonies and mother country was thought of mainly in terms of trade, the function of colonies being to supply raw materials and to buy in return manufactured goods.[2] The orthodox view is expressed by Montesquieu, who in this is not original, but states in simple language what most people believed:

---

[1] For Burke as New York agent see Hoffman, op. cit.
[2] V. T. Harlow, *The Founding of the Second British Empire*, 1952, pp. 159–62.

L'objet de ces colonies est de faire le commerce à de meilleures conditions qu'on ne le fait avec les peuples voisins, avec lesquels tous les avantages sont réciproques. On a établi que la métropole seule pourrait négocier dans la colonie; et cela avec grande raison, parce que le but de l'établissement a été l'extension du commerce, non la fondation d'une ville ou d'un nouvel empire.[1]

Montesquieu points out that this system is based on the principle of monopoly, and that the ancient world offers no exact parallel to the modern phenomenon he is describing:

Ainsi, c'est encore une loi fondamentale de l'Europe, que tout commerce avec une colonie étrangère est regardé comme un pur monopole punissable par les lois du pays : et il ne faut pas juger de cela par les lois et les exemples des anciens peuples, qui n'y sont guère applicables.[2]

He explains that the colonies gain an important advantage in return for this monopoly:

Le désavantage des colonies, qui perdent la liberté du commerce, est visiblement compensé par la protection de la métropole, qui la défend par ses armes, ou la maintient par ses lois.[3]

In Montesquieu there is no vision of an imperial system based on free trade or on a system of independent colonial status. Adam Smith had not yet written the *Wealth of Nations*, and, indeed, when this was published in 1776, no politician of importance was ready to put its ideas into practice.[4] Again, the theory of the constitution, which taught that the legislative power was lodged in King, Lords and Commons, did not envisage the establishment of an independent legislature and executive in the colonies, which would have upset the system of balanced government reputed to exist. George III was a constitutional monarch in the eighteenth-century sense of the word: he admired and tried to preserve the balanced constitution. In the quarrel with America he maintained that he was trying to save the constitution: he refused to countenance the American demand for legislative independence and for an imperial link through the Crown alone, and could thus claim that he was 'fighting the balance of the legislative'. As we shall see, Burke and the Rockinghams agreed in essentials with the King's ideas on the constitutional problem, and for this reason found it difficult to oppose him without appearing factious. Although, as we have seen, they were developing new ideas on the nature of the constitution, and which, if pushed to their logical conclusion would have removed the King from politics, the very fact that they were trying to reduce the influence of the

---

[1] E.L., xxi, 21.   [2] *Idem.*   [3] *Idem.*   [4] Harlow, op. cit., p. 199.

Crown made them all the more reluctant to see the Crown alone acting as the sole bond holding together the Empire. It was only when the Crown was placed outside politics, when modern cabinet government was developed, that such an imperial connection could work smoothly. Montesquieu had no vision of what was to be known as dominion status. He was a man of the eighteenth century, and was unable to foresee what the nineteenth and twentieth centuries would learn through experience. The most important part of this experience was that which centred around the American and Irish problems in the eighteenth century. In his *Notes sur l'Angleterre* Montesquieu had written,

Je crois que si quelque nation est abandonnée de ses colonies, cela commencera par la nation anglaise.[1]

But he did not develop this point, which is little more than a *pensée*. Even if he had developed it there is nothing to indicate that he might have been able to suggest a solution to the imperial problems which confronted England after 1763.[2]

When the Rockingham administration was formed in July 1765 it was almost immediately faced with the urgent problems of the colonies. For some time the amount of independence that was enjoyed by the provincial legislatures, and the economic growth of the colonies, had been making the relations between them and Britain uneasy. When, in 1763, the colonies were removed from all fear of the French in Canada, the need of defence by Britain was less urgently felt. George Grenville, during his administration, tried to revise the relations between Britain and America, by insisting on a strict application of the existing commercial regulations; and when he tried to raise money from America by means of the Stamp Act, all the latent differences between the colonies and the mother country appeared. It was with the disturbances in America that followed Grenville's measures that the Rockinghams were confronted in 1765.

Lord Rockingham and those who later composed his ministry had not opposed Grenville's measures on America in 1763-64. The problem of the relationship with the colonies was not thrust upon men's notice in a serious way until the effects of Grenville's legisla-

[1] *Œuvres* (Pléiade), i, p. 883.

[2] For discussion of the fundamental imperial problem see: Sir Lewis Namier, *England in the Age of the American Revolution*, 1930; G. H. Guttridge, *English Whiggism and the American Revolution*, California, 1942; E. Robson, *The American Revolution*, 1955; C. H. McIlwain, *The American Revolution*, New York, 1923; R. L. Schuyler, *Parliament and the British Empire*, New York, 1929.

tion were seen. Grenville had simply attempted to revise some already existing laws, and in passing the Stamp Act his ministry were acting within their legal rights to legislate for the colonies.

The Rockingham ministry's first reaction to American violence was not one of sympathy, and orders were given for the disturbances to be repressed while a policy was being formulated.[1] They were eager to enlist Pitt's support; but he refused to communicate his ideas, and the policy eventually arrived at could be claimed by the Rockinghams as their own. If they were unable to receive support within Parliament from Pitt, there was another source which they proved very eager to accept. The disturbances in America were reflected in England by a national agitation among the merchants, whose trade had been affected since the disturbances began. This section of the public, which was well represented in Parliament, proved a valuable support for the ministry. Dowdeswell and Burke were active in arranging meetings and consultations with the merchants; and it was after such meetings that the ministry decided to repeal the Stamp Act.[2] At the same time, however, the ministry were unable to accept the implication that the British Parliament had no right to tax the colonies. To avoid this implication, the repeal of the Stamp Act was preceded by the Declaratory Act, which confirmed the right of Britain to legislate for the colonies. These measures, introduced in February 1766, were the occasion of lively debates, of which only fragments survive, though in the *Annual Register* there is a masterly summary, possibly written by Burke.[3]

The ministerial policy was, naturally enough, opposed by George Grenville, who, defending his own previous policy, said that it was not only right, but also expedient, to tax the colonies. The ministers were also opposed by Chatham, whose argument was more subtle: he declared that Parliament never had the right to impose taxes, taxes having always been freely granted by the subject. He maintained that to impose taxes would be to infringe the natural right of property. His appeal was to the fundamental law of the constitution, which it was beyond the power of Parliament to alter. At the same time he maintained that Parliament was sovereign over all 'external' taxation, by which he meant trade regulations. Thus, though he

---

[1] C. R. Ritcheson, *British Politics and the American Revolution*, Oklahoma, 1954, pp. 41–42.
[2] L. S. Sutherland, 'E. Burke and the first Rockingham administration', EHR, 47 (1932), pp. 46–72.
[3] *Annual Register*, 1766, chap. vii.

supported the repeal of the Stamp Act, he refused to countenance the Declaratory Act.[1] The policy of the Rockinghams can be seen as a compromise between the opposing policies of Grenville and Chatham: in theory they agreed with Grenville, but in practice with Chatham. This has been variously judged as the best that could be done at the time, or as a piece of miserable shuffling, which, if it repealed the offending Stamp Act, passed the Declaratory Act, which opened the way for later grievances.[2] It must be allowed, however, that their policy required some courage, carried as it was against the formidable opposition of Chatham, and in spite of a misunderstanding with the King, who would have preferred modification to repeal.[3] Indeed, the Rockinghams were rather proud of their American policy, and never tired of giving it as an example of their 'consistency'.[4] Also, they could consider this policy as consistent with their Whiggism. They thought of the Glorious Revolution as the time when the Whigs had stood for the sovereignty of Parliament (i.e. the King in Parliament) as against the sovereignty of the King alone. In passing the Declaratory Act they were reaffirming the legislative supremacy of Parliament, and to this extent could claim that they were following Whig tradition. What they did not seem to notice, however, was that their Whiggism upheld the supremacy of Parliament not against the Crown—as in 1688—but against the American subjects. The Rockinghams' Whiggism was not like that of Chatham, which reached back to the doctrines of Locke and taught that the subjects had natural rights against their governors. The Rockinghams disliked anything that savoured of radicalism, and their object was not to discuss the constitution in terms of natural rights, but rather to maintain the *status quo*, the mixed and balanced system of government of the eighteenth century, and the electoral system weighted in favour of the aristocracy. Thus, while the Declaratory Act reaffirmed the supremacy of Parliament, this supremacy, as far as the Rockinghams were concerned, must be preserved intact on all sides, from below as well as from above.[5]

Burke's policy on America was formed from the necessity of taking some kind of action during a period of violent disturbances in the colonies. He does not appear to have drawn his policy on this

---

[1] P.H., xvi, pp. 97–108.
[2] See J. Brooke, *The Chatham Administration*, 1956; R. Pares, Review of Brooke, EHR, 72 (1957), pp. 333–37.
[3] See above, p. 69.   [4] Albemarle, op. cit., ii, p. 80.
[5] For this paragraph see Guttridge, op. cit., chap. i.

question from political thinkers, and, indeed, it was said, on the ministerial side, during the debates on the repeal:

> They observed it was necessary to clear away from the question, all that mass of dissertation and learning, displayed in arguments which have been brought from speculative men, who have written upon the subject of government. That the refinements upon that subject, and arguments of natural lawyers, as Locke, Selden, Puffendorf, and others, are little to the purpose in a question of constitutional law.[1]

Such authorities are irrelevant, it is maintained, because 'it is absurd to apply records from the earliest times to our present constitution', for 'the constitution is not the same'. It was also said that analogies with the colonies of antiquity were 'a mere useless display of learning'.[2] Montesquieu is not mentioned as one of the 'speculative men' whose learning is irrelevant to the problem; but we have seen that he has no help to offer on this subject, which was essentially a new one.

The Rockingham administration was succeeded by that of Chatham, and it was in 1767 that Charles Townshend, contrary to the policy of his fellow-ministers, declared that there was no difference between internal and external taxation, and introduced the series of taxes associated with his name. These taxes were resisted by the colonies, who now likewise rejected the distinction between internal and external taxes, and, becoming more exasperated and more radical, soon reached the stage where they wanted complete independence from the legislature of England, though they were willing to retain their loyalty to the Crown. At this time the Rockinghams did not play a conspicuous part in American affairs, though Burke himself spoke against the Townshend duties, and predicted that not a single shilling would be gained from the colonies.[3] The truth was that the Rockinghams were embarrassed by the violence of the American rebels and the radical nature of their demands, and thus were no longer willing to give them unqualified support.[4] They were quite clear on one point, however: to remain faithful to the policy they had formed while in office. Thus Lord Rockingham writes,

> The Declaratory Bill, which *we* brought in to fix and ascertain the rights of this country over its colonies, is what I must and shall ever adhere to. The exerting of that *right* is a matter which ought to be well considered, and the ability of the colonies ought to be the first postulatum ground to go upon.[5]

---

[1] *Annual Register*, 1766, p. 39.   [2] *Idem.*   [3] *Cavendish's Debates*, i, p. 39.
[4] See Dowdeswell's memorandum to Rockingham, Dowdeswell MSS., William Clements Library, Ann Arbor, quoted by Guttridge, op. cit., pp. 66–68.
[5] Albemarle, op. cit., ii, p. 80.

We see here a hardening of the attitude of the Rockinghams. Burke, like his leader, insists on the consistency of their policy, and—until they thought independence inevitable—their policy remains essentially the same.

In 1768 and 1769 the Rockinghams were eager to form some sort of united opposition, but this was difficult because of disagreement on American affairs. We have seen that the Middlesex elections and the subsequent petitioning did much to bring different sections of the opposition together. At the same time discussion of American policy could hardly be avoided, and when, in September 1769 Grenville's 'man of business', Whately, sounded Burke on the attitude of the Rockinghams to America, the reply is something of a surprise: Whately having said that if the repeal of revenue laws was proposed the Grenvilles would oppose, Burke replied,

> that as for himself, he hardly thought he should oppose; most probably he should absent himself; for his friends, many of them agreed in his principles, and some of them did not go so far.[1]

Thus at this time Burke and Rockingham appear to have been more interested in forming a strong opposition to dislodge Grafton than in serving the cause of America, which, as we have noted, was now too radical in outlook for most of the followers of Rockingham.

In March 1770 Lord North, now head of administration, proposed the repeal of all the Townshend duties, except that on tea, thus making concessions in a direction that the Rockinghams could not oppose, and also revealing weaknesses in the opposition, who differed among themselves on this question. Burke did not speak in this debate.[2] He did, however, make various references to America during 1770, his policy being simply a continuation of that of 1765-66:

> I shall not now enquire into the right of Great Britain to tax her colonies, 'all that is lawful is not expedient', and, I believe the inexpediency of taxing our colonies, even supposing it to be lawful, is now evident to every man in this Kingdom.[3]

Again, speaking in November, Burke said of the colonies that 'their support must be purchased by the removal of every cause of discontent', and adds,

> This is the only charm which can draw their affection, which can cement and unite the different members of the empire, and make it act, as if inspired by one soul.[4]

[1] *Grenville Papers*, iv, p. 449.   [2] The debate is in *Cavendish's Debates*, i, p. 483 seq.
[3] P.H., xvi, p. 725; Cf. P.H., xvi, p. 1003.   [4] P.H., xvi, p. 1044.

Thus the Rockinghams, though they disliked the radicalism of the Americans, were forced to trim their sails to the prevailing demands. But American policy was not a major item in the Rockingham creed at this time: we can see this from the *Present Discontents*, which, though it mentions 'influence and corruption' has nothing to say on America.

In 1772 and 1773 American affairs did not play an important part in parliamentary debates, nor did they afford much opportunity to the now disunited and discredited opposition to attack the ministry. Indeed, the Rockinghams were in essentials in agreement with the policy of Lord North at this time, and one of their supporters, Lord Dartmouth, became Secretary of State for the Colonies. However, in March 1774, following reports of the Boston riots, Lord North introduced a series of Coercive Acts against the colonies, and the Rockinghams began to think that at last they had an opportunity to become active again in opposition.[1] They were hindered, however, in that they were disunited among themselves, not all of them being prepared to sympathize with the colonists;[2] but they were in general agreement that the ministry were incompetent to deal with American affairs, and that the Rockingham policy of 1765–66 had been the right one. This policy is the basis of Burke's great speeches on America delivered in 1774 and 1775. In these speeches Burke is essentially summarizing and idealizing the Rockingham policy.

Burke's first major work on America is his great speech on *American Taxation*, delivered on April 19, 1774. In this speech, Burke, while maintaining the supremacy of Great Britain over the colonies, lays great stress on the importance for the legislator to attempt only what is expedient, and what is acceptable to the opinions and feelings of the colonists. Townshend made the mistake of trying to legislate against the grain, and the result of his taxes was that they 'filled the minds of the colonists with new jealousy, and all sorts of apprehensions',[3] leading them to quarrel with both the old and the new taxes, and to question the nature of their relationship with Great Britain. This policy, Burke thinks, was based on a misunderstanding of human nature, for,

no commodity will bear three-pence, or will bear a penny, when the general feelings of men are irritated, and two millions of people are resolved not to pay.[4]

This insistence on the importance of the collective feelings of the

---

[1] Albemarle, op. cit., ii, pp. 240–1.   [2] Ibid., ii, pp. 241–3.
[3] *Works*, i, p. 386.   [4] Ibid., p. 392.

people has an obvious kinship with the doctrine of the *esprit général*, though, as yet, the kinship does not amount to borrowing. Burke calls his principle simply one of 'expediency', using the terminology of the debates of 1765–66. It is in terms of expediency that he defends the traditional mercantile system, in the context of which the colonies were governed. He does not pretend that the system of monopoly is perfect; but he defends it as being compensated by certain advantages, such as the benefit of British capital and British institutions.[1] But the really important point, in Burke's opinion, is that the colonies were happy with this system until Grenville began to tamper with it. In this Burke is being unfair to Grenville, and he is minimizing the friction which was not unknown between Britain and the colonies before 1763.

If Burke devotes part of his speech to urging the importance of following the expedient, he also devotes much space to attacking attempts to apply abstract theory to the practical problems of politics, and much of what he says is simply a repetition of what he had said in the *Observations* of 1769:

> The spirit of practicability, of moderation, and mutual convenience, will never call in geometrical exactness as the arbitrator of an amicable settlement. Consult and follow your experience.[2]

In a more famous passage he says,

> leave America, if she has taxable matter in her, to tax herself. I am not here going into the distinction of rights, not attempting to mark their boundaries. I do not enter into these metaphysical distinctions; I hate the very sound of them.[3]

It is only by governing America in a way that respects the character and temper of the people, that respects their traditions, that we can hope for a revenue of any kind. Burke mentions that one of the advantages of his policy is that it does not disrupt the traditional pattern of imperial relations: the imperial rights of Great Britain and the 'privileges which the colonists ought to enjoy under these rights' are for him 'the most reconcilable things in the world'. The British Parliament, he says, has two capacities: one as 'the local legislature of this island, providing for all things at home, immediately, and by no other instrument than the executive power'. The other,

> and I think her nobler capacity, is what I call her *imperial character*; in which, as from the throne of heaven, she superintends all the several inferior legislatures, and guides and controls them all, without annihilating any.[4]

---

[1] Cf. E.L., xix, 27, paragraphs 33, 35.　　　　　[2] *Works*, i, p. 431.
[3] Ibid., p. 432.　　　　　[4] Ibid., p. 434.

The supreme power is to be held in reserve, to be used, for example, only in the case of disputes between the colonies, and for organizing the trade of the Empire.

Burke's ideas on imperial relations as expressed here are commonplace, in that they are based on the Navigation Laws. His insistence on the difference between the right and the expedient originates in the debates of 1765–66. But once he is in possession of this principle of expediency, Burke deepens it and examines its implications. He sees that the most important implications of the principle are that politics must be based on an understanding of human nature, and of the temper and character of the governed, and that this temper and character is to some extent determined by tradition and past experience. All these ideas, highly suggestive of the *esprit général*, are more or less present in the speech on *Taxation;* but it is not possible to say whether Burke was thinking of Montesquieu's theory at the time. It is, however, in Burke's speech on *Conciliation*, delivered in the following year, that we see the clearest influence of this doctrine on Burke.

The great speech on *Conciliation* was delivered on March 22, 1775. This year was, at least at first, an exciting one for the opposition, for Lord North's Coercive Acts were an obvious target for attack, and at this time Chatham, who had been absent from Parliament for some time, returned and opposed the ministry. However, he refused to ally himself with the Rockinghams, and even went so far as to attack the Declaratory Act.[1] The Rockinghams also suffered from the lack of support from public opinion, and especially from the merchants who had supported them in 1766. Thus as a small opposition group they cut a rather sorry figure, and their opposition appeared factious. But they made one great effort in opposing the ministry on American policy, and their greatest spokesman was Burke, in his speech on *Conciliation*. This is fundamentally the same as the speech on *Taxation*, but Burke tries to make it more than a mere piece of ordinary political propaganda: he attempts to analyse the temper and character of the Americans which has caused the revolt in the colonies; and he adopts, for this end, the historical method of Montesquieu.

Burke's attitude to the problem is that of a sociologist: he condemns abstract theory and urges an empirical approach:

Because after all our struggle, whether we will or not, we must govern America according to that nature, and to those circumstances; and not according to our own

[1] P.H., xviii, pp. 149–60.

imaginations; nor according to abstract ideas of right; by no means according to mere general theories of government, the resort to which appears to me, in our present situation, no better than arrant trifling.[1]

He then proceeds directly to an analysis of the empirical facts which the legislator must first consider. Burke first considers the question of the population of the colonies, their trade, agriculture and fisheries, and with an array of facts and figures, traces the increase of the prosperity of the colonists since the beginning of their settlements. He admires the growth of the colonies, which has taken place with the minimum of interference from the legislature:

> through a wise and salutary neglect, a generous nature has been suffered to take her own way to perfection.[2]

Turning more closely to the character of the colonists, Burke finds that the predominating feature is a love of freedom: they have a 'fierce spirit of liberty' which 'is stronger in the English colonies probably than in any other people of the earth'.[3] The important point—and this is where Burke comes closest to Montesquieu—is that this national spirit emanates

> from a great variety of powerful causes; which, to understand the true temper of their minds, and the direction which this spirit takes, it will not be amiss to lay open somewhat more largely.[4]

There follows a remarkable analysis of the various causes, physical and moral, which combine to produce this national spirit of liberty. Burke applies to a practical political problem the technique of Montesquieu's historical method which, until this time had been applied only, in a scholarly way, to the past.

The first cause of this spirit of liberty Burke finds in the fact that the colonists are the descendants of Englishmen, and that they migrated at a time when liberty was the most prominent feature of the English national character: the liberty they possess in the colonies is therefore 'liberty according to English ideas, and on English principles'.[5] Mere abstract liberty does not exist: 'Liberty adheres in some sensible object; and every nation has formed to itself some favourite point, which by way of eminence becomes the criterion of their happiness'.[6] In the ancient commonwealths liberty depended mainly on the right of electing magistrates,[7] and sometimes 'on the balance among the several orders of the state'.[8] But in England

---

[1] *Works*, i, p. 456.   [2] Ibid., p. 462.   [3] Ibid., p. 464.   [4] *Idem*.
[5] *Idem*; Cf. E.L., xix, 27, paragraph 35.   [6] *Idem*; Cf. E.L., xi, 2.
[7] *Idem*; Cf. E.L., ii, 2.   [8] *Idem*.

the essential point on which liberty depended was that the people themselves had control of public revenue: the great struggles of the seventeenth century between King and Parliament were mainly for the right to control public expenditure. Burke sees the colonists applying arguments of this kind, which had been used in England before 1688, and he stresses that his examination of this is objective:

> I do not say whether they were right or wrong in applying your general arguments to their own case. . . . The fact is, that they did thus apply those general arguments.[1]

He does not commit himself as approving or disapproving of the colonists' arguments: he is simply analysing causes.

The second factor that Burke considers as a cause of the American character is their form of government: they had provincial assemblies elected on a fairly broad basis and,

> this share of the people in their ordinary government never fails to inspire them with lofty sentiments and with a strong aversion from whatever tends to deprive them of their chief importance.[2]

Montesquieu had shown that the laws and institutions of a nation could be traced to the general spirit; but he also shows that these laws and institutions, once formed, in turn influence the spirit which produced them. This is the theme of one of the chapters of the *Esprit des lois* devoted to the British constitution.[3] Here Montesquieu shows that the institutions of England tend to reinforce the spirit of liberty which produced them. Burke's analysis of the influence of American institutions on the American character embodies similar principles.

Another factor analysed by Burke as contributory to the formation of the American character is their religion. This he finds relevant especially in the north, where the people are Protestants, and mainly Dissenters. He stresses the point, very obvious in the eighteenth century, that Dissenters were impatient of authority, religious and political. If in the north the factor of religion is important, in the south the spirit of freedom among the colonists is increased by the presence of slaves. Burke maintains that the effect of the institution of slavery is to make the masters proud and jealous of their freedom. He abstains from making a moral judgement: he is writing as a sociologist seeking causes, and not as a moralist:

> I do not mean, Sir, to commend the superior morality of this sentiment, which has at least as much pride as virtue in it; but I cannot alter the nature of man. The fact is so.[4]

[1] Ibid., p. 465. [2] *Idem.* [3] E.L., xix, 27. [4] *Works*, i, p. 467.

H

After briefly considering the importance in the colonies of education as a factor which influenced the general character of the people, Burke concludes his analysis with consideration of a physical factor: the colonies are separated from Britain by three thousand miles of ocean, and 'No contrivance can prevent the effect of this distance in weakening government'.[1] With possible reminiscences of Montesquieu's *Romains* Burke writes,

Nothing worse happens to you than does to all nations who have extensive empire; and it happens in all the forms into which empire can be thrown. In large bodies, the circulation of power must be less vigorous at the extremities.[2]

He concludes, after giving a number of examples of such empires, 'This is the immutable condition, the eternal law, of extensive and detached empire'.[3]

In this analysis of the character of the colonies the resemblance of Burke's method to that of Montesquieu is striking. We have noted similarities of detail, but these are less important than the fact that Burke applies and understands Montesquieu's method. Like Montesquieu, Burke attempts to consider sociological data objectively, and to separate moral judgements from the task of seeking causes. Thus Burke, though he disapproves of slavery,[4] confines himself to stating that the existence of slavery in the colonies is an empirical fact, and as such has an effect on the character of the colonists. Montesquieu, likewise, though he condemns slavery, attempts to make his analysis of it objective, and his failure to be completely objective calls from him the cry:

Je ne sais si c'est l'esprit ou le cœur qui me dicte cet article-ci.[5]

Burke never tires of stressing his objectivity: 'I do not mean to commend either the spirit in this excess, or the moral causes which produce it'.[6] For him the question is, 'not whether their spirit deserves praise or blame, but—what, in the the name of God, shall we do with it?'[7] There are three possible solutions to the problem:

To change that spirit, as inconvenient, by removing the causes. To prosecute it as criminal. Or, to comply with it as necessary.[8]

Each of these possibilities he examines in detail.

Burke's consideration of the first proposition is of particular interest. Montesquieu had pointed out that as existing laws were the

---

[1] Ibid., pp. 468–9.   [2] *Idem*. Cf. *Romains*, chap. 6.   [3] Ibid., p. 469.
[4] For Burke's true opinion of slavery see *Works*, v, p. 524 seq. (*Sketch of the Negro Code*), written in 1788.
[5] E.L., xv, 8.   [6] *Works*, i, p. 469.   [7] *Idem*.   [8] Ibid., p. 472.

product of the *esprit général* they could only be changed if the *esprit général* were itself changed, and this involved changing the factors that are its cause.[1] Montesquieu summarizes his theory thus:

> Ainsi, lorsqu'un prince veut faire de grands changements dans sa nation, il faut qu'il réforme par les lois ce qui est établi par les lois, et qu'il change par les manières ce qui est établi par les manières : et c'est une très mauvaise politique de changer par les lois ce qui doit être changé par les manières.[2]

This is exactly the principle we find in Burke, when he says that the plan 'to change the spirit . . . by removing the causes' is 'the most like a systematic proceeding'.[3] In considering this plan he quickly surveys the physical and moral causes he had already enumerated as sources of the spirit of liberty. The population of the colonies cannot be diminished, and the ruin of their trade would be contrary to England's interests. The other factors of descent, religion, education, cannot be changed. With regard to slavery, which he had given as a factor, Burke is on less certain ground when—for the sake of the symmetry of his argument, one feels—he says that this likewise cannot be changed: he says that there had been plans to enfranchise slaves, but he was never really in favour of it: 'Slaves are often much attached to their masters. A general wild offer of liberty would not always be accepted'.[4] He is on firmer ground when he says that if enfranchisement is to take place it would be more natural for it to come from the Americans themselves. However, even if these various factors, including slavery, could be changed, Burke points out that there is one fundamental physical factor which is unchangeable:

> But let us suppose all these moral difficulties got over. The Ocean remains. You cannot pump this dry; and as long as it continues in its present bed, so long all the causes which weaken authority by distance will continue.[5]

The causes, physical and moral, remaining unchangeable, the spirit will remain the same:

> the spirit infallibly will continue; and, continuing, will produce such effects as now embarrass us.[6]

Burke rejects the second plan for dealing with the American spirit of liberty by attempting to 'prosecute that spirit . . . as criminal', on the grounds that 'I do not know the method of drawing up an indictment against a whole people'.[7] Burke does not develop the full implications of this remark: he does not consider, for example, the

---

[1] Cf. above, p. 22. [2] E.L., xix, 14. [3] *Works*, i, p. 472.
[4] Ibid., p. 475. [5] *Idem*. [6] *Idem*. [7] Ibid., p. 476.

hypothetical case of a nation of cannibals. But he is writing political propaganda, where his aim is to persuade that the governors must follow the demands of the governed, and he passes on at once to the last alternative: 'to comply with the American spirit as necessary; or, if you please, to submit to it as a necessary evil'.[1] However, for Burke, granting the Americans what they want, complying with their natural spirit is not an evil but a duty. He brushes aside all consideration of legal rights, the 'great Serbonian bog' of discussion, and he places the question on the level of moral rights:

> The question with me is, not whether you have a right to render your people miserable; but whether it is not your interest to make them happy. It is not, what a lawyer tells me I *may* do; but what humanity, reason, and justice tell me I ought to do.[2]

Even if the colonists had 'sealed a regular compact of servitude', Burke says, 'I should hold myself obliged to conform to the temper I found universally prevalent in my own day'.[3] Therefore, for Burke, to follow the temper and spirit of the people would appear to be the same thing as obeying the higher moral law. He does not face the difficulties which such a statement involves, but this is mainly because he is writing as a propagandist and not as a political philosopher eager to present a logically coherent argument. It should be noted, however, that Burke's conception of the general spirit of the Americans as 'a generous nature' which has 'been suffered to take her own way to perfection'[4] helps to explain why he identifies following this spirit with moral duty. We have seen that Montesquieu too has great faith in human nature, and counsels the legislator to follow the general spirit at practically all costs. Montesquieu had also advised the legislator to keep in sight the Natural Law, and, if necessary, gradually to change the *esprit général*. Burke understood this, and his remarks on Agricola in the *Abridgment of English History* show that he believed that the general spirit could be changed.[5] In the speech on *Conciliation*, however, he is much more rigid in his insistence on the fact that the legislator must follow the character and inclinations of the people. The Rockinghams found that this was the most profitable theme to develop for the purposes of opposition; even though they disapproved of American radicalism.

The remainder of Burke's speech is devoted to his ideas on the imperial relationship, with which we are already sufficiently familiar.

---

[1] *Works*, i, p. 478.   [2] Ibid., p. 479.   [3] Ibid., p. 480.
[4] Ibid., p. 462.   [5] See above, pp. 51–2.

He still insists on the supremacy of Great Britain, but dislikes discussion of this legalistic point. He admits that the line between the authority of Great Britain and that of the provincial assemblies is not easily drawn, and is willing to make fairly large concessions, taking as model the example of Ireland. He has great praise to bestow on the system which bound together England and Ireland, which, in view of what was to happen in 1782, was hardly a felicitous example, and simply shows Burke's narrowness on imperial problems. Burke seems to think it is enough simply to grant the Americans what they want, without any legislative reorganization of the Empire, and all will be well:

> My hold of the colonies is in the close affection which grows from common names, from kindred blood, from similar privileges, and equal protection. These are ties, which, though light as air, are as strong as links of iron.[1]

Burke fails to indicate how exactly this is to be defined in terms of legislation, and there is a vagueness about his ideas on America which reveals his inability to grapple with the fundamentals of the problem. However, his propaganda theme of complying with the temper of the people, bolstered up with Montesquieu's technique of analysis of sociological phenomena, reveals great literary skill. But though his application of Montesquieu's method is more skilful than in the *Abridgment*, it is still, in places, rather rigid, especially where he is dealing with the factor of slavery. The total result is, however, impressive, and shows a considerable understanding of the American character. It is ironical that Burke, who understood so well the American character, should not have understood that it was incompatible with the form of parliamentary supremacy that the Rockinghams had been urging since 1766.

In spite of Burke's efforts and speeches, the Rockinghams were as far as ever from office; and when in June 1775 news that war had started with the colonies reached England, they reached the depths of despair, for, in resisting the colonies, Lord North had the force of public opinion behind him. In a letter written to Rockingham at this time Burke pours out his feelings: realizing that North has public support, Burke thinks that the opposition should take stock of public feeling and direct it into another channel:

> To bring the people to a feeling, such a feeling, I mean, as tends to amendment, or alteration of system, there must be plan and management. All direction of public humour and opinion must originate in a few. . . . I never yet knew an

---

[1] *Works*, i, p. 508.

instance of any general temper in the nation, that might not have been tolerably well traced to some particular persons.[1]

Thus, while in public Burke is preaching the importance of yielding to the general temper of the people, in private he sees the importance, for the Rockinghams, of changing it. On the one hand he minimizes the importance of the legislator, whereas on the other the legislator is the key to the situation. If Burke were writing as a pure theorist this contradiction would be difficult to explain; but as he was a politician and propagandist, a more cynical view is permissible. Burke believed that the Rockingham policy of 1766 was the best for America, and any arguments which could support this view were grist to his mill.

The policy of the Rockinghams at this time sank to an almost negative attitude. We find Burke writing,

A minority cannot make or carry on a war; but a minority, well composed and acting steadily, may clog a war in such a manner, as to make it not very easy to proceed.[2]

At the same time the most ardent supporters of the American cause in England were radicals, such as Parson John Horne and the members of the Society of the Supporters of the Bill of Rights, and the Rockinghams felt uncomfortable with such allies. More than ever they appeared a small aristocratic clique, without public support, and yet holding aloof from other Englishmen who sympathized with the colonists.

In November 1775 Burke introduced his second plan for conciliation.[3] There are signs here of a more flexible approach to the question of parliamentary supremacy: Burke says he had always wished to preserve the legislative supremacy of Great Britain over the colonies, but the blunders of North's government had made further concessions necessary. He maintains that the Parliament of Great Britain is the sovereign power over America and that,

the sovereignty was not in its nature an abstract idea of unity, but was capable of great complexity and infinite modifications, according to the temper of those who are to be governed, and to the circumstances of things; which being infinitely diversified, government ought to be adapted to them, and to conform itself to the nature of things, and not to endeavour to force them.[4]

Thus, though taxation is inherent in the supreme power in the state, it does not follow that it must reside in any particular power in that

---

[1] *Corr.*, ii, pp. 48–49.   [2] Ibid., ii, p. 55.   [3] P.H., xviii, p. 963 seq.
[4] Ibid., pp. 973–4.

state: Parliament can, by its own act, 'put the local power of the purse into other hands than its own, without disclaiming its just prerogative in other particulars'.[1] There is a great deal of face-saving here, for Burke was unwilling to see the repeal of the Declaratory Act, and at the same time he exploits anew the line taken in the speech on *Conciliation*, the importance of conforming to the temper of the people. But his essential views are unchanged.

Burke's second plan for conciliation being defeated, there seemed to be little hope for the Rockinghams. In the following year there was an increase in radicalism both in England and America, producing such works as Richard Price's *Observations on the Nature of Society*, Cartwright's *Take Your Choice*, and Paine's *Common Sense*. In July the Declaration of Independence was made. The Rockinghams, faced with the triumph of radicalism, found themselves in a very difficult situation, and after playing no very conspicuous part in Parliament, they withdrew from it in November. In this withdrawal they were not, however, unanimous, and Charles James Fox, who by this time was associated with them, remained in attendance.[2] It was during this period of abstention that Lord North introduced a bill to suspend the Habeas Corpus Act in cases of high treason. This measure tempted the Rockinghams to return to Parliament to defend what they regarded as one of the fundamental Whig liberties; but Burke was one of those who refused to return.[3] This refusal offended his constituents at Bristol and provoked from him the *Letter to the Sheriffs of Bristol*, which contains an important exposition of his American policy at this time.

It is worth noting briefly here another issue which arose in connection with Burke's election for Bristol, in the autumn of 1774. The question whether members should receive instructions was much discussed in the eighteenth century,[4] and in one of his speeches made to his constituents in 1774[5] Burke expresses his views on this question. Montesquieu had himself mentioned this problem, and was of the opinion that in England,

Il n'est pas nécessaire que les représentants, qui ont reçu de ceux qui les ont choisis une instruction générale, en reçoivent une particulière sur chaque affaire, comme cela se pratique dans les diètes d'Allemagne.[6]

---

[1] Ibid., p. 974.
[2] Lord John Russell, *Memorials and Correspondence of C. J. Fox*, 4 vols., 1853, i, pp. 144–54.
[3] Ibid., p. 154.
[4] E. and A. G. Porritt, *The Unreformed House of Commons*, 2 vols., Cambridge, 1909, i, pp. 263–6.
[5] *Speech at the Conclusion of the Poll, Works*, i, pp. 442–9.   [6] E.L., xi, 6.

He thinks that,

> Le corps représentant ne doit pas être choisi non plus pour prendre quelque résolution active, chose qu'il ne ferait pas bien; mais pour faire des lois ou pour voir si l'on a bien exécuté celles qu'il a faites, chose qu'il peut très bien faire, et qu'il n'y a même que lui qui puisse bien faire.[1]

Burke is in agreement with Montesquieu. He says that the member should always consider the interests, welfare and opinions of his constituents, but, in the last resort, his decisions should depend on his own independent judgement:

> But *authoritative* instructions; *mandates* issued, which the member is bound blindly and implicitly to obey, to vote, and to argue for, though contrary to the clearest conviction of his judgment and conscience,—these are things utterly unknown to the laws of the land, and which arise from a fundamental mistake of the whole order and tenor of our constitution.[2]

Thus, once again, Burke stresses the importance of the independence of the legislator, who should not blindly follow the inclinations of the people.

It is in the *Letter to the Sheriffs of Bristol* that we find the clearest exposition of Burke's ideas on the task of the legislator. He writes,

> In effect, to follow, not to force the public inclination; to give a direction, a form, a technical dress, and a specific sanction, to the general sense of the community, is the true end of legislature.[3]

This is in agreement with Montesquieu, though, as it stands, it tends to minimize the rôle of the legislator. Montesquieu had written, 'C'est au législateur à suivre l'esprit de la nation', but he at once makes the reservation, 'lorsqu'il n'est pas contraire aux principes du gouvernement'. Burke minimizes such reservations here probably because he is writing for propaganda purposes, as in the speech on *Conciliation*. There follows, in the *Letter*, a passage which, though long, is worth quoting, as it is an excellent summary of Burke's American policy at this time:

> instead of troubling our understandings with speculations concerning the unity of empire, and the identity or distinction of legislative powers, and inflaming our passions with the heat and pride of controversy, it was our duty, in all soberness, to conform our government to the character and circumstances of the several people who composed this mighty and strangely diversified mass. I never was wild enough to conceive, that one method would serve for the whole; that the natives of Hindustan and those of Virginia could be ordered in the same manner; or that the Cutchery Court and the grand jury of Salem could be regulated on a similar

[1] E.L., xi, 6.   [2] *Works*, i, p. 447.   [3] Ibid., ii, p. 27.

plan. I was persuaded that government was a practical thing, made for the happiness of mankind, and not to furnish out a spectacle of uniformity, to gratify the schemes of visionary politicians.[1]

In this passage we have Burke at his best and his worst on the problem of America: his refusal to contemplate the question of the surrender of parliamentary sovereignty; and his understanding of the practical nature of political problems, requiring an understanding of the temper and character of the people. Once again Burke affirms his belief in an empirical approach to politics, and his dislike of abstractions. He still tends to reduce the rôle of the legislator merely to following the spirit of the people:

If any ask me what a free government is, I answer, that, for any practical purpose, it is what the people think so; and that they, and not I, are the natural, lawful, and competent judges of this matter.[2]

Abstract liberty has no relevance to political problems; the real liberty one finds in states is 'variously mixed and modified, enjoyed in very different degrees', and it is 'shaped into an infinite diversity of forms, according to the temper and circumstances of every community'.[3] Burke believes that we cannot expect to find liberty in its pure metaphysical form in society; but that we do find free institutions. Montesquieu had shown, likewise, that liberty has many forms, inherent in different institutions.[4]

Although Burke recommends that the legislator should follow the spirit of the people, he finally feels obliged to admit that a certain degree of restraint must be placed on this spirit by the legislator. However, 'the degree of restraint it is impossible . . . to settle precisely': it ought to be discovered 'by cautious experiments, and rational, cool endeavours, with how little, not how much, of this restraint, the community can subsist'.[5] Thus Burke recommends a careful empirical trial-and-error approach to political questions.

In his condemnation of abstractions in politics Burke is not so much following Montesquieu as drawing on commonplaces of political thought. But he obviously owes a great deal to Montesquieu, especially in his insistence that the general spirit must be followed, and his technique of analysing this spirit in terms of physical and moral factors.

Burke's *Letter to the Sheriffs of Bristol* had been written to justify the abstention of the Rockinghams from Parliament. This abstention had not been a success, and in April 1777 they returned, and

---

[1] Ibid., pp. 28–29. [2] *Idem.* [3] Ibid., p. 30.
[4] E.L., xi, 2. [5] *Works*, ii, pp. 30–31.

continued to attack the government as best they could on the old charges of 'corruption' and 'influence' of the Crown.[1] Once again, their cause seemed hopeless, and in September Burke admitted that he had lost interest in politics, not having looked at a newspaper for a month.[2] By November, however, they began to hope that the moment was near when their opposition could prove effective, and the Duke of Richmond wrote to Lord Rockingham outlining a programme of attack:

> If we push enquiries this winter upon the misconduct of the war; if we bring to light the infamous jobs that are carrying on; if we call forth the attention of the nation to the losses, to the expenses; I do not despair but that the bad successes which must attend another campaign, and chiefly the little advances our armies can make, will by that time operate to some effect.[3]

The cause of all the disasters he finds simply in the 'overgrown influence of the Crown'.[4]

Events reached a crisis when in December 1777 news of the defeat of the British army at Saratoga arrived. The opposition could now count on public opinion being indignant against the government; but unfortunately the consequences of the American victory were to cause a fresh disagreement between the Rockingham and Chatham wings of the opposition. In February 1778 Lord North introduced a number of Conciliatory Propositions granting America practically everything asked, short of independence. Burke and his friends accepted these proposals with much ill-humour, complaining that they should have been introduced sooner.[5] At the same time, the Rockinghams were trimming their own policy to America, and disliking North's proposals, which amounted to a connection with America through the Crown alone, they felt their way towards granting America independence. On December 5 one of their number, David Hartley, moved a series of motions asking for some form of federal alliance with America.[6] But the Rockinghams did not remain for long at this stage. In March 1778 it became known that an alliance had been formed between France and America; and shortly after this the Rockinghams reconciled themselves to American independence. Their policy was announced in the Lords by the Duke of Richmond on April 7, when he was opposed by Chatham, who on this occasion made his last speech in Parliament.[7]

---

[1] P.H., xix, 125 seq.   [2] Albemarle, op. cit., ii, p. 314.   [3] Ibid., ii, p. 318.
[4] *Idem.*   [5] P.H., xix, p. 762 seq.
[6] Ibid., pp. 549–60; Cf. G. H. Guttridge, *David Hartley, M.P., An Advocate of Conciliation,* 1774–83, Berkeley, California, 1926.
[7] P.H., xix, pp. 1012 seq.

On April 10 Fox announced the same policy in the Commons, urging that independence be granted to America, and the war with France continued.[1]

It may be true that by this time the independence of America was inevitable; but the main motives of the Rockinghams in pressing for it were that a connection through the Crown alone would be dangerous in that it would increase the patronage at the disposal of the King, leading to more 'corruption' and 'influence'. When Lord North introduced his Propositions in February Burke said that,

> he saw the drift of the whole; the ministers thought to pay their court, by extending the prerogative, in proportion as they had lessened the empire; and that this war (which was pretended to be made to prevent the King's having a revenue in America independent of Parliament, and to assert the power of the House of Commons, to tax all the British dominions) now terminated in a surrender of the right of taxation, and of all other parliamentary rights to advise or check the power of the Crown.[2]

Fox, speaking on April 10 put the matter in even clearer terms: he said that the dependency of America was of very little importance to anyone except to the ministers, since it placed at their disposal an enormous number of jobs. He added that,

> The three estates of Parliament could no longer be the security and defence of our constitution, than when they remained in an equipoise with regard to one another.[3]

He regretted that the power of the Crown had for some years been growing, and this was dangerous to the constitution. Thus the debate on the American problem shifted to the old question of the influence of the Crown. As the war became more unpopular and public opinion began to express itself in petitioning, the Rockinghams felt that an effective opposition was once again possible. The battle they waged at this time was in essentials the same as in 1769 and 1770: their main object was to dislodge the ministry, and to rally the public behind them. The failure of North's policy in Ireland at this time added to the strength of the opposition, and indeed, everything was criticized by the opposition in terms of the influence of the Crown. The problem of America thus becomes subordinated to the older question of 'influence' and the activities of Burke and the Rockinghams after 1778 will be treated in the next chapter. By 1778 they had said all they had to say on the problem of America.

[1] Ibid., pp. 1082–5.   [2] Ibid., p. 779.   [3] Ibid., pp. 1082–3.

We have seen that Burke's ideas on America had their origin not in the writings of political theorists, but in the response of the first Rockingham administration to urgent practical problems, which they considered within the framework of accepted ideas on the nature of the constitution and imperial relationships. These accepted ideas could be found in Montesquieu, who taught that the balance of the constitution should be preserved, and that trade monopoly was normal practice with colonies. It is not until 1774 that the Rockinghams made American policy a major article in their creed, and in his great speeches of 1774 and 1775 Burke deepens the implications of the Rockingham American policy of 1766. It is with the help of Montesquieu's ideas on historical method that Burke analyses the American character, in which desire for liberty is the outstanding feature. Burke exploits Montesquieu's doctrine of the *esprit général* to strengthen the Rockingham policy of conciliation in the colonies, but in so doing he is led to minimize the rôle of the legislator in politics, and to exaggerate the importance of following the inclinations of the people. In this he was not entirely sincere, for at the same time he was stressing to Lord Rockingham the fact that the general temper of the people could be managed by skilful politicians, and, besides, Burke did not really intend to follow the inclinations of the Americans, who by this time were more radical than the Rockinghams could tolerate. Burke applies Montesquieu's analysis in a superficial and procrustean way, turning a blind eye on the radicalism of the colonists. It is brilliant propaganda, and it is fairest to Burke to judge it as such. It is a clever adaptation of Montesquieu to propaganda purposes. We find similar echoes of Montesquieu in the *Letter to the Sheriffs of Bristol*, where Burke likewise emphasizes the importance of legislating according to the general character of the people. However, though Burke borrows ideas from Montesquieu, the fundamental problem of America—that of the imperial relationship—was not solved for Burke by Montesquieu, his ideas being derived from the policy of Lord Rockingham in 1765-6. Montesquieu simply aids Burke to give literary form to these ideas.

CHAPTER VI

THE BRITISH CONSTITUTION: FROM THE DECLINE OF THE NORTH ADMINISTRATION TO THE ELECTIONS OF 1784 (1778–1784)

THE years from 1778 to 1784 are of the greatest importance in the history of the British constitution, and of the greatest interest for the study of the theory of the constitution as expounded by Montesquieu. After the American victory at Saratoga the opposition intensified their attacks on the ministry, and in this they had public opinion behind them. North was eager to resign, or at least to come to terms with the opposition; but the King insisted that he should remain in office, until, with the defeat of the British army at Yorktown, it proved no longer possible to avoid dismissing a ministry whose policy was thoroughly discredited. With defeat in America, threatened revolt in Ireland, war with France and Spain, and discontent at home, the King was forced to part with Lord North, and the only possible alternative at this time was Lord Rockingham, who in March 1782 became for the second time head of administration. The Rockinghams now had an opportunity to put into practice the constitutional ideas they had been cherishing for some time. This gave rise to a great deal of constitutional discussion, which became acute especially when, after the death of Rockingham in July 1782, his followers tried to force on the King a ministry of their own choosing. The King was able to resist this, and exercised his constitutional rights in appointing Lord Shelburne to succeed Rockingham; but the collapse of the Shelburne ministry in February 1783 raised the problem again, and the followers of Rockingham, now under the nominal leadership of the Duke of Portland, in coalition with Lord North, stormed the closet, and the King found himself with a ministry forced upon him. The dismissal of the Coalition in December 1783, and the appointment of Pitt as head of the new ministry, raised the debates on the constitution to their highest level, and they continued until the dissolution of Parliament in March 1784. The elections which followed confirmed the victory of Pitt and the King over the opposition. It was also a triumph of one idea of the constitution over another: a triumph of the balanced and mixed constitution described by Montesquieu over the new ideas that Burke and his friends had been advocating for some time. We shall see that the problem was discussed in terms of the mixed constitution, and that Montesquieu is more than once referred to as an authority.

The news of the defeat of the British army at Saratoga, arriving in December 1777, gave the opposition an opportunity to attack the ministry, though, as we have seen, that attack was weakened by the concessions that North was willing to make.[1] In the early part of 1778 Lord North was eager to resign, and to allow Chatham, or Chatham and Rockingham together, to form a ministry; but the King would not hear of this, the furthest concession he was willing to make being to strengthen the ministry by enlisting the support of part of the opposition.[2] Negotiations to strengthen the ministry in this way were begun, but were unsuccessful, the opposition groups following Chatham and Rockingham refusing to serve under North.[3] The King regarded this refusal as an attempt to deprive him of his constitutional right to choose his own ministers, and his correspondence of this time is full of references to 'a set of men who certainly would make me a slave for the remainder of my days': he declared that he would never be 'shackled by those desperate men', and even threatened to abdicate.[4]

An interesting commentary on the attitude of the Rockinghams at this time is afforded by an exchange of correspondence between Fox and Richmond early in the following year. Fox was perturbed by the refusal of the Rockinghams to accept the King's terms in 1778, and on January 24, 1779, he wrote to Richmond asking for what amounted to a definition of the Rockingham policy. He reproaches Rockingham with thinking that they 'can best serve the country by continuing in a fruitless opposition', and asks,

is it, or is it not, a fair and open declaration that you will not have anything to do with any ministry that is *not entirely* of your own framing?

He also asks whether, if a coalition were again proposed, and the more objectionable of the present ministers dismissed, he would object if some of his friends took office.[5] This letter was sent to Rockingham, and was seen by Burke.[6] The reply, written by Richmond, can be taken as the considered policy of the Rockinghams. Richmond denied that their policy is to take office only if they come in as a whole, 'and the King compelled to a kind of submission which

---

[1] See above, p. 104.   [2] *Correspondence of King George the Third*, no. 2219 seq.
[3] Lord John Russell, op. cit., i, p. 178 seq.; Albemarle, op. cit., ii, p. 353 seq.
[4] *Correspondence of King George the Third*, nos. 2226, 2232.
[5] The letter is in Russell, op. cit., i, p. 206 seq.   [6] Ibid., p. 213.

you think is not to be expected, and can never be forced'. The main
point made by Richmond is that they should refuse to take office
unless they first understand to what policy the King is willing to
agree. If the King invited Lord Rockingham to form a ministry
then it could be taken for granted that he would agree with Rockingham's policy; but if a coalition were to be formed, it would be
necessary for Rockingham to understand what policy he was
expected to support. Otherwise,

> it is merely an offer of places without power, under a bargain to screen those
> whom we have been so long condemning.[1]

These arguments seem to have convinced Fox, and the Rockinghams
retained their solidarity. The sessions of 1778 and 1779 were spent
mainly in attacking the mishandling of the war by the government.
It was in 1779 that the discontent of the people reached its height,
and the debates during the session which opened on November 25
are of the greatest importance on constitutional issues.

The speeches of the Rockinghams during these debates show how
little their ideas had changed since 1770. Lord Rockingham in the
Lords, and Lord John Cavendish in the Commons led the attack on
the ministry.[2] Rockingham saw the failure of the ministerial policy
as the result of 'a baleful and pernicious system' of 'unconstitutional
control and advice', and the remedy must be 'new councils and new
counsellors'; besides, 'the King must give his confidence to those he
apparently trusted'. In this Rockingham was supported by Shelburne,
who said that there was no possibility of defeating the 'system of
secret advisers' until 'Parliament ceased to support every measure
indiscriminately which came recommended by the servants of the
Crown'. But at the same time he denounced all those who had
'party views'. In the Commons Lord John Cavendish spoke in the
same vein as the Rockinghams in the Lords. A more vigorous
attack, however, was launched by Fox, who attacked the proposition
that 'the King was his own minister'. There was a certain inherent
contradiction in the eighteenth-century constitution which, while it
made the King head of the executive, yet held ministers responsible
to Parliament.[3] Fox exploits this contradiction in an attempt to
embarrass the ministry. He said that the doctrine that the King
was his own minister was dangerous to the constitution as it 'tended
to take responsibility from the shoulders of the ministers and place
it on a personage who could do no wrong, and could not be called

---

[1] Ibid., p. 219.   [2] The debates are in P.H., xx, pp. 1020-92; 1092-1156.
[3] Cf. Sir Lewis Namier, *Monarchy and the Party System*, Oxford, 1952.

to account'.[1] Fox, with typical outspokenness, went so far as to
remind his hearers what had happened to James II in 1688 when
'ministers were forgotten, and the prince alone was punished'.[2]
Burke was prevented by hoarseness from speaking at any length in
this important debate; but he stated that he was in full agreement
with Fox.[3] The logical conclusion of Fox's attitude would have
been for the monarch to retire from politics and to allow the ministers to assume full executive powers; and this, as we have seen, was
the Rockingham policy's implications since as early as 1767.[4] The
reply given to Fox is extremely interesting, coming from the
Attorney General, Wedderburn. He says that the King is head of the
executive, and, as such, is alone responsible for appointing executive
officers. Wedderburn speaks in terms of the mixed and balanced
constitution:

> If the prince were debarred of such a choice, the nobles would acquire a most
> dangerous ascendency over the Crown: or the Commons, encircling the King,
> like a spider's web, with a ministry of their own choosing, would reduce us to the
> very lowest state of anarchy and confusion.[5]

In complete contradiction to the Rockinghams, who held that
the King should give his confidence to the ministers, Wedderburn
holds that Parliament ought to give their confidence to ministers of
the King's choice. As for Fox's contention that the King was his
own minister, and that therefore executive officers were not responsible to Parliament, Wedderburn said that it was 'a doctrine which
had never come to his ears before', and 'language contrary to the
constitution'.[6] He maintained that the right of choosing ministers
lay with the Crown alone, the two Houses of Parliament having the
right to impeach ministers. Wedderburn was here expounding
sound constitutional doctrine, whereas Fox was trying to formulate
a new doctrine, unsupported by any constitutional authority. In
Montesquieu we can find support for what Wedderburn says, but
none for Fox.[7]

An important aspect of this problem is whether impeachment was
the only means of control Parliament had on the executive power.
When Rockingham and Cavendish moved what amounted to
motions of censure on the North ministry, calling for 'new councils
and new counsellors', this was opposed by some of the ministers as
unconstitutional, and it was suggested that impeachment was the

[1] P.H., xx, pp. 1116–28.   [2] Ibid., p. 1124.   [3] Ibid., pp. 1132–7.
[4] See above, chap. iv.   [5] P.H., xx, p. 1140.   [6] Ibid., pp. 1140–1.
[7] E.L., xi, 6, paragraphs 43–44.

only means of control that Parliament had over the executive.
Thus Lord Thurlow, in reply to Rockingham said,

> to come in with a side wind, without notice, without evidence, or any one
> species of proof whatever, to propose a removal, without a pretence of direct or
> implied guilt, was a mode of proceeding he would never accede to. It was an
> outrage on the constitution.[1]

In the Commons the same defence was made by Dundas, North and
Jenkinson. It was by this time established constitutional practice that
no ministry could carry measures through Parliament unless they had
the support of both Houses. It was, however, one thing to
say that the ministers must have the confidence of Parliament, and
another to say that Parliament had the right to call for a removal of
ministers. The only right recognized by the theory of the constitution, when a minister had lost the confidence of Parliament, was that
of impeachment. Montesquieu, as we have seen, realized that the
King, even against his will sometimes, must choose ministers
acceptable to Parliament; but he does not say that Parliament can
call for removal of ministers.[2] In practice this was not a great step
to take; but it had not been taken in theory, and there were no clear
precedents for it. It was therefore easy for the ministers to refute the
arguments of the opposition, especially in the imprudent formulation
given to them by Fox. In Wedderburn and the ministers we find a
rigid literal interpretation of the constitution; in Fox and the
Rockinghams we find what can probably be regarded as an over-
statement of the spirit of the constitution. However, it is in Lord
North that we find a more moderate view, avoiding the extremes
of both Fox and Wedderburn:

> An hon. gentleman . . . asked him, what he would do when he should find him-
> self deserted by his friends in Parliament? He was prepared to answer him; he
> would instantly retire; for whenever the majority of the House should disapprove
> of a minister's conduct he must give way. Like a torrent their disapprobation must,
> and ought, to sweep ministers before it. For God forbid, exclaimed his lordship,
> that there should be a voice in the nation stronger than that of Parliament![3]

Although North was able to maintain his majority throughout
the debates, largely consisting of what amounted to motions of
censure, that took place in the first weeks of the session, he was
uncomfortable in maintaining this majority, and early in December
1779 there were once again negotiations for a new ministry, the
Rockinghams being approached by Lord Thurlow on behalf of the

---

[1] P.H., xx, p. 1087.   [2] See above, p. 66.   [3] P.H., xx, p. 1109.

I

King. However, the negotiations were totally unsuccessful, no part of the opposition wanting to associate itself with the now totally discredited North ministry.[1]

By this time the opposition felt that they had public opinion firmly behind them. Reform associations were springing up, and, opposed to the expense of the war, they demanded enquiry into the expenditure of public money. On December 30 a meeting was held at York, and a petition agreed to; after this the movement spread rapidly.[2] At first Lord Rockingham was very timid of giving his support to the reform movement, for the reformers wanted not only reform of expenditure, but also reform of Parliament, and the latter was against the aristocratic ideals of the Rockinghams. Eventually, however, Lord Rockingham overcame his scruples, and gave the reformers his support, though he insisted, as in 1769, that the radical demands be avoided, and reform be concentrated on economy. With this Burke was in agreement, and he threw himself into the work of drawing up a plan for economical reform. The Rockinghams were not unanimous, however, Fox and the Duke of Richmond supporting the more radical demands of the reformers.

On December 15, 1779, Burke gave notice of his Plan of Public Reform and Economy, in which he attacked the 'fatal influence of the Crown' and outlined his proposal to reduce influence equal to the places of fifty members of Parliament. On February 11 he made his great speech on Economical Reform, and the remainder of the session found him taking his bill clause by clause through the committee stage. One great success was gained when on March 13 the clause abolishing the Board of Trade was carried with a majority of eight votes. However, the next clause of the bill was defeated, and Burke in disgust said he was indifferent as to the fate of the remaining clauses.[3]

Burke's aim in introducing his economical reform measures was not so much to save public money as to reduce the patronage of the Crown.[4] In the *Present Discontents* he had opposed a place bill; but now, more logically, he pressed for a reduction in the number of places. In Parliament he was challenged with inconsistency.[5] To this he replied that 'At that time influence was not carried to the extent to which it had been carried since.'[6] In any case, in the

---

[1] See Russell, op. cit., i, pp. 237–40; *Correspondence of King George the Third*, no. 2916.
[2] See G. S. Veitch, *The Genesis of Parliamentary Reform*, 1913; H. Butterfield, *George III, Lord North, and the People*, 1779–80, 1949.
[3] P.H., xx, p. 1293 seq.; xxi, p. 1 seq.　　　[4] Ibid., xxi, p. 63.　　　[5] Ibid., p. 234.
[6] Ibid., p. 384.

Discontents it was a general place bill he had opposed, whereas now he was aiming at the removal of certain clearly defined placemen. The ministers opposed the reform measures mainly on the grounds that it was unconstitutional for Parliament to interfere with the King's Civil List, which would amount to encroachment of the legislative on the executive power. To this Burke and Fox replied that the power of the Crown was a trust for the people, and the Civil List a voluntary grant from the people.[1] Thus at this point Burke is willing to use Lockian arguments of trusteeship which he was unwilling to use when dealing with the problem of America. At this stage of the argument the ministers could regard themselves as attempting to preserve the balance of the constitution, keeping the King's executive power intact, whereas Burke and Fox could be considered as trying to alter this balance. To Burke the ministers are guilty of 'Jacobitism' which 'elevates Kings into the ranks of gods, and contends that the people were made for them, not they for the people',[2] whereas to Fox the ministerial argument was 'a new and damnable doctrine, and infamous to a degree'.[3] A great deal of time was spent debating to what extent the legislative power was competent to criticize the executive. Thus, when on March 8, 1780, Shelburne moved for an enquiry into the removal of the Marquis of Carmarthan and the Earl of Pembroke from the lieutenancies of their respective counties, this was opposed on the grounds that it would subvert the prerogative of the Crown if every appointment or dismissal were subject to parliamentary control and examination.[4] On March 13 Fox put this much-vexed question to the Speaker, who ruled that, the necessity of the case being shown, Parliament had a right to interfere with the public part of the Civil List.[5] It was largely to clarify this issue that Dunning's motion that 'the influence of the Crown has increased, is increasing, and ought to be diminished' was moved on April 6. This motion also contained the clause that Parliament was competent to examine and correct abuses in the expenditure of the Civil List.[6] This was regarded by the opposition as a great victory; but in fact it was only a victory on a theoretical point. When Burke renewed his efforts on economical reform he found that he had no real support in Parliament. Such hopes as the opposition had were blasted by the Gordon riots in June, at the end of the session, which brought all reform movements under suspicion. In the General Election that followed the Rockinghams found their

---

[1] Ibid., p. 203 seq. [2] Ibid., p. 204. [3] Ibid., p. 216.
[4] Ibid., p. 217 seq. [5] Ibid., p. 258 seq. [6] Ibid., p. 347 seq.

powers and numbers reduced, Burke himself losing his seat for Bristol.[1]

When the new Parliament met at the end of October the ministry found itself strengthened by the change in public opinion, and the news of the victory of the British army at Charleston gave some hope that the war would soon be finished with victory for Great Britain. During this session the opposition continued to attack the ministry on the conduct of the war and to press for economical reform; but without success. It is interesting that at this time quotations from Montesquieu begin to appear in the debates. Thus in February, in a debate on one of Burke's reform measures, John Courtenay, supporting the ministry, quotes from the *Esprit des lois* xix, 27.[2] The opposition were unable to arouse public opinion, and at the end of the session the *Annual Register* notes the 'total indifference to the desperate situation of affairs' common among the people.[3] It was not until the news of the disastrous defeat of the British army at Yorktown reached England in November 1781 that the opposition found the tide turning in their favour. The parliamentary session began on November 27, and the opposition launched a series of vigorous attacks on the ministry, culminating in March 1782 in a number of near-defeats for the ministry. In the meantime, North was once again eager to resign, and it was becoming more obvious to the King that a change of ministry was inevitable. Thurlow was sent to negotiate with Lord Rockingham, who insisted on having *carte blanche* in the composition of a new ministry.[4] On March 18 North wrote to the King,

> Your Majesty is well apprized that, in this country, the Prince on the throne, cannot, with prudence, oppose the deliberate resolutions of the House of Commons: your royal predecessors (particularly King William III and his late Majesty) were obliged to yield to it much against their wish in more instances than one.[5]

The King replied that he was 'hurt' by what North had said, and he found it difficult to resign himself to the new administration.[6] The Rockinghams had not forgotten the lesson they learned in 1766, and they conducted an almost complete purge of placemen who had served under Lord North. The King refers to this:

> At last the fatal day is come which the misfortunes of the times and the sudden change of sentiments of the House of Commons have drove me to, of changing the

---

[1] Thereafter he sat for Malton (Yorks.).
[2] P.H., xxi, pp. 1277–9.
[3] *Annual Register*, 1781, p. 137 seq.
[4] *See Correspondence of King George the Third*, no. 3551 seq.
[5] Ibid., no. 3566.
[6] Ibid., no. 3567.

ministry, and a more general removal of other persons than, I believe, ever was known before: I have to the last fought for individuals, but the number I have saved, except my Bedchamber, is incredibly few.[1]

The Rockinghams were, however, not entirely successful in their attempt to fill all places with men professing loyalty to them alone. They were not numerous enough to achieve this, and the second Rockingham administration was in reality a coalition with Lord Shelburne, who was one of the Secretaries of State in the new government.

On March 20, 1782, North announced that the ministry was at an end. The new ministry did not begin auspiciously, for the King's hostility to Lord Rockingham was quite undisguised.[2] Besides, the Rockinghams were uncomfortable in the coalition with Lord Shelburne, who was a follower of their old enemy Lord Chatham, and, we are told,

Charles Fox told Lord Shelburne that he perceived this administration was to consist of two parts—one belonging to the King, the other to the public.[3]

The terms on which the Rockinghams insisted were those that might be expected: peace in America, even at the price of independence, economical reform to reduce the influence of the Crown.[4] The new administration was, however, too short for all of this programme to be carried out; but they did manage to carry out the essential points of Burke's reform plan. When the King sent a message to the Commons recommending reform, Burke, with more enthusiasm than judgement, treated the House to a lyrical rhapsody on the virtues of George III: the King was now free from 'secret influence', and the message was 'the best of messages to the best of peoples from the best of Kings'. The King, he said, now 'wished, chose, and desired to depend upon an independent Commons' House of Parliament, for the support of his person and family'.[5]

It was a great blow to the Rockinghams when their leader died on July 1, 1782. The latent hostility between the Fox and Shelburne sections of the ministry reached a crisis very soon. The King appointed Shelburne head of the new ministry; but this was resisted by Fox and his friends, who attempted to force the King to accept the Duke of Portland as Rockingham's successor. In an interview with the King Fox said that,

the only means of securing the support of those whom he believed to be the

[1] Ibid., no. 3593.   [2] Russell, op. cit., i, p. 304 seq.   [3] Ibid., p. 292.
[4] Albemarle, op. cit., ii, pp. 452–3.   [5] P.H., xxii, pp. 1269–71.

firmest friends to his Majesty's government, was to appoint some person to succeed Lord Rockingham, in whom that description of persons could place their confidence.[1]

But the King insisted in appointing Shelburne. Portland, in a letter to Fox is more outspoken, and shows that they had no scruples about storming the closet:

> Confidence I conceive to be wholly out of the question; power must be taken as its substitute, and unless you can possess that, and convince the public of your possessing it, both your honour and duty to the country dictate your retreat.[2]

But the King refused to yield, and shortly afterwards a number of Fox's supporters resigned, including Portland, Burke and Lord John Cavendish. To their great displeasure Conway and Richmond refused to resign on what they considered an unconstitutional and factious pretext.[3] Fox maintained that the reason for his resignation was disagreement on American policy, but he had difficulty in putting his case convincingly.[4] The disappointed minority now directed furious attacks against Shelburne: Fox described him as a man who stood for increasing the power of the Crown, while at the same time pretending to diminish it. Burke, supporting Fox, insisted that the King should have chosen as minister someone like Lord Rockingham, and described Shelburne as 'a wolf disguised', 'a Catiline', 'a Borgia'.[5] In reply to these attacks Shelburne defended his principles: he reprobated the idea of government by 'party' or 'faction', for if the country were to be so governed 'the constitution must necessarily expire'.[6] As for the King,

> he declared that he never would consent that the 'King of England should be a King of the Mahrattas', among whom it was a custom for a certain number of great lords to elect a peshaw, who was the creature of an aristocracy, and was vested with the plenitude of power, while the King was, in fact, nothing more than a royal pageant, or puppet.[7]

He thus insists on the constitutional right of the King to choose his own ministers; if the Fox-Portland group were to have their way, he said, 'the monarchical part of the constitution would be no more'.[8] This speech was made on July 10 and on the following day Parliament was prorogued.

The King's speech on the opening of the new session, on December 5, called for the temper and moderation of Parliament.[9] In this Fox saw an opening for attack, and on the following day he complained

[1] Russell, op. cit., i, p. 436.   [2] Ibid., p. 330.   [3] P.H., xxiii, p. 167.
[4] Ibid., p. 173.   [5] Ibid., p. 183.   [6] Ibid., p. 192.
[7] Idem.   [8] Idem.   [9] Ibid., p. 203 seq.

that if the appeal from the throne were followed Parliament would
tamely acquiesce in all ministerial measures. He was in the position
common to opposition politicians in the eighteenth century, fearing
that the legislative power was being corrupted by the executive. He
complained that 'ministers were become the monitors of Parliament',
and continued,

> This was what he termed the most insidious attack that could be formed, in his
> mind, against the constitution, for it was aiming to inspire the opinion that the
> period was arrived which Montesquieu predicts to be the fall of the British liberty—
> when the legislature shall become more corrupt than the executive government.[1]

He added, however, that 'we were not yet come to this period'.
Burke spoke in the same vein, saying that 'the executive government
was not appointed to control the legislature, nor to teach them their
duty'.[2] We shall see that the ministerial side soon appeal to Montesquieu to support their point of view.

It was during Shelburne's short administration that the combined
opposition of Fox and North was formed. It is now generally
realized that this coalition is not as surprising as has been formerly
supposed, for the real enemies of the Rockinghams had been Chatham
and Shelburne, who repudiated all idea of 'party'.[3] Besides, as we
have seen, North's ideas on the limitations of the power of the King
were moderate, and not unacceptable to Fox and Burke. On
February 14 Fox and North had a meeting to discuss policy. They
agreed that economical reform had gone far enough, and that, as to
electoral reform, each man should follow his own views. Fox
declared that the King should not be his own minister, and North's
reply is revealing:

> If you mean there should not be a government by departments I agree with
> you; I think it is a very bad system. There should be one man, or a cabinet, to
> govern the whole. Government by departments was not brought in by me. I
> found it so, and had not vigour and resolution to put an end to it. The King
> ought to be treated with all sort of respect and attention, but the appearance of
> power is all that a King in this country can have. Though the government in my
> time was a government by departments, the whole was done by the ministers,
> except in a few instances.[4]

However, no matter what Fox and North might think of the
practice of the constitution, they could not deny that the King had
the theoretical right to choose his own ministers. Thus Fox, speaking
on March 6, 1783, in reply to the proposition that 'the King had a

[1] Ibid., p. 277.   [2] Ibid., p. 272.
[3] Cf. J. Brooke, *The Chatham Administration*, 1956, p. 293.
[4] Russell, op. cit., ii, p. 38.

right to choose his own ministers', said that 'he rested on the spirit of the constitution' and 'not on the letter of it'. He declared that ministers must possess the confidence not only of the King, but also of Parliament.[1]

After the collapse of Shelburne's ministry in February 1783, the King found himself in unprecedented difficulty in forming an administration. Fox and North were now in alliance under the nominal leadership of the Duke of Portland, and there was no one else capable or willing at this time to form an administration. After nearly six weeks of trying almost every expedient the King finally had to resign himself to coming to terms with Fox and North. The new ministry was formed on April 2, the King being forced to give full freedom to Portland in appointing ministers.[2]

The most important constitutional issue of the new administration was that implied in Fox's East India Bill, which was to lead to the dismissal of the Coalition, and thus to the great debates of the early part of 1784. Before proceeding to these debates, however, we shall pause at an interesting debate that took place in the Lords on June 3, and which shows that the speakers of this time were familiar with Montesquieu, and were prepared to use him as an authority on the constitution. The Duke of Richmond introduced a motion for a committee on the independency of judges, objecting to the recent practice of the Crown in increasing judges' salaries, and in paying extra emoluments to judges chosen for commissions. This practice, Richmond asserted, was contrary to the statute of 13 William III, by which judges held their situations *quamdiu se bene gesserint*, which had as its object to guarantee the independence of judges from the influence of the executive. He also objected to judges sitting in the Lords, and in his support quoted from the *Esprit des lois* passages to show that liberty depended on the separation of powers. The reply to Richmond came from Lord Stormont, who showed that he too had read Montesquieu, and indeed, understood him better than Richmond. Stormont said,

the president was not so ignorant of the English constitution, as not to know, that a judicial was blended with a legislative power of that House; and that their lordships sat there, acting, as occasion required, in both capacities.

Further quotations from Montesquieu follow.[3]

[1] P.H., xxiii, p. 596.
[2] See Russell, op. cit., ii, p. 42 seq.; *Correspondence of King George the Third*, vi, p. 325 seq.; Cf. D. G. Barnes, *George III and William Pitt, 1783–1806*, Stanford University, 1939.
[3] For this debate see P.H., xxiii, pp. 959–983.

Fox's East India Bill proposed to place the affairs of the Company under the direction of seven commissioners, to be appointed in the first instance by the ministers for four years, and thereafter by the Crown. The bill was attacked furiously in the name of the constitution, some speakers saying that it increased the influence of the Crown, some that it diminished the influence of the Crown, and Pitt arguing ingeniously that it did both:

> This was a paradox; but he explained it thus: it increased the influence of the Crown in the end; but in the meantime, it increased only the influence of the present ministers, independent of the Crown; and should they be driven from their places, they would carry this influence with them into private life, and it would be exerted against the Crown.[1]

The most comprehensive indictment, however, of the Coalition comes on December 15, from Lord Abingdon, who to support his attack, quotes copiously from Montesquieu. Abingdon reprobates the idea of 'subverting the constitution of this country by placing the executive power of government in the hands of a mountebank secretary of state', who 'does not shrink back from declaring, that he is not the King's minister, but the minister of the people'. This is an attempt to 'set up a middle power between the King and people', a plan

> to wrest the reins of government out of the hands of the executive power, and to place it in the hands of a self-created demagogue, supported by a factious and desperate cabal.[2]

Abingdon points out that their policy is contained in the *Present Discontents*, a policy which, 'whilst it pulls the influence of the Crown down to the ground, it sets up another influence ten times more destructive to the constitution. The influence of an aristocracy.'[3] Abingdon then moved that the judges be summoned to give their advice on certain points of law arising out of the East India Bill. The first point is whether the commission proposed by Fox constituted an unconstitutional executive power, and he quotes Montesquieu:

> Now, my lords, in putting this query to the judges, I find myself no less upheld therein by the spirit of the constitution, than confirmed by the letter of the law: by the spirit of the constitution as handed down to us by the very ingenious and learned author of the Spirit of Laws.[4]

He quotes two passages to the effect that the executive power is

---

[1] Ibid., pp. 1404–5.   [2] Ibid., xxiv, p. 137.   [3] Ibid., p. 139.
[4] Ibid., p. 140.

lodged in the monarch, and not in a committee of the legislature.[1] Also, he quotes from Montesquieu to show that the King has the right to veto bills.[2]

After this the debates in the Commons became more heated, especially when it was learned that the King, through Lord Temple, was bringing pressure to bear on the Lords to have the East India Bill rejected. On December 17 Fox said,

> The deliberations of this night must decide whether we are to be freemen or slaves; whether the House of Commons be the palladium of liberty, or the organ of despotism; whether we are henceforth to possess a voice of our own, or to be only the mere mechanical echo of secret influence.[3]

It is ironical that after for years having attacked a secret influence which was largely non-existent, the charge should now have a basis in reality in that the King was using Lord Temple as intermediary to convey his opinion to the Lords. In Fox's speech we find the usual attack on the placemen who serve the King first rather than the ministers, and he quotes George Grenville as having said on a similar occasion,

> 'I will never again . . . be at the head of a string of janissaries, who are always ready to strangle or dispatch me on the least signal'.[4]

Fox denies that he is trying to upset the balance of the constitution; but maintains that he is attempting to keep the power of the Crown within its proper boundaries, and with reference to influence, he says,

> A great writer has said, that the English constitution will perish, when the legislative becomes more corrupt than the executive power. Had he been as sound a judge of the practice as of the theory of government, he might have added, with still greater truth, that we shall certainly lose our liberty, when the deliberations of Parliament are decided—not by the legal and usual—but by the illegal and extraordinary exertions of prerogative.[5]

The bill was defeated in the Lords, and on December 19 a new ministry under Pitt was set up. Between the formation of the Pitt ministry and March 24 the struggle between government and opposition was mainly on constitutional principles. In the course of these remarkable debates the ministry suffered a number of defeats, and one of the most important questions debated was whether a ministry could continue in office when it clearly did not command a

---

[1] E.L., xi, 6, paragraphs 36–37. [2] Ibid., paragraphs 42–43.
[3] P.H., xxiv, p. 206. [4] Ibid., p. 213. [5] Ibid., p. 216.

majority in Parliament. Fox and North appealed to the precedent set when Carteret resigned and was replaced by Pelham: Fox said,

the first . . . was supported by the secret advisers of the Crown; but the Commons properly addressed the Crown to state that he only could be a minister with effect who had the confidence of the people.[1]

Pitt and Dundas replied to this, asking what ground there was for supposing the ministers did not have the confidence of the people, and repudiating suggestions of secret influence.[2] On January 16 the opposition moved for the removal of the ministers, and this was carried by a majority of twenty-one votes. In this debate Fox stressed the distinction between the theory and the practice of the constitution: the King, he said, has the right to appoint ministers, but it is imprudent for him to appoint ministers who do not have the confidence of Parliament; the King, again, has the right to veto bills, but not in the indirect way the King vetoed the East India Bill.[3] The defence of Pitt and his colleagues was to hold fast to the letter of the constitution, to insist on the King's right to appoint ministers, and to invite the opposition to impeach if they could make a case.[4] Pitt, speaking on January 26, said,

he hoped he should not give offence when he declared, that a minister might . . . act constitutionally, by remaining in office after that House had declared their disapprobation of him.[5]

Fox pointed out that a ministry without support of Parliament was in an impossible position in that it could not carry any measures.[6] In the stormy debates that followed, Dundas and Pitt consolidated their arguments. Dundas appealed over the head of Parliament to the people, pointing out that a large number of petitions had been received from different parts of the kingdom thanking the King for dismissing the Coalition.[7] Pitt became more intransigeant:

With regard, however, to the resignation of ministers, he saw no reason for it. If that House insisted upon their going out, there were two constitutional means open to them, either by impeachment to proceed against them for their crimes, if they had committed any, or by an immediate address to the Crown to desire their removal. The removal of ministers lay with the Crown and not with that House.[8]

On February 20 he carried the argument a stage further, when he said that, 'Grant only this, that this House has a negative in the appointment of ministers, and you transport the executive power

[1] Ibid., p. 287.   [2] Ibid., pp. 291–4.   [3] Ibid., p. 366–7.
[4] Ibid., p. 369 seq.   [5] Ibid., pp. 432–3.   [6] Ibid., pp. 434–7.
[7] Ibid., p. 473.   [8] Ibid., p. 483.

into this House'.[1] This he sees as contrary to the balance of the constitution:

> For in truth, Sir, if the constitutional independence of the Crown is thus reduced to the very verge of annihilation, where is the boasted equipoise of the constitution? Where is that balance among the three branches of the legislature which our ancestors have measured out to each with so much precision? Where is the independence—nay, where is even the safety of any one prerogative of the Crown, or even of the Crown itself, if its prerogative of naming ministers is to be usurped by this House?[2]

The debate continued, and on March 1 Fox maintained that the Commons were 'possessed of the power of putting a negative on the choice of ministers', and he referred to the precedent of Walpole's resignation in 1742, when he still had the confidence of the Crown.[3] Pitt clarified his position by saying that he would never agree that the disapproval of the Commons should *ipso facto* compel the King to dismiss ministers. He repeated that the proper course for the opposition to follow was to impeach, if they could, or to address the Crown.[4] These debates were brought to an end when the King dissolved Parliament. Since the passing of the Septiennial Act of 1716 it was law that there should be a new Parliament every seven years, and this had generally been respected as a convention whereby Parliament had a right to live for this time, though the right of dissolution still lay technically with the King. In March 1784 the King disregarded this convention and dissolved Parliament. By this time the King and Pitt were certain that fresh elections would turn the scale in their favour, and in this they were proved correct.[5]

During Pitt's ministry from December 1783 to March 1784, a number of attempts had been made to come to terms with the opposition. Immediately after his appointment Pitt had tried to win over Fox, but without success.[6] In January 1784 there was a meeting at Saint Alban's Tavern to attempt to conciliate the ministry and opposition; but Portland refused to negotiate with Pitt unless the latter first resigned.[7] Another attempt at conciliation, through Lord Sydney, reached a similar deadlock: the Portland-Fox connection were willing to accept office only on their own terms, which amounted to storming the closet.[8] The King and Pitt refused to accept such terms, and defended what they considered the constitutional rights of the Crown as head of the executive power.

The main problem of these years of short ministries was that of the

---

[1] P.H., xxiv, p. 663.   [2] Ibid., p. 663.   [3] Ibid., pp. 687–89.   [4] Ibid., p. 709.
[5] See W. T. Laprade, *Parliamentary Papers of John Robinson, 1774–1784*, 1922.
[6] See Barnes, op. cit., p. 71.   [7] Ibid., p. 80.   [8] Ibid., p. 81 seq.

relation of the legislative and executive powers. It is easy to see that
the King and Pitt were holding fast to the letter of the constitution,
as described by Montesquieu and as implied in the Revolution
Settlement. This theory, and this constitution, placed the King at
the head of the executive power, leaving the choice of ministers at
his sole disposal. In theory the only way in which the ministers
could be checked by the legislative power was through impeachment. These arguments could be supported—and were supported—
by passages from the *Esprit des lois*, xi, 6. At the same time, the
practice of the constitution did not leave the legislative and executive
powers in the sort of deadlock that resulted during these years of
crisis. In the *Esprit des lois*, xix, 27, Montesquieu had described how
the constitution normally functions: the King must choose ministers
having enough support in Parliament to carry measures through both
Houses, and this sometimes involves choosing ministers personally
disagreeable to him. But Montesquieu does not advance the doctrine
that the legislative power has the right to choose ministers, or even
to demand the withdrawal of a minister, otherwise than by impeachment. Portland and Fox were going beyond any recognized
constitutional authority when they tried to storm the closet several
times in these years. Thus, if Pitt seems rather old-fashioned and
inflexible in his constant appeal to the strict letter of the constitution,
the opposition seem much more modern in their attitude. This
modernity is only superficial, however, for, as in 1770, the solidarity
of the Portland-Fox group had hardly anything in common with
modern political parties. The majority which they commanded, in
coalition with Lord North, during these years, was not a faithful
reflection of public opinion. Besides, the 'party' was beginning to
show signs of internal weakness. In 1783 Richmond had remained in
office with Shelburne, and refused to serve under the Coalition.
Also, some of their numbers, notably Fox, entertained ideas more
radical than Lord Rockingham would have considered fitting.

During the debates that took place under Pitt's short administration from December 1783 to March 1784, Burke did not speak very
often; but he was in full agreement with Fox and Portland. By
March 1784 the cause for which the opposition had fought was lost,
and the opposition themselves were thoroughly discredited in
public opinion. However, during the first session of the new
Parliament Burke moved, on June 14, for a Remonstrance to the
Crown, objecting to the dissolution of the late Parliament. This was
rejected without debate, and, indeed, it must have seemed rather

untimely, since the cause was already lost. But Burke attached a great deal of importance to his effort and published the Remonstrance with notes. It is, in a sense, the last word in the series of debates we have been following.[1]

The late Parliament, he complains, was dismissed because it showed a spirit of independency, and the result of the dissolution has been that Parliament is ready to support any measures introduced by the ministers. Here we have, then, the familiar opposition theme of the legislature being corrupted by the executive power. But what Burke principally objects to is a passage in the King's speech of December 5, 1782, where it was requested that the Lords and Commons should behave with moderation and said that the King had acted to preserve the balance of the constitution.[2] To this Burke replies,

> It were desirable that all hazardous theories concerning a balance of rights and privileges (a mode of expression wholly foreign to parliamentary usage) might have been forborne.[3]

He believes that Lords and Commons have each their rights and privileges, and they know and respect the prerogatives of the Crown; but he refuses to admit a 'balance' of those rights, privileges and prerogatives:

> nor are they able to discern to what object ministers would apply their fiction of balance; nor what they would consider as a just one. These unauthorized doctrines have a tendency to stir improper discussions; and to lead to mischievous innovations on the constitution.[4]

In place of idle speculations on the balance of these rights Burke recommends that the practice of the earlier part of the century be followed. It has been supposed that Burke is here attacking the generally accepted theory of the balanced constitution.[5] This seems, however, unlikely, in that a few years later he is to describe the constitution in these very terms of balance, and is to make allusion to Montesquieu at the same time.[6] What he is objecting to in the Remonstrance is the rigid literal interpretation of the constitution, which would reduce the Commons to merely registering the edicts of the Crown. He explains what he means by the term 'balance' as used in the Remonstrance:

---

[1] The Remonstrance is in *Works*, ii, pp. 249–76.
[2] See ibid., p. 252; Cf. P.H., xxiii, pp. 203–10.
[3] *Works*, ii, p. 255.   [4] Ibid., p. 256.
[5] R. Pares, *King George III and the Politicians*, Oxford, 1954, pp. 31–32.
[6] *Works*, iii, p. 1 seq. (*Appeal from the New to the Old Whigs*, 1791, Cf. below, p. 165).

it is a contrivance full of danger, for ministers to set up the representative and constituent bodies of the Commons of this kingdom as two separate and distinct powers, formed to counterpoise each other, leaving the preference in the hands of secret advisers of the Crown.[1]

He is here referring to the dissolution, which was, in fact, an appeal by the King over the head of Parliament. The 'balance' which Burke objects to is the 'new doctrine' that Parliament and people may be played off one against the other by the 'secret advisers of the Crown', and has nothing to do with the familiar doctrine of Montesquieu. Burke is, in fact—as during the debates on America—fighting to preserve Parliament from both King and people, conceiving that the balance (in the sense used by Montesquieu) can be upset on more sides than one. Burke was thus, in a sense, defending the traditional constitution from radical tendencies.

After the Remonstrance of June 1784, Burke is no longer concerned with the practical problems of the relations of the legislative and executive powers in the constitution. The cause was lost, and Burke was never again to see the Portland-Fox group given office.[2] After 1784 his attention was absorbed by the problem of India and the Impeachment of Warren Hastings, and then by the French Revolution and Ireland. It was during the French Revolution that he found himself with the task of defending the British constitution against forces of radicalism, but it was the theory rather than the practice of the constitution he had to defend. We shall see that in this defence of the theory of the constitution he turned to the authority of Montesquieu.[3]

The period of crisis, which we have been examining, reveals the latent weakness of the eighteenth-century constitution, which in theory was based on separate and independent powers. Until a more satisfactory way of binding together the executive and legislative powers could be found, friction of this kind was to be expected. The solution to the problem was not to be found until the rise of cabinet government in the modern sense, and in which the policies of both the King and Burke are irrelevant: the King is pushed out of politics; but eighteenth-century 'parties' are replaced by modern organized parties from which representatives are elected by reformed constituencies. The victory of the King and Pitt in 1784 was a victory for the traditional constitution of the eighteenth century. It

---

[1] *Works*, ii, p. 259.
[2] In the summer of 1794 the Portland wing of the group were absorbed into Pitt's ministry, but the Fox wing went into opposition, Cf. below, p. 144.
[3] See below, chap. viii.

was, paradoxically, however, during Pitt's administration after 1784 that the power of the Crown began to decline, thus opening the way for the modern form of parliamentary government. But the decline of the power of the Crown was not the result of deliberate attacks on it; it was rather accidental, owing to administrative reforms introduced by Pitt for the sake of greater efficiency, and because of the declining health of George III after 1788.[1] With the decline of the power of the Crown and the beginning of parliamentary reform, the constitution described by Montesquieu is no more, and the arguments of both Pitt and Burke are irrelevant.

[1] See Pares, op. cit., chap. vi.

CHAPTER VII

BURKE AND INDIA

FROM the beginning to the end of his parliamentary career Burke was, in one way or another, concerned with East Indian affairs. At the time when he entered Parliament it was becoming obvious that the relations between the State and the East India Company were in need of some kind of revision.[1] Though this problem did not play any important part during the first Rockingham administration, it was the object of Chatham's attention shortly after the formation of the new administration in July 1766. Chatham wanted a parliamentary enquiry into the affairs of the Company; and during his administration Acts were passed giving the State a larger measure of control over the Company as well as a share in its profits. The Rockinghams opposed these measures on the grounds that the State ought not to violate the Company's chartered rights.[2] However, their opposition was factious, largely the result of Chatham's recent dismissal from office of their supporter Lord Edgcumbe.[3] Besides, some of Rockingham's supporters and friends—and notably Burke's cousin William and brother Richard— were at this time gambling on the East India stock market, and resisted any government interference which would threaten the Company's revenue. During the next few years William and Richard Burke continued to speculate in this way, and they became involved in the collusive transfer of stock in connection with the Company's elections in 1769. It is not clear to what extent Edmund was actively collaborating with his cousin and brother in these dealings; but it is certain that when in the summer of 1769 there was a collapse in the price of East India stock all the Burkes were financially ruined. These transactions did much damage to the reputation of the Burkes; and Edmund Burke's first contacts with Indian affairs were thus by no means auspicious.[4]

[1] On the general problem of the relation of the State to the Company see: H. H. Dodwell, 'British India', vol. v of *The Cambridge History of India*, 1929; L. S. Sutherland, *The East India Company in Eighteenth Century Politics*, Oxford, 1952.
[2] D. A. Winstanley, *Lord Chatham and the Whig Opposition*, Cambridge, 1912, p. 94; H. Walpole, *Memoirs of the Reign of George III*, ed. G. F. R. Barker, 4 vols., 1894, ii, p. 288 seq.
[3] Cf. above, p. 70; see J. Brooke, *The Chatham Administration, 1766–1768*, 1956, pp. 61–62.
[4] Sutherland, op. cit., pp. 155–6; 188 seq.; Dixon Wecter, *Edmund Burke and His Kinsmen*, Boulder, 1939; Sir Philip Magnus, 'The Character and Private Life of Edmund Burke', *English Studies*, 1949, pp. 25–42; see also, Magnus, *Edmund Burke*, 1939.

In 1772 and 1773 the problem of the relation of the Company to the State was again of leading political importance. The Company was suffering from divisions in India and at home, and in 1772 two parliamentary committees were set up to investigate into the alleged abuses of the Company. In 1773 Lord North's Regulating Act was passed, giving the State more control over the Company at home and in India. During this time the Rockinghams were working out a policy on India. On October 28, 1772, Lord Rockingham wrote to Burke, indicating some possible lines of attack on the government. Rockingham feared that North's measures would increase the amount of patronage at the Crown's disposal; and he gave expression to humanitarian feelings for the natives of India, who, it was commonly believed at this time, were suffering from British misrule.[1] The line which the Rockinghams took in their speeches at this time was that of the iniquity of the government's attempt to violate chartered rights, and they opposed any form of parliamentary enquiry into the conduct of the Company.[2] Burke was not yet ready to stand forth as champion of the natives of India, though the Rockinghams sympathized with their alleged sufferings. At this time India was not a major cause for Burke and his friends, who, after the passing of the Regulating Act, turned their attention to America.

It was not until late in 1777, and then for personal and party reasons, that the Rockinghams again became active in Parliament on Indian affairs. Lord Pigot, who was one of their supporters, had in 1775 gone out to Madras as Governor, with instructions from the Company to reverse the policy of his predecessor Wynch, recalled for supporting the Nawab of Arcot, who had annexed the kingdom of the Rajah of Tanjore. When Pigot attempted to implement his instructions he was deposed by the Council of Madras, put in confinement and, to the embarrassment of his enemies, died.[3] When news of this arrived in England the opposition were not slow to exploit it against the government, and Burke was foremost among those who launched an attack on the government's policy in Madras and the Carnatic. He also attacked the alleged alliance between the ministry and the Nawab of Arcot, and he enlarged his attack to include Warren Hastings, Governor of Bengal, who was at this time a supporter of Pigot's opponents in Madras.[4] It is important to note that at this time William Burke was in the employment of

[1] Fitzwilliam MSS. (Sheffield); quoted in Sutherland, op. cit., pp. 241–2.
[2] P.H., xvii, pp. 461–3; 567–8; 818–23; 834–7; 900–2.
[3] Sutherland, op. cit., p. 271; pp. 317–9.
[4] See P.H., xix, pp. 284–7.

the Rajah of Tanjore, and that once again we see in Burke an entanglement of public and private interests.[1]

As the North administration declined on account of the American war, the opposition took advantage of the ministry's weakness on Indian policy. In March 1780 the Company's charter being due to expire, North moved that it should be given notice of its dissolution. To this there was furious opposition, especially from Fox and Burke, who did not want to see the East Indian patronage falling into the hands of the government.[2] North yielded to opposition pressure and prolonged the life of the Company. But by this time the alleged abuses of the Company were a public scandal, and in 1781 two parliamentary committees of enquiry were set up. A Select Committee, under General Smith, and including Burke as its most active member, was formed to consider the state of the administration of justice in Bengal, Bihar and Orissa, and also general questions of British rule in India. It issued, from 1781 to 1783, eleven reports, of which the ninth and eleventh were written by Burke.[3] A Secret Committee also was formed, under Henry Dundas, and it had the task of enquiring into the causes of the war in the Carnatic. It issued six reports.[4]

It was during the time that he served on the Select Committee that Burke learned to consider Indian affairs as a serious imperial problem, and at the same time he mastered the enormous wealth of material he was later to use in the impeachment of Warren Hastings. An important source of his information was Philip Francis, who, having just returned from India in 1781, became a member of the same committee. Francis, with two other councillors, had been sent out to Bengal in 1774 under the terms of the Regulating Act, to join Warren Hastings, the Governor, and Barwell who was on the Council. There followed a spectacular clash between Hastings and Barwell on the one side, and the new councillors on the other. Hastings had undertaken the colossal task of attempting to find a solution to what was by this time an urgent problem: the problem of reconciling the interests of the Company with those of the decadent Indian empire. The central authority of the Moghul empire had decayed, and subordinate kingdoms were in a state of chaos, the weak native rulers of Bengal being propped up by the military power of the Company. The weakness and instability of

---

[1] Sutherland, op. cit., pp. 327–8. [2] P.H., xxi, pp. 309–19. [3] *Works*, vol. iv.
[4] For the Reports of the Secret and Select Committees see *Reports from Committees of the House of Commons reprinted by order of the House*, v–viii, 1803.

Indian rulers, along with the corrupt practices which had grown up
among the Company's servants, made the problem extremely
complicated, and there were no constitutional precedents which
could give any guidance, though at this time the problem was
considered as administrative rather than constitutional. Clive, in
1765, had already made an attempt to reconcile the native interests
with those of the Company by assuming the *Diwani* or revenue
administration, and yet allowing native officials to continue the
actual functions of collecting and administrating. By the time
Hastings was appointed Governor, in 1771, this practice was corrupt
and discredited. The Company authorized Hastings to 'stand forth
as Diwan', which amounted to investing the Company with the full
administrative functions of Bengal, and this also involved the
assumption of judicial functions. Hastings was convinced that the
native institutions were corrupt and could be rejuvenated only by
the Company assuming full responsibility. At the same time he
respected the traditions and customs of the natives and, whenever
possible, tried to preserve Indian laws. He set up two Supreme
Courts of Appeal for the natives, and, at his own expense, employed
an eminent scholar, N. B. Halhed, to make a translation of the
Hindu Code.[1] His attitude to these problems has been much admired
by modern historians.[2]

The struggle between Hastings and the hostile majority in the
Council was partly a struggle of personalities and partly of political
principles. With the personal clash we are not here concerned; but
the conflict of principles is of cardinal importance. Francis was a
man of theory, with no sound knowledge of the practical problems
of Indian administration. He was shocked at the idea of a trading
company assuming political power, and on this point he quoted the
authority of Montesquieu:

> Of all despotic governments there is none which oppresses itself more than where
> the Prince declares himself proprietor of the soil and heir of all his subjects. It
> always follows that the cultivation of the earth is abandoned; but if, besides this,
> the Prince is a merchant, every species of industry is ruined.[3]

Francis took little care to relate such ideas to facts. From political
theorists, however, little could be learned to help those dealing with

---

[1] N. B. Halhed, *A Code of Gentoo Laws*, 1776.

[2] See: S. Weitzman, *Warren Hastings and Philip Francis*, Manchester, 1929; A. Mervyn
Davies, *Warren Hastings, a Maker of British India*, 1935; M. E. Monckton-Jones, *Warren
Hastings in Bengal 1772–1774*, Oxford, 1918; Keith Feiling, *Warren Hastings*, 1954; G. W.
Forrest, *Selections from the State Papers of the Governors-General of India: Warren Hastings*,
Oxford and London, 1910.   [3] Weitzman, op. cit., p. 74; Cf. E.L., v, 14.

what was essentially a new problem: that of establishing an imperial relationship with an oriental empire. In this task Hastings relied not on theory but on vast practical administrative experience, his sense of justice and expediency. Francis, on the other hand, full of abstract ideas on the sufferings of the natives of India, wanted a return to something equivalent to the 'dual system' of Clive, which he believed would free the natives from British tyranny. He does not, however, face the fundamental issue that the native institutions were decayed; and thus he misunderstood the nature of Hastings' reforms.[1]

When in 1781 Francis returned from India, having failed in his attempt to discredit Hastings, he tried to find support among the opposition, and particularly from Burke. He had, indeed, been trying for some time to interest Burke more closely in East Indian affairs,[2] but it was not until late in 1781, when Francis became a member of the Select Committee, that he began to influence Burke. It is in his contacts with Francis that we can trace Burke's renewed activity in the cause of India.[3] It is now established that most of the information imbibed by Burke and his fellow committee members from Francis is untrustworthy; but it is important to understand the fundamental generosity of Burke's impulse to oppose what he thought a despotic rule imposed on the natives of India. Burke was by no means the only person to be perturbed by accounts of British misrule in India, and the committees of 1772 had been animated by similar ideas.

The collapse of the North administration in 1782 gave the Rockinghams an opportunity to take the Indian problems in hand. Burke and Dundas, speaking for the Select and Secret Committees respectively, were particularly active in Parliament.[4] Among other things Hastings was recalled, though on a technical point the Company was able to defy Parliament, and Hastings remained at his post until 1784. The great event of this time, as far as Burke was concerned, was Fox's East India Bill, introduced in November 1783, which inspired one of Burke's most celebrated speeches. It is in this speech, delivered on December 1, that we find his first major contribution to the problem of India in the eighteenth century. This speech is also of interest in that Burke applies once again the technique of analysis that he had already used in the American

---

[1] On Francis' ideas see Weitzman, op. cit., chap. iii.
[2] See letter from Francis to John Bourke, Nov. 30, 1774, J. Parkes and H. Merivale, *Memoirs of Sir Philip Francis*, 2 vols., 1867, ii, pp. 18–19.
[3] See Weitzman, op. cit., chap. v.   [4] P.H., xxii, pp. 1275–1333.

speeches. We have seen that this technique was learned from Montesquieu.

In the American speeches Burke had found it necessary to deal with arguments on legal rights; and he is confronted with somewhat similar arguments on India. One of the arguments he had used earlier against state interference in the affairs of the Company was that such interference would be against the Company's chartered rights. This argument was turned against the Fox-North ministry who themselves were now proposing to subject the Company to a greater degree of control from the State. In reply to such arguments Burke admits that the rights of man are 'sacred things', but such rights are not to be confused with the rights of the East India Company: the charter of the Company established certain rights of monopoly, which have nothing to do with the type of rights found in Magna Charta. The Company's charter established various rights and privileges; but these were a trust, and as such, were accountable to Parliament, which granted them. Burke contends that the Company have abused their trust, and therefore the contract between them and Parliament is broken. Burke could claim that his attitude to the problem of India was consistent. Since 1766 the Rockinghams had refused to contemplate parliamentary interference in India, because this would violate chartered rights; but Burke now maintained that the contract guaranteeing these rights had been broken by the Company, and therefore Parliament was justified in revising its relations with the Company, by formulating a new charter.[1]

Having thus disposed of the argument of chartered rights, Burke proceeds to consider the question historically and empirically. He is convinced that the Company have abused their trust; but the question of whether the Company's powers should be changed must be considered with full reference to all the facts:

> I do not presume to condemn those who argue *a priori*, against the propriety of leaving such extensive political powers in the hands of a company of merchants. . . . I feel an insuperable reluctance in giving my hand to destroy any established institution of government, upon a theory, however plausible it may be. My experience in life teaches me nothing clear upon the subject.[2]

In order to justify interference in the affairs of the Company it is not sufficient to show that there are abuses in its administration, for there are necessarily abuses in all governments. It must be shown that several conditions are fulfilled: that the object affected is 'great

[1] *Works*, ii, p. 176 seq. [2] Ibid., ii, pp. 179–80.

and important'; that the abuse is 'a great abuse'; that it is 'habitual and not accidental'; that it is 'utterly incurable in the body as it now stands constituted'.[1]

Burke then begins his survey of India, and the way in which it is governed by the Company. He is conscious that he is approaching the subject methodically, and writes:

> The attention, Sir, which I wish to preserve to method will not be considered as unnecessary or affected. Nothing else can help me to selection out of the infinite mass of materials which have passed under my eye; or can keep my mind steady to the great leading points I have in view.[2]

The method is similar to that in the American speeches, and he begins with a consideration of geographical factors. He pays particular attention to the population of the country, and describes how this population is composed of various orders and classes. This is complicated, he says, by various religions, manners and hereditary employments. He then gives an account of the political and commercial policy of the Company, which amounts to an indictment of both. Burke stresses that the legislator has a duty:

> there we are placed by the Sovereign Disposer; and we must do the best we can in our situation. The situation of man is the preceptor of his duty.[3]

Burke's attack on the administrative policy of the Company draws on an enormous wealth of detail, mainly from the reports of the Select Committee. In this attack he makes reference to abuses which he alleges were perpetrated under the direction of Warren Hastings. Burke had always contended that the legislator should respect the inclinations of the people; but here he contends that the rule of the Company is based on principles exactly the opposite.

In its mastery of historical, geographical and other details, and its refusal to argue simply in terms of theoretical rights, this speech represents Burke's empirical approach to political problems. The legislator must try to make the people happy; and this can be done only by respecting the traditions and customs of those he governs. In all this Burke is, as in his speeches on America, close in spirit to Montesquieu; but to see the full development of these arguments as applied to India we must examine his speeches on the impeachment of Warren Hastings.

After the defeat of Fox's Bill and the fall of the Coalition, Indian affairs began to occupy Burke more than ever, and until the French Revolution, became the main object of his speeches. He devoted

---

[1] Ibid., p. 180.   [2] Ibid., p. 183.   [3] Ibid., p. 197.

some of his energy to opposing Pitt's East India Bill;[1] but the greatest cause of these years was the impeachment of Hastings. On July 30, 1784 Burke moved for papers relative to the conduct of Warren Hastings; in January 1785 he protested against the absence from the King's speech of any mention of India; and in the following month he delivered his great speech on the debts of the Nawab of Arcot.[2] In June Hastings, who had resigned his post as Governor-General in January, arrived in England; and on June 20 Burke gave notice that he would introduce a motion respecting the conduct of a gentleman just returned from India. Shortly after this Burke, Gilbert Elliot and others were engaged in drawing up articles of impeachment. It is unnecessary to follow here the detailed preliminaries to the impeachment, which finally opened on February 13, 1788, and lasted until 1795.[3]

It would be beyond the scope of the present study to attempt anything like a detailed examination of the voluminous material available concerning the impeachment of Warren Hastings.[4] Burke's sources were mainly the information supplied by Francis, and the reports of the Select Committee, rather than political thinkers like Montesquieu. However, Burke does more than accumulate charges against Hastings: he endeavours to base these charges on political principles, and he takes a great deal of trouble to make these principles quite clear in his speeches. As we shall see, these principles are the same as those he expressed in his speeches on America.

It is in his speech on the third day of the trial, on February 15, 1788, that Burke takes most pains to express the principles lying behind his charges against Hastings. He is concerned mainly with the problem of the duty of the legislator to the peoples of India: the problem confronting him is not merely the guilt or innocence of Hastings, but 'whether millions of mankind shall be made miserable, or happy'.[5] Other constitutions, he says, are content to make 'good subjects'; the British constitution is also concerned with the question of 'good governors'.[6]

The way in which Burke treats this question reflects his ideas on the duty of the legislator. We have seen that he had already

---

[1] P.H., xxiv, pp. 1290–1316. [2] P.H., xxv, pp. 163–258; *Works*, iii, p. 122 seq.
[3] See Weitzman, op. cit., chap. vi.
[4] The most important materials are the following: *Minutes of the Evidence taken at the Trial of Warren Hastings*, 11 vols., 1788–94; E. A. Bond (ed.), *Speeches of the Managers and Counsel in the Trial of W. Hastings*, 4 vols., 1859–61; *The History of the Trial of W. Hastings, Esq.*, 1796.
[5] *Works*, vii, p. 9. [6] Ibid., p. 11.

expressed such ideas in the *Abridgment of English History*, the *Present Discontents*, and in the American speeches, and we noted that the influence of Montesquieu was present in each case. Burke, like Montesquieu, insisted that a people must be governed according to their temper and character. In the speeches on the impeachment we find similar ideas. Thus, speaking of the Hindus, Burke says, 'If we undertake to govern the inhabitants of such a country, we must govern them upon their own principles and maxims, and not upon ours'.[1] It is the duty of the legislator to understand their ideas, and not to attempt to force them into British ways of thinking. Burke is particularly interested in what he calls 'opinion', meaning the temper and character of the people:

> We know what the empire of opinion is in human nature. I had almost said that the law of opinion was human nature itself. It is, however, the strongest principle in the composition of the frame of the human mind; and more of the happiness and unhappiness of mankind resides in that inward principle than in all external circumstances put together.[2]

If this is true among us, he says, 'it has a pure, unrestrained, complete, and despotic power amongst them'.[3] He explains what he means: 'The variety of balanced opinion in our minds weakens the force of each', for in Europe the laws of religion, the laws of the land, and the laws of honour often differ; but in India they are all

> united and consolidated in one invariable system, and bind men by eternal and indissoluble bonds to the rules of what, amongst them, is called his *caste*.[4]

Burke's analysis of the general spirit of the inhabitants of India is very similar to what Montesquieu says about China, where the legislators 'confondirent la religion, les lois, les mœurs et les manières: tout cela fut la morale, tout cela fut la vertu'.[5] The result is that 'la Chine ne perd point ses lois par la conquête':

> Les manières, les mœurs, les lois, la religion y étant la même chose, on ne peut changer tout cela à la fois. Et comme il faut que le vainqueur ou le vaincu changent, il a toujours fallu à la Chine que ce fût le vainqueur: car ses mœurs n'étant point ses manières; ses manières, ses lois; ses lois, sa religion; il a été plus aisé qu'il se pliât peu à peu au peuple vaincu, que le peuple vaincu à lui.[6]

This is exactly the same opinion as that expressed by Burke with reference to India. Burke writes,

> We must not force them into the narrow circle of our ideas; we must extend ours to take in their system of opinions and rules, and the necessities, which result from both; all change on their part is absolutely impracticable.[7]

---

[1] Ibid., p. 44. [2] *Idem.* [3] *Idem.* [4] *Idem.*
[5] E.L., xix, 17. [6] E.L., xix, 18. [7] *Works*, vii, p. 44.

Thus in both India and China the general spirit is remarkably rigid and intolerant of change: it follows that the nations which conquer these countries will find it practically impossible, without tyranny, for a new system of laws or rules to be introduced. Montesquieu had indicated one of the most serious consequences of this solidarity of laws, religion and customs:

Il suit encore de là une chose bien triste : c'est qu'il n'est presque pas possible que le christianisme s'établisse jamais à la Chine.[1]

In such a rigid system, any attempt to introduce a new religion would be tantamount to changing laws and customs as well. Burke, likewise, realizes the importance of not changing the religion of such a people, though his approach to this aspect of the problem is cautious:

The policy, civil or religious, or, as theirs is, composed of both, that makes a people happy, and a state flourishing (putting further and higher considerations out of the way, which are not now before us) must undoubtedly, so far as human considerations prevail, be a policy wisely conceived in any scheme of government.[2]

He then proceeds to demonstrate that the Hindu religion has been conducive to good government: this is 'confirmed by all observation'.[3] He contrasts the effect of the 'paternal, lenient, protecting arm of a native government, formed on the long connection of prejudice and power' with the 'effects resulting from the rapacity of a foreign hand'.[4] In order to illustrate this point Burke begins an historical survey of India, under the various conquerors who had preceded British rule. His aim is not to give 'an history of the furious military achievements of a barbarous invader' but to give an idea of 'the principles of policy, which prevailed in these several revolutions'.[5] He approaches the history of India with a view to seeing whether the conquerors of that country ruled in accordance with the spirit of the people.

It is unnecessary to follow Burke in the account he gives of India under Hindu rule, Arab rule, Tamerlane, Akber, then the independent Soubdahs of Bengal, and, finally, under the British. The essential point that emerges from this survey is that,

through all these revolutions in government, and changes in power, an Hindu polity, and the spirit of an Hindu government, did more or less exist in that province with which he was concerned, until it was finally to be destroyed by Mr. Hastings.[6]

Burke thus idealizes the past history of India, and blackens the period

---

[1] E.L., xix, 18.   [2] *Works*, vii, p. 47.   [3] Ibid., p. 47.
[4] Ibid., p. 48.   [5] Ibid., p. 51.   [6] Ibid., p. 55.

of British rule, concluding that Hastings was the greatest tyrant that country had ever known. Speaking of Tamerlane, for example, Burke says that he was 'no barbarian', and that those who submitted to him did not submit like slaves to a conqueror, but,

admitted a great, supreme emperor, who was just, prudent, and politic, instead of the ferocious oppressive lesser Mahommedan sovereigns, who had forced their way by the sword into the country.[1]

Under Tamerlane and his successors the subordinate heads of the various Indian dominions retained most of their rights; but under Hastings they were 'called wretches' and 'treated as such'. Thus Burke concludes that until Hastings began to rule, and in spite of various conquests, 'the Hindus were a favoured, protected, gently treated people'.[2] This, he says, is because though the central government might rise or fall, the subordinate rulers were left to govern their people according to immemorial custom and with respect for their feelings and inclinations.[3]

In his speech on the fourth day of the trial Burke develops some of these ideas, and pays special attention to the history of India since the beginning of British rule. The year 1756 introduced

a new nation from the remotest verge of the western world, with new manners, new customs, new institutions, new opinions, new laws, into the heart of Asia.[4]

As this new nation was to play the part of legislator, it obviously offered a challenge to the ideas they had on this subject. Burke does not consider this in terms of the conquest of India: he is reluctant to discuss the question of whether the conquest was right or wrong, preferring to accept it as an empirical fact:

There is a sacred veil to be drawn over the beginnings of all governments. Ours, in India, had an origin, like those, which time has sanctified by obscurity. Time, in the origin of most governments, has thrown this mysterious veil over them; prudence and discretion make it necessary to throw something of the same drapery over more recent foundations.[5]

In the *Vindication of Natural Society* Burke had shown his dislike of speculations on the origin of governments, and we have seen that this dislike was shared by Montesquieu.[6]

Thus Burke passes over the origin of British government in India to what he considers a more important question, the establishment of good laws. He defines what he conceives to be the duty of a legislator sent from Britain:

[1] Ibid., p. 52.   [2] Ibid., p. 54.   [3] *Idem.*
[4] Ibid., p. 58.   [5] Ibid., p. 60.   [6] See above, p. 40 seq.

when a British governor is sent abroad, he is sent to pursue the good of the people, as much as possible in the spirit of the laws of this country, which in all respects intend their conservation, their happiness, and their prosperity.[1]

What he means is that Hastings 'ought to govern on British principles, not by British forms'.[2] His meaning is that the spirit and principle of justice and liberty are everywhere the same, but the letter differs according to circumstances. Burke insists on the unchangeable character of justice, and singles out for attack the part of Hastings' defence where it had been said that 'actions in Asia do not bear the same moral qualities which the same actions would bear in Europe'.[3] Burke says that the duties of man are governed by 'their relation to the great Governor of the Universe' and by 'their relation to mankind', and not by 'climates, degrees of longitude, parallels not of life but of latitudes'.[4] It is in this speech that we find one of Burke's most explicit references to the higher Natural Law, which is the law of God:

> No man can lawfully govern himself according to his own will, much less can one person be governed by the will of another. We are all born in subjection, all born equally, high and low, governors and governed, in subjection to one great, immutable, pre-existent law, prior to all our devices, and prior to all our contrivances, paramount to all our ideas and all our sensations, antecedent to our very existence, by which we are knit and connected in the eternal frame of the Universe, out of which we cannot stir.[5]

A conqueror must act in the light of this higher law, and Burke goes so far as to call conquest an 'immediate designation of the hand of God'.[6] Obedience to the higher law will, therefore, it seems, take the form of respecting the spirit and established customs of the conquered race.

Burke's ideas on the duty of the legislator are the same as those of Montesquieu. Montesquieu's ideas on this subject are expressed in the *Esprit des lois*: when a people are conquered,

> le droit que le conquérant a sur lui suit quatre sortes de lois : la loi de la nature, qui fait que tout tend à la conservation des espèces; la loi de la lumière naturelle, qui veut que nous fassions à autrui ce que nous voudrions qu'on nous fît; la loi qui forme les sociétés politiques, qui sont telles que la nature n'en a point borné la durée; enfin la loi tirée de la chose même.[7]

He adds that there are four ways of governing such a state:

> il continue à le gouverner selon ses lois, et ne prend pour lui que l'exercice du gouvernement politique et civil; ou il lui donne un nouveau gouvernement

[1] *Works*, vii, p. 92.   [2] Ibid., p. 93.   [3] *Idem*.   [4] Ibid., p. 94.
[5] Ibid., p. 99.   [6] Ibid., p. 100.   [7] E.L., x, 3.

politique et civil; ou il détruit la société et la disperse dans d'autres; ou enfin il extermine tous les citoyens.[1]

The first of these methods is 'conforme au droit des gens que nous suivons aujourd'hui', whereas the last was the method of the Romans,

> sur quoi je laisse à juger à quel point nous sommes devenus meilleurs. Il faut rendre ici hommage à nos temps modernes, à la raison présente, à la religion d'aujourd'hui, à notre philosophie, à nos mœurs.[2]

The similarity of Montesquieu's ideas to those of Burke is obvious. Both thinkers turn away from the notion that the conqueror can do as he pleases to the idea that the conqueror has a duty to govern according to the established opinions of the conquered people. The guiding principle in both thinkers is here the principle of Natural Law; and we have seen that Burke found such ideas in his early study of the classics.[3]

However, not all that Burke says is in agreement with Montesquieu. In one of his speeches he refers to Montesquieu, to contradict him, on the question of whether there are more females born in the East than in the West.[4] More serious, he disagrees with Montesquieu's contention that oriental governments are arbitrary. In his speech on the fourth day of the trial he says,

> I have been endeavouring to inform myself at all times on this subject; of late my duty has led me to a more minute inspection of them, and I challenge the whole race of man to show me any of the oriental governors claiming to themselves a right to act by arbitrary will.[5]

Burke offers this as an empirical generalization, and presents us with a formidable array of facts, showing that the laws of India are based on the Koran, the Institutes of Tamerlane, *Fetfa* (precedents), written codes, *Kanon* (statutes), and *Rage ul Malk* (Common Law). Such laws are incompatible with arbitrary power; and Burke relates how Tavernier, 'a traveller of power and consequence' gives instances of governors having been punished because they abused their trust and aspired after arbitrary power.[6] It follows, according to Burke, that Hastings is guilty, whether judged by British or Indian law: 'Let him run from law to law'—he can find no refuge from justice.[7]

Burke's statement that the government of India had never been

---

[1] *Idem.*   [2] *Idem.*
[3] See above, pp. 56–7. Such ideas were commonplace by the eighteenth century, Cf. Grotius, *Le Droit de la guerre et de la paix*, trans. J. Barbeyrac, 2 vols., Leyden, 1759, Book III, ch. xv, § vii.
[4] *Works*, viii, 261.   [5] Ibid., vii, p. 105.   [6] Ibid., p. 114.   [7] Ibid., p. 118.

despotic was not allowed to pass unchallenged; and in the defence, on February 14, 1792, authorities were quoted to the effect that Burke was mistaken:

> Mr. Burke had said, that there was never such a thing as arbitrary power in India. Mr. Law, on the contrary, read extracts from Bernier, Catrou, Gibbon, Montesquieu, Dow, Major Rennel, and many other unexceptionable writers, in order to prove, that previous to our establishment in India, its history is a history of the treasons, murders, poisonings, cruelties, and despotism of the rankest kind; each author stating that the lands, lives, and properties of every man in India depended solely upon the will of the Sovereign.[1]

Burke was not given an opportunity to reply to this until the reply to the defence which he delivered in May 1794. He complains that the defence

> have thought proper, my lords, to enter into an extended series of quotations from books of travellers, for the purpose of showing that despotism was the only principle of government acknowledged in India,

and, 'after citing a long line of travellers to this effect, they quote Montesquieu, as asserting the same facts'.[2] Burke rejects this idea. In the first place, he points out how absurd it is for a man who had spent twenty-five years in India, fourteen of them as Governor-General, to call in 'a long line of the rabble of travellers, to inform you concerning the objects of his own government'. He adds,

> Good God! would not one rather have expected to hear him put all these travellers to shame by the authority of a man who had resided so long in the supreme situation of government; to set aside all these wild, loose, casual and silly observations of travellers and theorists.[3]

He then sets to work to produce reliable evidence to prove that the Indians have native laws, rights, and property, and he summarizes his purpose thus:

> in short, I mean to prove that every word which Montesquieu has taken from idle and inconsiderate travellers is absolutely false.[4]

Burke's proof consists of an historical survey of Indian laws and customs, ranging from the original Hindu inhabitants to the immediate predecessors of the British. It is, however, Montesquieu's documentation that Burke is attacking, and not Montesquieu's method. It is, indeed, Montesquieu's historical method and the doctrine of the *esprit général* that Burke applies throughout the trial

---

[1] *The History of the Trial of W. Hastings, Esq.*, 1796, Part v, p. 3. The passage quoted from Montesquieu was E.L., xvii, 5, quoted in E. A. Bond, op. cit., ii, p. 540.
[2] *Works*, vii, p. 488.   [3] Ibid., p. 489.   [4] Ibid., p. 491.

of Hastings. His admiration for Montesquieu was not in any way diminished: in 1791 he had penned his greatest eulogy of the President, and in 1795, after the conclusion of the impeachment and the acquittal of Hastings, we find Burke flattered to receive in his home the grandson of Montesquieu.[1] Admiration for Montesquieu's general principles is not incompatible with belief that his documentation is often inaccurate.[2]

In his works on India Burke is under the influence of Montesquieu's historical method and his doctrine of the *esprit général*. However, in these works Burke is not so consciously imitating Montesquieu as in his earlier works on America. The application of ideas from Montesquieu to political problems now comes more naturally to Burke. This may be partly because the subject matter required a broad historical treatment, and involved the essential problem of the duty of the legislator. The question of Natural Law also arose, and in this Burke is, like Montesquieu, a believer in the existence of a higher standard of justice anterior to all positive law.

Burke's application of Montesquieu's method to the problem of India is not unworthy of the master, though it is ironical that Burke, who reproached Montesquieu for using unreliable sources, was blind to the inaccuracy of the information he accepted on the authority of Francis. Thus, if he shares some of Montesquieu's virtues, he also shares his shortcomings.

[1] See above, pp. 37–8.
[2] Cf. above, p. 14, and see M. Dodds, *Les Récits de voyages, sources de l'*Esprit des lois *de Montesquieu*, 1929.

CHAPTER VIII

BURKE AND THE FRENCH REVOLUTION

BETWEEN 1765 and 1789 Burke was much more concerned with practical politics than with abstract theory; and it is not until he begins to write on the French Revolution that he becomes a political philosopher in the proper sense of the word. He believes that the French Revolution is based on a theory—the theory of the rights of man—and that this theory is false. The object of his writings on the French Revolution is to demolish this theory; and in its place he offers his own political philosophy. Burke's opponents argue on the plane of abstract theory, and he is obliged to meet them on their own ground. In a sense it might appear that Burke is returning to the kind of literary and philosophical writing that interested him before 1765, when he wrote the *Vindication of Natural Society* and the *Tracts on the Popery Laws*. Indeed, in these early works we find some of the essential ideas later developed in the works on the French Revolution, notably his dislike of theories of natural right, his defence of empiricism, and his ideas on Natural Law. However, although Burke is thus in a sense fulfilling his early promise as a political philosopher, it would be a mistake not to stress the fact that his writings on the French Revolution grow directly out of his political career with the Rockinghams. We have seen that, as propagandist for the Rockinghams, Burke was always ready to have recourse to political theory; but such theory was usually in the nature of a rationalization or idealization of his political experience. There were times, however, when Burke had to take political theory seriously for its own sake, and especially when combating radical reformers. The Rockinghams were an aristocratic group with no love for parliamentary reform; and it was the task of Burke, as their spokesman, to put their point of view and defend them against arguments used by radicals. The radical arguments were those of natural right, derived largely from Locke, but throughout the eighteenth century among the commonplaces of every political pamphleteer. On at least one occasion—on May 7, 1782—Burke gave a fairly full statement of his objections to reform based on such arguments; and in this speech we have the essentials of the arguments he uses when writing on the French Revolution.[1] It

[1] This speech is on the question of parliamentary reform, see *Works*, vi, pp. 144–53; Cf. the *Letter on the Duration of Parliaments*, in *Works*, vi, pp. 1–5 (1780).

was not, however, until the Revolution that this kind of radicalism which Burke had always opposed achieved a great victory in a European state, and this victory in France gave a new lease of life to English radicalism.[1] Burke thereupon was alarmed and felt obliged to give a much more complete and coherent exposition of his views on this subject. In a sense he was fulfilling the literary and philo-sophical career he began with the publication of the *Vindication of Natural Society*; but at the same time he is giving a full and coherent statement of the Rockingham hostility to radicalism.

It is important to stress the truth of Burke's remark in a letter to Calonne, where he is speaking of the *Reflections*,

In reality, my object was not France, in the first instance, but this country.[2]

When the news of the first manifestations of the French Revolution reached England there were many who greeted it with rapturous joy. One of the foremost admirers of the Revolution was Charles James Fox, who, with a small group of followers, had never really shared the Rockingham dislike of radicalism. Fox, referring to the fall of the Bastille, exclaimed, 'How much the greatest event it is that ever happened in the world, and how much the best!',[3] and he called the draft of the new French constitution 'the most stupen-dous and glorious edifice of liberty, which had been erected on the foundations of human integrity in any time or country'.[4] Burke himself received the news with mixed feelings, confessing that 'the spirit it is impossible not to admire'.[5] However, he soon decided that the Revolution was completely evil and in a letter written in November to Charles-François de Pont gives the essentials of his arguments against the philosophy of the Revolution.[6] By this time Burke had realized the affinity between the ideas of the French revolutionaries and the English radicals. English newspapers of the time were full of accounts of the events that were taking place in France, including the debates of the National Assembly.[7] It was natural for Burke to dislike the stress that the French were placing on

[1] See S. MacCoby, *English Radicalism*, 5 vols., 1935–55, vol. ii; G. S. Veitch, *The Genesis of Parliamentary Reform*, 1913; W. T. Laprade, *England and the French Revolution*, 1789–97, Baltimore, 1909; P. A. Brown, *The French Revolution in English History*, 1918; A. Cobban, *The Debate on the French Revolution*, 1789–1800, 1950.

[2] October 25, 1790, quoted in C. de Parrel, 'Burke and Calonne', *French Quarterly*, 11 (1929), 11–18.

[3] Lord John Russell, *Memorials and Correspondence of C. J. Fox*, 4 vols., 1853, ii, p. 361.

[4] P.H., xxix, p. 249.

[5] *Historical Manuscripts Commission*, Thirteenth Report, Appendix, Part viii (Charlemont MSS., vol. ii), pp. 105–6. [6] *Corr.*, iii, pp. 102–121.

[7] See for 1789–90: The *Courier de Londres; London Chronicle; Whitehall Evening Post; St. James's Chronicle*.

L

metaphysical arguments on the rights of man and the importance
they attached to theoretical problems of government.[1] At the same
time he was aware of the enthusiasm the events in France kindled
among English radicals. One of the clearest manifestations of this
kind of enthusiasm was on the meeting of the Revolution Society
in November 1789. This was a body of Dissenters who met an-
nually to celebrate the Revolution of 1688; and on this occasion
Dr. Richard Price preached a sermon entitled *A Discourse on the
Love of our Country*, in which he not only praised the principles of
the French Revolution, but also identified them with the principles
which had inspired the Revolution of 1688. The Revolution Society
sent an address to the French National Assembly, and opened correspondence with societies in Dijon and Lille.[2] Price's sermon was
widely read and discussed, and other radical societies followed the
Revolution Society in sending an address to the National Assembly
and in corresponding with French political societies. For our purpose
it is particularly interesting that Price's sermon provoked many
replies, and that long before Burke published his *Reflections* (November 1790) there had been a voluminous pamphlet literature on the
problems raised by Price.[3] Some of Price's opponents use arguments
similar to those employed by Burke, showing that the latter was
very often simply drawing on arguments which were commonplace.[4] Burke's views on the French Revolution led to his famous
quarrel with Fox, and to Burke's temporary isolation from his
former colleagues, now under the Duke of Portland. But though
Burke was described as 'a man decried, persecuted, and proscribed;
not being much valued, even by his own party',[5] his isolation was
more apparent than real, and the main body of Portland's followers
were in agreement with Burke by 1792.[6] The truth is that Burke
was expressing the opinions of a vast section of his fellow-countrymen
who 'were seriously alarmed by the dangerous and rapid progress
of democracy in France'.[7] His became the great voice of English
conservative opinion, and the battle which raged around the
Reflections mainly in the name of Burke and Thomas Paine, was

[1] Particularly in the debates of August 1789 on the declaration of rights: see J. Mavidal,
E. Laurent and others, *Archives parlementaires*, Ser. 1, 82 vols., viii, 214 seq.
[2] Veitch, op. cit., chapter vi.
[3] Reviews and extracts of such pamphlets are given in the *Critical Review* and *Gentleman's
Magazine*, for 1789–90.
[4] Cf. below, p. 145 seq.
[5] W. Windham, *The Windham Papers*, 2 vols., 1913, i, p. 97.
[6] For Burke's relations with his former colleagues see H. Butterfield, 'Charles James Fox
and the Whig Opposition', *Cambridge Journal of History*, 9 (1949), pp. 293–330.
[7] J. Courtenay, *Philosophical Reflections on the Late Revolution in France*, 1790, p. 2.

really the culmination of the struggle which had been going on all
through the eighteenth century between conservatism and radicalism.
Eighteenth-century radical thought always drew on theories of
abstract rights; and there was also a tradition of conservative thought,
reaching back to the seventeenth century, and, indeed, beyond.[1]
Burke makes full use of this conservative tradition, and, in a
sense, he fights over again a battle which had already been fought
many times. He is fully aware that he is greatly indebted to tradition
for his arguments against the French revolutionaries, and at one
point in the *Reflections* says,

> I assure you I do not aim at singularity. I give you opinions which have been
> accepted amongst us, from very early times to this moment, with a continued and
> general approbation, and which indeed are so worked into my mind, that I am
> unable to distinguish what I have learned from others from the results of my own
> meditation.[2]

We shall see that much of Burke's philosophy can be traced to
the English Common Law tradition. He also gives us another
hint of the sources of his ideas when he says in his *Letter to a Member
of the National Assembly*,

> We continue, as in the last two ages, to read, more generally than I believe is
> now done on the continent, the authors of sound antiquity. These occupy our
> minds.[3]

We have already mentioned Burke's early admiration for Cicero;[4]
in his writings on the French Revolution he owes much to classical
sources, and especially to the Stoics.

Our examination of the influence of Montesquieu on Burke at
this time must clearly take account of these other important influences on his thought. Indeed, since Burke himself believes that he is
unable to distinguish what he has learned from others from what is
of his own invention our task must appear difficult. However, in
our attempt to discover his debt to Montesquieu we shall be helped
by the fact that we know what aspects of Montesquieu's thought he
found most attractive in his earlier works. It will also be helpful if
we know something of Montesquieu's reputation in France and
England at the time of the Revolution: this will show us that at the
time when Burke was the champion of conservatism in England
Montesquieu was being attacked by radicals because of the empirical
and conservative nature of his thought. The enemies of Burke were
also the enemies of Montesquieu, and this is a line of approach worth

[1] J. G. A. Pocock, *The Ancient Constitution and the Feudal Law*, Cambridge, 1957, pp. 21–43.
[2] *Works*, ii, pp. 370–1.   [3] Ibid., p. 541.   [4] See above, pp. 56–7.

following, as it will reveal something of the affinity of the thought of the two thinkers.

It is true that certain aspects of Montesquieu's thought were admired by the French revolutionaries. Montesquieu was considered an authority on republics: the article REPUBLIQUE in the *Encyclopédie* was largely inspired from Montesquieu; and the *Chronique de Paris* published in May, 1793, a series of articles on 'Montesquieu républicain'.[1] However, the general spirit of the Revolution was hostile to Montesquieu, and attacks on him at this time are common.[2] One of his admirers at this time was probably expressing the general view when he wrote,

> C'est sans doute une maladresse de se donner pour disciple de Montesquieu dans un temps où on le réfute d'une manière aussi victorieuse que laconique.[3]

Another writer predicted that the opponents of the doctrines of natural right and enemies of the Revolution would have recourse to Montesquieu: 'jamais ce nom n'aura été proclamé avec plus d'éclat; ceux qui l'auraient autrefois fait brûler, le canoniseraient aujourd'hui'.[4] The same writer thinks that although in his day Montesquieu was 'un génie bienfaisant', he is also 'un génie coupable, lorsqu'il défend l'aristocratie'.[5] He criticizes Montesquieu for his preoccupation with empirical facts and his conservatism:

> Il semble avoir omis deux parties essentielles de son ouvrage, son commencement et sa fin; la première, destinée à montrer les droits de l'homme naturel, le contrat spécial ou tacite de toute société . . . : la seconde, consacrée à enseigner les moyens de perfectionner les gouvernements.[6]

Such criticism of Montesquieu is widespread not only among the more radical reformers of the time, but also among moderates like Mounier, who says of Montesquieu that, 'cet auteur ... n'a jamais assez oublié qu'il était noble français, membre d'un parlement', and that 'cet écrivain, en cherchant l'esprit des institutions, a toujours tâché de justifier tout ce qu'il a trouvé établi'.[7] One of the most representative attacks published at this time on Montesquieu was

---

[1] See F. A. Aulard, *Histoire politique de la Révolution française*, 5th ed., 1921, p. 9.

[2] See E. Carcassonne, *Montesquieu et le problème de la constitution française au XVIIIe siècle*, 1927; G. Bonno, *La Constitution britannique devant l'opinion française de Montesquieu à Bonaparte*, 1931; A. Masson, 'Naissance et fortune de l'"Esprit des lois"', *Revue des Deux Mondes*, Oct. 15, 1948; B. Mirkine-Guetzévitch, 'De l'"Esprit des lois" à la démocratie moderne', in Mirkine-Guétzévitch (ed.), *Bicentenaire de l'"Esprit des lois"*, 1948.

[3] Anon., *Le Disciple de Montesquieu*, 1789, p. 33.

[4] [P.-A. Grouvelle], *De l'autorité de Montesquieu dans la Revolution présente*, n.p., 1789, pp. 10–11.   [5] Ibid., p. 14.   [6] Ibid., p. 20.

[7] *Nouvelles observations sur les Etats-généraux de France*, n.p., 1789, pp. 212–4.

that in the *Lettres de M. Helvétius au Président de Montesquieu et à M. Saurin, relatives à l'aristocratie et la noblesse*.[1] These letters were in fact not written by Helvétius;[2] but they are particularly interesting in that they were known in England. We find Sir Samuel Romilly asking for a copy of the work,[3] and it is reviewed in the *Gentleman's Magazine*, where we read that Montesquieu's principles 'have been embraced and urged by the aristocratic party in France'.[4]

If Burke had read the pseudo-Helvétius letters he would have found that Montesquieu was attacked, in the first place on account of his empiricism and conservatism:

> un écrivain qui voulait être utile aux hommes devait plus s'occuper de maximes vraies dans un meilleur ordre de choses à venir que de consacrer celles qui sont dangereuses, du moment que le préjugé s'en empare pour s'en servir et les perpétuer.[5]

Also, Montesquieu is attacked on account of his having praised the British constitution. It was, indeed, common at this time to attack the British monarchy: Sieyès, for example, refers to the House of Lords as 'un monument de superstition gothique' and the constitution in general as 'un échafaudage prodigieux de précautions contre le désordre'.[6] In the pseudo-Helvétius letters we read,

> L'exemple du gouvernement anglais vous a séduit. Je suis bien loin de penser que cette constitution soit parfaite . . . La liberté même dont la nation anglaise jouit est-elle bien dans les principes de cette constitution plutôt que dans deux ou trois bonnes lois qui n'en dépendent pas, que les Français pourraient se donner et qui, seules, rendraient peut-être leur gouvernement plus supportable.[7]

Montesquieu is also attacked for what he says about the French constitution, and the author complains that, 'C'est par des usurpations héréditaires que nous sommes gouvernés'.[8] The best reply to these attacks is to be found in the writings of Burke on the Revolution: Burke defends the empirical and conservative approach to politics, and at the same time he defends the British and French constitutions.

If the French revolutionaries considered Montesquieu as an enemy, Burke showed that he was aware that there was little in

---

[1] Paris, 1789.

[2] R. Koebner, 'The Authenticity of the letters on the "Esprit des lois" attributed to Helvétius', *Bulletin of the Institute of Historical Research*, 24 (1951), pp. 19–43. The author of the letters was M.-L. de La Roche.

[3] Sir Samuel Romilly, *Memoirs of the Life of Sir Samuel Romilly*, 2nd ed., 3 vols., 1840, i, p. 373 (Letter of Oct. 1789).

[4] Jan. 1790, p. 67.   [5] *Œuvres* (Nagel), iii, p. 1103.

[6] E.-J. Sieyès, *Qu'est-ce que le Tiers Etat?* ed. E. Champion, 1888, pp. 61–62.

[7] *Œuvres* (Nagel), iii, p. 1104.   [8] Ibid., p. 1540.

common between their philosophy and that of the author of the *Esprit des lois*. In a letter to a friend he says,

> You say, my dear Sir, they read Montesquieu—I believe not. If they do they do not understand him. He is often obscure, sometimes misled by system; but on the whole, a learned and ingenious writer, and sometimes a most profound thinker. Sure it is they have not followed him in any one thing they have done. Had he lived at this time, he would certainly be among the fugitives from France.[1]

But, on the other hand, Burke believes that writers like Voltaire and Rousseau played an important part in bringing about the Revolution:

> With regard to the other writers you speak of, I do believe the directors of the present system to be influenced by them! Such masters! Such scholars! Who ever dreamt of Voltaire and Rousseau as legislators? The first has the merit of writing agreeably, and nobody has ever united blasphemy and obscenity so happily together. The other was not a little deranged in his intellects, to my almost certain knowledge.[2]

If Burke sees in Montesquieu the very antithesis of the spirit of the Revolution, it is Rousseau that he sees as the main source of the abstract theory which he is concerned to refute. It is true that Rousseau was not the uncompromising theorist of natural right Burke would have us believe, and that there was an empirical side to Rousseau's teaching. But Rousseau's more zealous French disciples did not notice the two sides to Rousseau, and so it is with Burke, who is more interested in refuting the theory of the rights of man, no matter what its source, than in giving a scholarly and exact interpretation of Rousseau.[3] He would certainly, however, have found in Rousseau a passage which regrets that Montesquieu was too much concerned with the nature of governments as they are and not enough with what they ought to be.[4] In his early literary works Burke had admired Montesquieu and attacked Rousseau: we find the same attitude in his writings on the French Revolution.

We have seen that in his earlier works the most striking of Burke's debts to Montesquieu was his use of the historical method. Burke had applied this method in the *Abridgment of English History*, where he was dealing with the past, and in his speeches on America and India where he was concerned with the present. We might expect to see

---

[1] J. Prior, *Memoir of the Life of Edmund Burke*, 2nd ed., 2 vols., 1826, ii, p. 50.
[2] *Idem.*
[3] For the two sides of Rousseau's thought, as seen by a contemporary of Burke see *Mémoire de M. le comte de Lally-Tolendal ou seconde lettre à ses commetans*, 1790, p. 7.
[4] *The Political Writings of J. J. Rousseau*, ed. C. E. Vaughan, 2 vols., Cambridge, 1915, ii, p. 147.

in his writings on the French Revolution yet another example of his use of this method; but this is not so, and instead of seeking for physical and moral causes which produced the Revolution, he writes, almost in despair,

> All circumstances taken together, the French Revolution is the most astonishing that has hitherto happened in the world. The most wonderful things are brought about in many instances by means the most absurd and ridiculous; in the most ridiculous modes; and, apparently, by the most contemptible instruments.[1]

Burke is thus compelled to accept the hypothesis that the Revolution was brought about by the influence of political theorists, and especially by Rousseau. One might be tempted to say that Burke did not want to apply the historical method to the French Revolution because he did not want to discover historical causes, for to explain is to some extent to excuse, and Burke was not interested in giving a cool objective analysis of the Revolution as an historical phenomenon: his intention was to combat it as a menace to mankind on account of the theory it embodied. It is not, however, sufficient to say that Burke did not apply the historical method for this reason. He does not apply Montesquieu's historical method because he no longer believes in it. There are a number of explicit utterances in his writings on the Revolution which make quite clear his views on this subject. To begin with, he objects to the idea that states are subject to scientific laws of growth and decay like physical bodies:

> But commonwealths are not physical but moral essences. They are artificial combinations, and, in their proximate efficient cause, the arbitrary productions of the human mind.[2]

It must be said at once that Montesquieu had not assumed that states were physical bodies, and he makes it quite clear that though laws and institutions are to a large extent determined by physical factors, they are the product of 'la raison humaine' of the legislator.[3] But, on the other hand, Montesquieu had taught that states decay and decline: he had analysed the decline of Rome, and felt that the political philosopher could formulate, as a general law, that all states follow this pattern. He wrote of the British constitution: 'Comme toutes les choses humaines ont une fin, l'état dont nous parlons perdra sa liberté'.[4] It is this sort of historical determinism that Burke now opposes: he is faced with the claims of the French revolutionary philosophers who maintain that the British constitution, like the French monarchy, is effete and doomed to decay.

---

[1] *Works*, ii, p. 284.
[2] Ibid., v, p. 153.
[3] See above, p. 16 seq.
[4] E.L., xi, 6.

Burke's reply to this sort of diagnosis of states is to attack the methodology of his opponents:

> I doubt whether the history of mankind is yet complete enough, if ever it can be so, to furnish grounds for a sure theory on the internal causes which necessarily affect the fortune of a state. I am far from denying the operation of such causes: but they are infinitely uncertain, and much more obscure, and much more difficult to trace, than the foreign causes that tend to raise, to depress, and sometimes to overwhelm a community.[1]

It follows from this that the historian must resign himself to ascribing a great deal to 'mere chance' or to 'the occasional interposition and the irresistible hand of the Great Disposer'.[2] Thus,

> A common soldier, a child, a girl at the door of an inn, have changed the face of fortune, and almost of nature.[3]

All this amounts to a negation of the lesson taught by Montesquieu in the *Romains*, a work which Burke now—though not in the same context—mentions in unflattering terms as one of the textbooks of the French revolutionaries.[4] Thus Burke retreats from the conception of history he had held up to this time, and which had, following the teaching of Montesquieu, eliminated the part played by mere chance and Divine Providence, and attempted to trace events to physical and moral causes. Indeed, we might wonder if Burke's use of Montesquieu's historical method was ever absolutely wholehearted. In the *Abridgment of English History* he had shown a tendency to lapse into references to Divine Providence;[5] and in his American and Indian speeches he was not a philosopher or historian, but primarily a propagandist, using Montesquieu's method as means to an end. In any case, it is certain that in the last resort he is hostile to Montesquieu's historical method. He is now interested in the moral content of history: it is not to be studied for the purpose of discovering scientific laws of human behaviour, but for the wisdom it embodies,

> In history a great volume is unrolled for our instruction, drawing the materials of future wisdom from the past errors and infirmities of mankind.[6]

He believes that the state, as a moral essence, will flourish as long as the moral qualities of its citizens are pure: there is no question of inevitable decay as in the physical world. Burke therefore cannot accept Montesquieu's doctrine that all states, including the British constitution, inevitably decay.

---

[1] *Works*, v, p. 153.   [2] Ibid., p. 154.   [3] *Idem.*
[4] Ibid., v, p. 249.   [5] See above, pp. 54–5.   [6] *Works*, ii, p. 412.

At this point it must be pointed out that there is something of an inconsistency in Montesquieu's teaching. If on the one hand he teaches that states inevitably decay; on the other hand he always insists that he is not a fatalist or 'spinosiste';[1] and the doctrine of the *esprit général* is inconsistent with the doctrine of the inevitability of the decay of states. His theory of the *esprit général* embodies a theory of progress, showing that whereas in primitive states the physical factors of climate and situation predominate and determine laws and institutions, in more advanced states it is possible for the legislator to shift the emphasis more and more to moral factors, thus showing that man is to a large extent master of his own fate.[2] Montesquieu shows that the corruption of states is to be explained not simply in terms of scientific law: this corruption was brought about by the corruption of their 'principles' of virtue, honour, or fear. In the last resort it depends on men themselves to keep the 'principles' pure: it is within the power of the legislator (except possibly in very primitive civilizations) to direct and emphasize the moral aspects of the *esprit général*, and to direct and maintain the purity especially of those aspects of the *esprit général* which form the 'principles' of the state. The state will survive as long as the moral principles behind it survive; and this is a question of morals, not of scientific law. Montesquieu the sociologist and historian looks at the history of the past and sees events forming certain well-defined patterns, including the pattern of decline and fall of states. But Montesquieu the moralist sees that, strictly speaking, these examples of decline and fall need not have happened: man is an intelligent being with free will, and he does not necessarily follow predictable patterns of behaviour. In the *Romains* Montesquieu speaks primarily as an historian, and the emphasis is on historical determinism; but in the *Esprit des lois* the emphasis on morals is strong, for Montesquieu is concerned not only with laws but also with the problem of whether laws are good or bad. Montesquieu's double approach to institutions and history, involving both moral idealism and historical determinism, leads him into certain contradictions, as when at one moment he says that the British constitution must necessarily perish, and at the next that no government need perish so long as its moral principles are kept pure. In looking back into the past and finding a pattern in historical events Montesquieu was on fairly safe ground, for at least he had facts on which he could base his inductions; but on looking into the future and predicting the fate of states he was

[1] E.L., i, 1; *Défense de l'Esprit des lois.*   [2] See above, p. 22 seq.

involving a different set of assumptions of a highly questionable nature. It was against this notion that the future could be predicted that Burke reacts with such violence.[1]

Burke's attack on historical determinism is part of his general attack on the mania for systems at the time of the Revolution. He maintains that states, being moral essences, are not subject to the universal laws of the physical world. The individual human being, considered from the physical point of view, has a body and therefore is 'subject to laws universal and invariable';[2] but this is not so of the state. Any theory which assumes that the behaviour of states can be predicted is fundamentally wrong, for, though there are inductive laws relevant to the moral world, Burke says that they are as yet unknown to us.[3] It follows from this that we do not possess the necessary knowledge to enable us to draw up comprehensive plans of reform: Burke says that the historian, looking into the past, is unable to see there any clear pattern of behaviour of states, and that much depends on mere chance or Divine Providence. How much more difficult is it, then, for the political speculator and reformer who looks into the future and tries to produce a plan for the society of tomorrow! This, according to Burke, is the predicament of French politicians, and their English admirers praise the new French constitution not for what it is, but for what it will become: 'They do not talk as politicians, but as prophets'.[4] These politicians do not understand that it is impossible to apply to the subject matter of politics a method which is applicable only to the physical sciences. The scientist· can formulate laws which will enable him to predict the behaviour of physical bodies; but the politician is denied any such privilege as far as non-physical bodies are concerned. Since the French philosophers insist in applying a method suitable only for bodies devoid of moral qualities it is not surprising that they are not interested in men as intelligent or moral beings. To these politicians a human being is thus simply an animal for experiment:

> These philosophers consider men in their experiments, no more than they do mice in an air pump, or in a recipient of mephitic gas.[5]

They are not interested in the moral aspects of the problems that confront them:

---

[1] For the problem of methodology discussed here Cf. Karl Popper, *The Poverty of Historicism*, 1957.
[2] *Works*, v, p. 153.   [3] Ibid., pp. 153–4.   [4] Ibid., iii, pp. 16–17.
[5] Ibid., v, p. 142.

But in these gentlemen, there is nothing of the tender, parental solicitude, which fears to cut up the infant for the sake of an experiment.[1]

They do not really understand the complexity of human nature or political problems, but suppose that men will conform their behaviour to schemes of reform drawn up on paper. Thus they treat legislation as a matter of arithmetic and pseudo-scientific calculation, dividing their country up into new administrative units, organizing finance and elections, but, in so doing, inevitably oversimplifying and misunderstanding human nature: 'They reduce men to loose counters, merely for the sake of simple telling'.[2] They are not interested in man as an individual with all his idiosyncracies:

It is remarkable, that, in a great arrangement of mankind, not one reference whatsoever is to be found to anything moral or anything politic; nothing that relates to the concerns, the actions, the passions, the interests of men. *Hominem non sapiunt.*[3]

In this they differ greatly from the legislators of the ancient republics, who 'had to do with men, and they were obliged to study human nature'.[4] But in France Burke sees with sorrow that 'an unfeeling heart, and an undoubting confidence, are the sole qualifications for a perfect legislator'.[5]

Burke's attack on the methodology of the French politicans involves a turning away from the historical method he had earlier employed, and borrowed from Montesquieu. But his main attack on the French is not so much against their interpretation of the past as against their attempts to formulate comprehensive plans for the future. It cannot be denied that Burke rejects Montesquieu's historical method as a means of interpreting the past; but in his attack on the attempts of the French revolutionaries to predict the future on pseudo-scientific principles he is not in disagreement with Montesquieu's real opinion on this problem. It is true that Montesquieu had formulated various laws about the future of states— and notably on the British constitution—but we have seen that this is not entirely consistent with the main body of his doctrine, and he believes that politics should be based on human nature. He believes that change should be slow and gradual, not a matter for sweeping reform. Burke, as we have seen, thought that Montesquieu was 'sometimes misled by system', and we are now able to understand the full significance of this remark. But Burke adds immediately

---

[1] Ibid., ii, pp. 436–7. [2] Ibid., p. 455. [3] Ibid., p. 452.
[4] Ibid., p. 454. [5] Ibid., p. 439.

that Montesquieu is, 'on the whole, a learned and ingenious writer,
and sometimes a most profound thinker'.[1] He sees in him the complete antithesis of the revolutionary spirit. The nature of the kinship
which Burke felt between his ideas and those of Montesquieu will
appear as we examine Burke's ideas on the revolutionary doctrine
of natural rights.

In the *Vindication of Natural Society* Burke had attacked the theory
of the social contract and natural rights by showing that abstract
theory was irrelevant in politics, which required an empirical
approach.[2] In his writings on the French Revolution Burke attacks
the theory of natural right in the same way, but with subtler and
more fully developed arguments. Some of the most celebrated
passages of Burke's writings are those where he attacks the abstract
theory of the French revolutionary philosophers. However, he
does not object to abstract theory as such, but only when it over-
steps its bounds: 'I do not put abstract ideas wholly out of any
question, because I well know that under that name I should dismiss
principles'.[3] He insists that abstract ideas, and notably those of
rights, exist on a metaphysical plane of thought which makes them,
in their pure form, irrelevant in ordinary life:

As to abstract rights of all kinds, he thought they were incorporeal, and unfit
for the body. They might be discussed in some other state; but they were totally
unfit for this life, and consequently could not be fit for argument. These abstract
ideas were too airy diet, and ill suited the mixed constitution of man, which was
composed of speculation and practice, of mind and body.[4]

It is interesting that Montesquieu, when making his most important
methodological pronouncements, stressed the fact that man was
part mind and part body. Montesquieu believed that if man were
purely physical he would conform to universal scientific laws, and if
purely intelligence he would conform to the higher moral law in its
abstract form; but as man is of mixed nature, neither the scientific
nor the metaphysical approach to politics will be successful. The
approach recommended by Montesquieu is that whereby the
legislator follows the *esprit général*, taking into account physical and
moral factors, and at the same time not forgetting that there is a
higher moral law which serves as guide.[5] Burke's point of view is
very close indeed to that of Montesquieu:

A statesman differs from a professor in an university; the latter has only the
general view of society; the former, the statesman, has a number of circumstances

---

[1] See above, p. 148.   [2] See above, p. 40 seq.   [3] *Works*, vi, pp. 113–14.
[4] P.H., xxix, pp. 1388–9.   [5] See above, pp. 23–4.

to combine with those general ideas, and to take into his consideration. . . . A statesman, never losing sight of principles, is to be guided by circumstances.[1]

Burke reproaches the French revolutionaries with misunderstanding human nature: if on the one hand they tend to treat man as subject to scientific laws and as a purely physical being, they also go to the other extreme and speak as though man could govern himself by metaphysical abstractions. In all this Burke sees an example of muddled thinking.

Burke points out that the French commit a grave error of logic in attempting to apply natural rights directly to the state of civil society. In the hypothetical state of nature men no doubt enjoy natural rights, such as the right of self-defence.[2] But in the state of civil society we move on a different plane of thought:

how can any man claim under the conventions of civil society, rights which do not so much as suppose its existence? rights which are absolutely repugnant to it? . . . Men cannot enjoy the rights of an uncivil and of a civil state together.[3]

In civil society men enjoy not hypothetical natural rights but civil rights, and the latter are the '*real* rights of men'.[4] Burke summarizes the civil rights of men thus: 'Whatever each man can separately do, without trespassing upon others, he has a right to do for himself'.[5] Turning aside from the hypothetical man, he says, 'I have in my contemplation the civil social man, and no other'.[6] He stresses the difference between natural and civil rights:

Government is not made in virtue of natural rights, which may and do exist in total independence of it; and exist in much greater clearness, and in a much greater degree of abstract perfection: but their abstract perfection is their practical defect. By having a right to everything they want everything.[7]

Burke defines government as 'a contrivance of human wisdom to provide for human *wants*', and among these wants he counts restraints on passions. Such restraints form no part of the theory of natural rights. Burke says that 'the restraints on men, as well as their liberties, are to be reckoned among their rights'.[8] But these restraints and liberties, he says, 'vary with times and circumstances, and admit of infinite modifications, they cannot be settled upon any abstract rule'.[9] His conclusion is that the task of the legislator is 'like every other experimental science, not to be taught *a priori*':[10] the legislator must adopt a cautious trial-and-error technique, avoiding sudden

---

[1] *Works*, vi, p. 114.   [2] Ibid., ii, p. 332.   [3] *Idem*.   [4] Ibid., ii, p. 331.
[5] Ibid., p. 332.   [6] *Idem*.   [7] Ibid., pp. 332–3.   [8] Ibid., p. 333.
[9] *Idem*.   [10] *Idem*.

change, and respecting institutions that have stood the test of time. The proper guide for the legislator is not metaphysics but prudence, 'the first in rank of the virtues, political and moral', and 'the director, the regulator, the standard of them all'.[1]

Burke takes some pains to demonstrate the shortcomings of the abstract reason of metaphysics when applied to politics, which he contrasts with the approach of the wise legislator, who takes prudence as his guide. Metaphysics tends to pursue simple truths to extremes: 'The excellence of mathematics and metaphysics is to have but one thing before you'.[2] The excellence of the moralist and the politician is, however, different:

> he forms the best judgement of all moral disquisitions, who has the greatest number and variety of considerations in one view before him, and can take them in with the best possible consideration of the middle results of all.[3]

Burke is here expounding the classical doctrine of the mean, and he never tires of repeating it. With particular reference to the doctrine of natural rights he says,

> The pretended rights of these theorists are all extremes: and in proportion as they are metaphysically true, they are morally and politically false. The rights of men are in a sort of *middle*, incapable of definition, but not impossible to be discerned. The rights of men in governments are their advantages; and these are often in balances between differences of good; in compromises between good and evil, and sometimes between evil and evil.[4]

Metaphysics, when applied to the subject matter of politics amounts to nothing more than 'clumsy subtlety' which deforms and over-simplifies human nature.[5] It is for this reason that he believes that 'the simple governments are fundamentally defective, to say no worse of them'.[6] It is in the mixed British constitution that he sees the best example of the mean in political institutions:

> The whole scheme of our mixed constitution is to prevent any one of its principles from being carried as far as, taken by itself, and, theoretically, it would go. . . . To avoid the perfections of extreme, all its several parts are so constituted, as not alone to answer their own several ends, but also each to limit and control the others.[7]

Burke's attack on metaphysical politics thus becomes a defence of the British constitution.

It is perhaps futile to attempt to find precise sources for Burke's attack on metaphysics and natural rights, for he is repeating much

---

[1] *Works*, iii, p. 16.   [2] Ibid., vi, p. 133.   [3] *Idem.*   [4] Ibid., ii, p. 335.
[5] Ibid., p. 331.   [6] Ibid., p. 334.   [7] Ibid., iii, p. 110.

that was commonplace at this time both in France and England. Many French politicians were of the opinion of Etienne Dumont, who refers to the debates on the Declaration of Rights as 'vaines disputes de mots, fatras métaphysique, bavardage assommant',[1] and it was the constant theme of moderate opinion in the National Assembly that 'Ce n'est pas des droits naturels ... qu'il faut s'occuper; c'est des droits civils, du droit positif propre à un grand peuple'.[2] The debates of July and August 1789 are thus mainly occupied with the reasons for and against publishing a declaration of rights; and there we find abundant criticism of the futility of attempting to apply metaphysics to politics, and we find reasoning in support of the empirical method which takes account of circumstances and traditions. One member of the National Assembly pointed out how vulnerable a declaration of natural rights would be to attack from their enemies:

> songez quelles armes nous donnerions à nos calomniateurs; comme ils triompheraient; comme ils diraient que sur cette égalité primitive qui ne serait pour eux que la confusion de la société, que sur le droit de nature qui ne serait, à les entendre, que le droit de la force, nous voulons établir la subvention de toute société.[3]

It is thus clear that the French foresaw in what terms they would be attacked by the champions of the old order. They may thus be said to have anticipated Burke's attack; but Burke was not the first English writer to publish a pamphlet against the principles of the French Revolution, and in pamphlets like *Observations on Dr. Price's Revolution Sermon*,[4] we find that the English were perfectly familiar with arguments based on the incompatibility of natural and civil rights, and the irrelevance of metaphysics to politics.

The originality of Burke's writings on the French Revolution does not lie so much in his inventing new ideas as in his ability to express with great eloquence and subtlety ideas which in one form or another were generally accepted by conservative opinion in England. He rises above the level of mere propaganda to become a political philosopher, and, not content merely to destroy his opponents' arguments, he has a positive as well as a negative side to his writings. Above all he gives a moral significance to his theory. It was certainly Burke's early interest in political philosophy that enabled him to think more profoundly about these problems than the average political pamphleteer of his time. He was able to go

---

[1] E. Dumont, *Souvenirs de Mirabeau*, 1832, p. 138.
[2] *Archives parlementaires*, viii, p. 323; Cf. ibid., pp. 214–16; 222–3; 280–1; 283–6; 321–2; 340–57.   [3] Ibid., p. 222.
[4] Reviewed in *Gentleman's Magazine*, Feb. 1790, p. 143 seq.

beyond the commonplaces of contemporary thought to the great political thinkers in whom these commonplaces had their origin, or in whom, at least, these commonplaces appeared in philosophical form. Thus, every opponent of the Revolution complained of the irrelevance of the abstract perfection of metaphysics, but Burke appears to be the only thinker who develops and deepens this argument by reaching back to the classical doctrine of the mean. It is interesting that Montesquieu admired this doctrine:

Je le dis et il me semble que je n'ai fait cet ouvrage que pour le prouver : l'esprit de modération doit être celui du législateur; le bien politique, comme le bien moral, se trouve toujours entre deux limites.[1]

When Burke expounds his doctrine of the mean he is simply using a commonplace of political philosophy rather than following Montesquieu; but it is surely Montesquieu he has in mind when he says that the object of the mixed British constitution was 'to avoid the perfections of extremes'.[2] Montesquieu had written, in the same context,

Comment dirais-je cela, moi qui crois que l'excès même de la raison n'est pas toujours désirable, et que les hommes s'accommodent presque toujours mieux des milieux que des extrémités?[3]

It is immediately after admiring the British constitution as an embodiment of the mean that Burke praises Montesquieu as the great philosopher who, having studied all the governments of the world, thought that that of England was the best.[4]

Burke does more than attack the French philosophers of the Revolution on account of their methodology: his most devastating attack is on their morality. Burke says that to understand them we 'must connect the morals with the politics of the legislators';[5] he accuses them of imitating Rousseau, who 'is a moralist or he is nothing',[6] and of attempting 'a regeneration of the moral constitution of man'.[7] The revolutionaries' doctrine of the rights of man has no moral content: in the pre-social state the abstract man of their theory has none of those social restraints without which society would degenerate into anarchy. Abstract rights

superseded society, and broke asunder all those bonds which had formed the happiness of mankind for ages. He would venture to say, that if they were to go back abstractedly to natural rights, there would be an end of all society.[8]

[1] E.L., xxix, 1.   [2] *Works*, iii, p. 110.   [3] E.L., xi, 6.   [4] *Works*, iii, p. 113.
[5] Ibid., ii, p. 538.   [6] Ibid., pp. 535–6.   [7] Ibid., p. 537.   [8] P.H., xxviii, p. 435.

But Burke does not believe that man is at his best as a savage living in the state of nature: it is only in civil society that man fulfils himself, for man is a social animal, and his true 'state of nature' is civil society.[1] Indeed, even out of civil society men need 'a sufficient restraint upon their passions'.[2] Civil society requires,

not only that the passions of individuals should be subjected, but that even in the mass and body, as well as in the individuals, the inclinations of men should frequently be thwarted, their will controlled, and their passions brought into subjection.[3]

Burke maintains that this is not understood by the French, who base their theories on the general will, which, when translated into practical terms, means the will of the majority to do whatever they like.[4] Over and above the will of the people Burke places duty: 'Neither the few nor the many have a right to act merely by their will in any matter connected with duty, trust, engagement, or obligation'.[5] Man's sense of duty does not come to him from any abstract natural rights, but through his instincts, for man is a moral as well as a social animal:

Dark and inscrutable are the ways by which we come into the world. The instincts which give rise to this mysterious process of nature are not of our making. But out of physical causes, unknown to us, perhaps unknowable, arise moral duties, which as we are able perfectly to comprehend, we are bound indispensably to perform.[6]

Burke believes that there is a moral order in the universe, to which all men are subject. In this we must take as our guide our 'untaught feelings',[7] beginning with the intimate feelings which exist in the family relationship:

We begin our public affections in our families. No cold relation is a zealous citizen. We pass on to our neighbourhoods, and our habitual provincial connections.[8]

In the French revolutionaries Burke finds the complete antithesis of this philosophy: not only do they disregard our natural instincts; they admire and take as their model J.-J. Rousseau, who was lacking in these instincts: 'they erect statues to a wild, ferocious, low-minded, hard-hearted father; a lover of his kind, but a hater of his kindred'.[9]

In insisting that our perception of the higher moral order comes

[1] *Works*, iii, p. 86. [2] Ibid., ii, p. 333. [3] *Idem*. [4] Ibid., iii, pp. 45, 76.
[5] Ibid., p. 76. [6] Ibid., p. 79. [7] Ibid., ii, p. 359.
[8] Ibid., p. 467. [9] Ibid., p. 538.

M

to us through our instinctive feelings Burke is not advancing an anti-rational claim for the emotions at the expense of reason.[1] He distrusts passion, but believes that our traditional instincts, such as love for our parents and our neighbours, are perfectly rational: 'under the direction of reason, instinct is always in the right',[2] and he believes that 'Government is made for the very purpose of opposing that reason to will and caprice'.[3] Since the higher moral order is an order of reason, it is, no doubt, possible for some profound thinkers to have an awareness of it through their reason; but this is not the lot of ordinary men:

> Profound thinkers will know it in its reason and spirit. The less enquiring will recognize it in their feelings and their experience. They will thank God they have a standard which, in the most essential point of this great concern, will put them on a par with the most wise and knowing.[4]

There is, then, in Burke's moral philosophy, a harmony between reason and instinctive feeling, and he believes it is natural for men to want instinctively that which is reasonable. The feelings of the people are always the best guide for the legislator, though he must guard against using this guide when people have had their passions roused and their true moral-social instincts clouded by passion.[5] However, Burke understands that there is always a sort of joint effort by the legislator and the people to achieve the best results in government, the feelings of the latter being followed only so far as the reason and judgment of the former think desirable.[6]

It is difficult, once again, to find precise sources for Burke's moral ideas. His idea of man as having moral and social instincts can probably be traced to his interest in the Stoics, though these ideas were well known in the eighteenth century. The similarity of Burke's ideas to those of Montesquieu, especially the story of the Troglodytes, is striking. Montesquieu, inspired by Stoic ideas, possibly through English sources, had demonstrated that civil society could not survive if based on will and unbridled self-interest. He showed that the true basis of society is a moral one: man's natural aptitude for virtue. Like Burke, he stressed the importance of the primary instinctive feelings, love for one's parents and one's neighbours. Again, like Burke, Montesquieu, in the *Esprit des lois*, combines a belief in a higher moral order—which is an order of

---

[1] C. Parkin, *The Moral Basis of Burke's Political Philosophy*, Cambridge, 1956, p. 115. I am generally indebted to this work for its excellent analysis of Burke's ideas on natural rights.
[2] *Works*, v, p. 136.				[3] Ibid., p. 122.				[4] Ibid., iii, p. 112.
[5] Ibid., ii, p. 555.				[6] Ibid., v, p. 119.

reason—with the belief that the legislator must follow the natural feelings of the people, as far as this is practicable. There is, however, nothing to show that Burke was writing with Montesquieu's theories in mind; and it is possible that both writers were simply drawing on a similar classical and eighteenth-century background of thought.[1]

In Burke's philosophy the best institutions are the result of the moral and social instincts of the people under the guidance of the reason of the legislator. However, man is an imperfect creature, and even the best and wisest legislator will distrust the power of his own reason and understand the importance of having recourse to the reason of others:

> We are afraid to put men to live and trade each on his own private stock of reason; because we suspect that this stock in each man is small, and that the individuals would do better to avail themselves of the general bank and capital of nations and of ages.[2]

Wise legislators will have recourse to 'the ancient, permanent sense of mankind',[3] which is embodied in established traditions, prejudices and institutions. In political arrangements, he says, 'mind must conspire with mind. Time is required to produce that union of minds which alone can produce all the good we aim at', and this normally 'requires the aid of more minds than one age can furnish'.[4] Whereas the French philosophers appealed to the rights of the individual and the general will of the people, Burke appeals to the wisdom embodied in traditional laws and institutions. This is the true value of history, he believes, and, as we have seen, he no longer treats it as a branch of science, but as an embodiment of the wisdom of the past. Above all Burke appeals to the wisdom of the British constitution as seen in its historical continuity.[5] It is in our constitution that we find the true moral order:

> Our political system is placed in a just correspondence and symmetry with the order of the world, and with the mode of existence decreed to a permanent body composed of transitory parts; wherein, by the disposition of a stupendous wisdom, moulding together the great mysterious incorporation of the human race, the whole, at one time, is never old, or middle-aged, or young, but, in a condition of unchangeable constancy, moves on through the varied tenor of perpetual decay, fall, renovation, and progression.[6]

Thus, behind the historical continuity of the constitution Burke

---

[1] For Montesquieu and Stoicism see A. S. Crisafulli, 'Montesquieu's story of the Troglodytes: its background, meaning and significance', PMLA, 58 (1943), pp. 372–92.
[2] *Works*, ii, p. 359.   [3] Ibid., p. 435.   [4] Ibid., pp. 439–40.
[5] Ibid., iii, p. 114.   [6] Ibid., ii, p. 307.

sees the higher moral order, the order of God. He believes that it is
'the awful Author of our being' who has 'disposed and marshalled
us by a divine tactic, not according to our will, but according to
His':[1] it is our duty to obey the law of God as expressed in the
constitution. Our obligations are 'not in consequence of any
voluntary pact';[2] our obligations depend on the place God has
appointed us to in the universe. At the same time, Burke does not
deny the importance of the social contract as applied to the British
constitution. But in his thought the social contract is not a mere
voluntary pact which can be revoked at will: both governors and
the governed are under the obligation to observe the higher moral
law as expressed in the constitution.[3] Burke sees the contract as a
moral and religious obligation: it is 'a clause in the great primaeval
contract of eternal society'.[4]

In appealing away from the theory of the sovereignty of the will
of the people to the traditional constitution, and in seeing this
constitution as the deposit of the wisdom of ages, Burke is continuing a very old tradition of English thought. During the constitutional struggles of the seventeenth century the opponents of the
theory of the Divine Right of Kings had similarly appealed to the
ancient constitution and the tradition of Common Law.[5] Burke's
thought reaches back to Coke and Hale; and, indeed, he was a great
admirer of the latter.[6] In idealizing the Common Law and the
traditional institutions Burke was simply continuing this same
tradition, and we find a similar idealization of the constitution and
the Common Law in Blackstone.[7] At the same time, on account
of the strong religious overtones of Burke's theories it is possible
that he may be indebted to thinkers like Hooker and Bishop Butler.[8]
It is therefore with great caution one must attempt to trace here any
influence of Montesquieu on Burke. The general similarity of their
thought is obvious enough: the same respect for traditional laws and
institutions, which are the result of the wisdom of the legislator and
the general collective feelings of the people, the whole being an
expression of the higher moral order. The similarity is probably
best explained by the fact that just as Burke was reaching back to
the tradition of English Common Law, Montesquieu represents a

---

[1] *Works*, iii, p. 79.   [2] *Idem.*   [3] Ibid., ii, p. 294.   [4] Ibid., p. 368.
[5] J. G. A. Pocock, *The Ancient Constitution and the Feudal Law*, Cambridge, 1957.
[6] *Works*, vi, p. 413.
[7] *Commentaries on the Laws of England*, 4 vols., Oxford, 1765–69, i, 40 seq.; Cf. Sir Ernest
Barker, *Essays on Government*, Oxford, 1945, pp. 136–39.
[8] See M. Enaudi, 'The British Background of Burke's Political Philosophy', *Political
Science Quarterly*, 49 (1934), pp. 576–98.

continuation of the French tradition of *droit coutumier*.[1] It does not appear, that, on the whole, Burke was indebted to Montesquieu for these ideas; and we shall find it more profitable to examine Burke's ideas on different types of government, especially on the French and British monarchies, where the influence of Montesquieu is most obvious.

Burke, rejecting the assumption of the theorists of natural right that all men are equal, rejects the idea of a classless society. He agrees with Aristotle that a democracy has much in common with a tyranny,[2] and admires the legislators of the ancient republics, who dealt not with abstractions, but with human nature:

> It is for this reason that Montesquieu observed very justly, that in their classification of the citizens, the great legislators of antiquity made the greatest display of their powers, and even soared above themselves.[3]

Montesquieu, in spite of this admiration—at least in the first eight books of the *Esprit des lois*—had never envisaged an absolute democracy, in which there were no social divisions; and in the passage referred to by Burke, he says,

> Dans l'état populaire, on divise le peuple en de certaines classes. C'est dans la manière de faire cette division que les grands législateurs se sont signalés; et c'est de là qu'ont toujours dépendu la durée de la démocratie et sa prospérité.[4]

As we have seen, one of the most common criticisms made of Montesquieu by the French revolutionaries was that he had upheld class distinctions. Burke thus ranges himself with Montesquieu and the lawgivers of classical antiquity against the French Revolution.

The French revolutionaries disliked Montesquieu mainly because they saw in him a supporter of the *Ancien régime*. In actual fact Montesquieu had been one of the most daring critics of the *Ancien régime* in his time; but it was the abuses rather than the old order itself he had attacked, his ideal being a monarchy based on the principle of intermediary powers. It is easy to see that Burke's view is, generally speaking, similar. He admits that the French constitution was full of gross abuses; but he thought it possible to renovate and repair it:

> Your constitution, it is true, whilst you were out of possession, suffered waste and dilapidation; but you possessed in some parts the walls, and, in all, the foundations of a noble and venerable castle. You might have repaired those walls; you might have built on those old foundations. Your constitution was suspended

[1] Cf. above, p. 25. [2] *Works*, ii, p. 396. [3] Ibid., p. 455. [4] E.L., ii, 2.

before it was perfected; but you had the elements of a constitution nearly as good as could be wished.[1]

However, Burke does not defend the French constitution in terms of intermediary powers. It is in the meeting of the States-General that he sees the starting-point of a return to the pristine purity of the constitution, and his remarks on the different orders are based not on Montesquieu (who does not mention the States-General) but on current political commonplaces. Burke, at the same time, speaks of the nobility and clergy, idealizing them, and drawing on his experiences while in France in 1773.[2] However, Burke is not very far from the spirit of Montesquieu, and on one point—that of the vendibility of offices in the parlements—he almost certainly has Montesquieu in mind. Montesquieu had written:

> Cette vénalité est bonne dans les états monarchiques parce qu'elle fait faire, comme un métier de famille, ce qu'on ne voudrait pas entreprendre pour la vertu; qu'elle destine chacun à son devoir, et rend les ordres de l'état plus permanents.[3]

Burke writes, speaking of the parlements,

> They possessed one fundamental excellence; they were independent. The most doubtful circumstance attendant on their office, that of its being vendible, contributed however to this independency of character. They held for life. Indeed they may be said to have held by inheritance. Appointed by the monarch, they were considered as nearly out of his power.[4]

Thus both Montesquieu and Burke defend the vendibility of offices in somewhat similar terms.

Montesquieu had defined the French constitution not only according to its form, but also according to its spirit. He says that the 'principle' of monarchy is honour. Burke, who informs us that from an early age he studied 'both the form and spirit of republics',[5] regrets that the French revolutionaries have extinguished the old spirit of honour which had played such an important part in the constitution. He said he had always thought the French 'a generous and gallant nation, long misled to your disadvantage by your high and romantic sentiments of fidelity, honour, and loyalty'.[6] But in the new constitution, 'Every person in your country, in a situation to be actuated by a principle of honour, is disgraced and degraded'.[7] It is in these terms that Burke laments that 'the age of chivalry is gone. That of sophisters, economists, and calculators, has succeeded; and the glory of Europe is extinguished for ever.'[8] Burke is very close

---

[1] *Works*, ii, p. 308. [2] Ibid., pp. 416–17. [3] E.L., v, 19. [4] *Works*, ii, p. 476.
[5] Ibid., iii, p. 37. [6] Ibid., ii, pp. 309–10. [7] Ibid., p. 322. [8] Ibid., p. 348.

to Montesquieu when he distinguished between the form and the spirit of the French constitution and makes honour its animating principle; but he goes beyond Montesquieu when he traces this honour back to the ancient chivalry, and makes it the essential spirit, not only of the French constitution, but of modern Europe.[1] He goes on to say that European civilization is based not only on this principle of honour, but also on the principle of religion.[2]

Burke's political theory, as expressed in his writings on the French Revolution, is in the last resort a defence of the British constitution. It was principally as an admirer of the British constitution that Montesquieu was known in England, and it is as the great thinker who had understood and praised the constitution of England that Burke holds up Montesquieu to our admiration in the famous closing passage of the *Appeal from the New to the Old Whigs*.[3] This work is full of references to the theory of the British constitution as a mixed and balanced form of government, and Burke's sources are the ordinary commonplaces of political theory along with the speeches which he quotes from the trial of Sacheverell.[4] But it is to the authority of Montesquieu that Burke appeals, in his defence of the British constitution against the French revolutionaries. He sees in Montesquieu

a genius not born in every country, or every time; a man gifted by nature with a penetrating, aquiline eye; with a judgement prepared with the most extensive erudition; with an herculean robustness of mind, and nerves not to be broken with labour; a man who could spend twenty years in one pursuit. Think of a man, like the universal patriarch in Milton, . . . a man capable of placing in review, after having brought together from the east, the west, the north, and the south, from the coarseness of the rudest barbarism to the most refined and subtle civilization, all the schemes of government which had ever prevailed amongst mankind, weighing, measuring, collating, and comparing them all, joining fact with theory, and calling into council, upon all this infinite assemblage of things, all the speculations which have fatigued the understandings of profound reasoners in all times!— Let us then consider, that all these were but so many preparatory steps to qualify a man, and such a man, tinctured with no national prejudice, with no domestic affection, to admire, and to hold out to the admiration of mankind, the constitution of England![5]

It is significant that this magnificent eulogy of Montesquieu should come at the end rather than at the beginning of Burke's career. As a young man Burke had been content to admire Montesquieu as the 'greatest genius' of the age. But it was only when Burke

[1] Ibid., p. 351. [2] *Idem.* [3] Ibid., iii, p. 113.
[4] Ibid., p. 1 seq. [5] Ibid., p. 113.

himself had spent a lifetime devoted to political problems, when he
had come to a stage in his career when he was compelled to re-
examine all his most cherished fundamental beliefs, that he was
capable of understanding the true greatness of Montesquieu's achievement. If Burke were, in his eulogy of Montesquieu, speaking as a
mere servile imitator his words would have little value. But Burke
speaks as one great mind who, having independently thought of
certain problems, is able to estimate the value of the contribution of
another mind to these same problems. He sees in Montesquieu not
so much a source of ideas as a fellow-worker in a great cause: the
defence of the old order against the abstract philosophy of the French
Revolution. It is thus that we have considered Montesquieu in this
chapter. Burke's ideas in his writings on the Revolution draw on
many sources, many of them traditions and classical commonplaces
which had worked themselves into his rich mind over a long period
of time. Montesquieu had been an important influence on the earlier
Burke, and though in the writings on the French Revolution the
historical method comes under Burke's censure, other, more important aspects of Montesquieu's thought are still present in his mind,
notably the doctrine of the *esprit général*, and the theories of the
French and British constitutions. However, Montesquieu's thought is
only one stream which at this time fertilizes Burke's mind, and we
have not attempted to deny the importance of other sources,
especially that of the tradition of English Common Law. We
have seen that Burke and Montesquieu are writers who often draw on
common traditions, and it is not surprising that the French revolutionaries should consider them both alike as enemies.

CHAPTER IX

BURKE AND IRELAND

BURKE, from his undergraduate days, was interested in the history of his 'poor country',[1] though during his youth spent in Dublin he does not appear to have taken any part in politics or political pamphleteering.[2] It was not until 1761 that he became in any way active in Irish politics. In that year his employer, William Gerard Hamilton, became Chief Secretary in Ireland, and Burke spent the parliamentary sessions 1761–2 and 1763–4 in Dublin. But after his appointment as Lord Rockingham's secretary in 1765, he did not take part in Irish politics for some time, and then only in so far as Irish and English affairs were related. He was active in connection with the proposals of the Irish parliament to tax absentees in 1773; he took part in supporting Irish demands for free trade in 1778; and he became involved in the affairs of Ireland which culminated in the Revolution of 1782. We find him again taking part in the trade laws controversy of 1785; but his greatest contribution to Irish politics belongs to his later years, during the period of the French Revolution. After 1789 Ireland, partly under French influence, was pressing for a consolidation of the independence it had won in 1782, and for certain measures of reform, and notably for Catholic emancipation. Burke played an important part in trying to preserve, while purifying, the Irish constitution, and also in pressing the case of the Catholics. But, at the same time, he tried to prevent Ireland from falling into the hands of radical reformers with French sympathies. These last years of the century were critical years for Ireland; and Irish affairs, along with the French Revolution, are the constant theme of the last seven or eight years of Burke's life. Thus Burke was occupied to a greater or lesser degree with Irish politics throughout his career. However, as the influence of Montesquieu on this part of Burke's career is usually very slight, it will be sufficient to deal with many of the Irish issues with the utmost brevity.

Montesquieu, as we have noted, never visited Ireland, though he was interested in Ireland and Irishmen.[3] His opinions on the Irish

---

[1] Samuels, op. cit., p. 98.
[2] Cf. G. Vincitorio, 'Edmund Burke and Charles Lucas', PMLA, 68 (1953), pp. 1047–55.
[3] See above, pp. 6–7.

problem in the eighteenth century are known from his conversation with Lord Charlemont in 1754. Charlemont relates,

> In the course of our conversations, Ireland, and its interests, have often been the topic; and upon these occasions, I have always found him an advocate for an union between that country and England. 'Were I an Irishman', said he, 'I should certainly wish for it; and, as a general lover of liberty, I sincerely desire it; and for this plain reason, that an inferior country, connected with one much her superior in force, can never be certain of the permanent enjoyment of constitutional freedom, unless she has, by her representatives, a proportional share in the legislature of the superior kingdom.[1]

It is interesting that we should have here Montesquieu's opinion on what was to become, by the end of the century, the fundamental Irish problem. We find that in the *Esprit des lois* Montesquieu also makes reference to Ireland, though not by name: speaking of England, he says,

> Il pourrait être qu'elle aurait autrefois subjugué une nation voisine qui, par sa situation, la bonté de ses ports, la nature de ses richesses, lui donnerait de la jalousie : ainsi, quoiqu'elle lui eût donné ses propres lois, elle la tiendrait dans une grande dépendance; de façon que les citoyens y seraient libres, et que l'état lui-même serait esclave.
>
> L'état conquis aurait un très bon gouvernement civil, mais il serait accablé par le droit des gens; et on lui imposerait des lois de nation à nation, qui seraient telles que sa prospérité ne serait que précaire, et seulement en dépôt pour un maître.[2]

As we have seen, Montesquieu considered it legitimate for a nation to hold its colonies under rigorous Navigation Laws which ensured the commercial monopoly of the mother country.[3] Ireland, however, he does not consider so much as a colony, as a conquered nation, and hence the note of disapproval when he mentions the rigour of the trade laws. From his conversation with Lord Charlemont we gather that he saw in a legislative union the solution which would give the Irish the same liberties as the English.

There are many aspects of Irish history which Montesquieu would have disapproved of: the manner of conquest, in which the native Irish were deliberately evicted from their land, was completely against the doctrine of the *esprit général*. However, considering the conquest as a *fait accompli*, Montesquieu admires the 'bon gouvernement civil' of Ireland, which is, of course, an English institution. But he disapproves, as we have just seen, of the harsh trade laws imposed on Ireland by the English; and we find that he also disapproves of penal laws. On the latter point we find that Montesquieu

---

[1] Francis Hardy, *Memoirs of the Earl of Charlemont*, 2 vols., 1812, i, p. 70.
[2] E.L., xix, 27. [3] See above, pp. 84–6.

was often quoted in Ireland. Thus, one speaker in the Irish House of Commons said,

> The wisest man who, I believe, has ever written on the subject of legislation, (I mean Baron Montesquieu) says, that penal laws as to religion, have never produced any other effect, than that of making the objects of them more persevering: Says he, 'The sure way to win the zealots in any religion is, to court them by favours—by the conveniences of life—by hopes of fortune. It is an established rule as to the changing of religion, that the invitations to the change must ever be more strong than the penalties.'[1]

Montesquieu does not mention the Irish penal system; but he must have been aware of its injustice, as he had so many friends who were Irish exiles.

If we turn to the Irish political scene in the eighteenth century[2] we shall find that reality confirms Montesquieu's remarks. Ireland, like America, was under Navigation Laws designed to preserve English trade monopoly. But in America these laws were felt less severely than in Ireland: they were often easily evaded in America; and, besides, America was fortunate in being rich in natural resources, of which England had need. But Ireland was close to England, and therefore constantly under the jealous eye of English commercial interests; and, besides, it was poor in natural resources. Every attempt of the Irish to establish an industry which would compete with England aroused English jealousy, and sooner or later such Irish industries were extinguished. It was forbidden for Ireland to export to England most agricultural products, the Irish were deprived of trade with the colonies, and the Irish woollen industry was forbidden to export to any country. The only industry which was tolerated was linen, which did not compete with England. Thus Montesquieu's remarks on the commercial tyranny of England over Ireland are fully justified.

As for his praise of the 'bon gouvernement civil' of Ireland, this can be accepted only with certain reservations. Ireland had, indeed, a constitution on the English model: a House of Commons and House of Lords, with a Lord Lieutenant to represent the Crown. However, the power of the Irish Parliament was limited by the law of Poynings[3] and the Declaratory Act of 6 George I. These enactments amounted to giving England the right to legislate for Ireland, and lodging judicial supremacy in England. The Irish Parliament

---

[1] *The Parliamentary Register; or History of the Proceedings and Debates of the House of Commons in Ireland* (1781–1800), 20 volumes, Dublin, 1784–1800, i, p. 253; Cf. E.L., xxv, 12.
[2] For eighteenth-century Ireland see W. E. H. Lecky, *A History of Ireland in the Eighteenth Century*, 5 vols., 1892; Vincent T. Harlow, *The Founding of the Second British Empire*, 1952.
[3] 10 Henry VII.

met only on alternate years, and lasted the duration of the life of the monarch, until 1768, when the Octennial Act was passed. The Irish Parliament could draft bills, but could pass them only when returned by the Privy Council of England, and if the latter altered them, the Irish Parliament could only reject or accept. Again, control of the Irish Parliament over revenue was limited, a large portion of it—the hereditary revenue—being beyond its control. There was no Habeas Corpus Act, no Mutiny Act, and the Irish judgeships were held only during pleasure. The lower House was elected only by Protestants of the Established Church, the Catholics, forming three-quarters of the population, having no vote, and the Dissenters, especially numerous in the north, being excluded by a Test. Of the three hundred members of Parliament, more than two-thirds were elected by boroughs and manors, and many by individuals. Until 1768 this system had worked by the expedient of the Lord Lieutenant making a bargain with the Undertakers, the powerful borough owners, who carried his business through Parliament in return for the patronage he offered them. This meant, in fact, that the Lord Lieutenant had to deal with a powerfully established oligarchy. This system had been broken in 1768 by Lord Townshend, and government was henceforth carried on as in England, by having a Court 'interest' established in Parliament, directly under control of the Lord Lieutenant, who introduced the innovation of residing continuously in Ireland. This Court 'interest' was, however, managed with a degree of corruption that did not exist in England, except in the imagination of frustrated opposition politicians. Whereas in England the cry 'corruption' and 'influence' was usually simply a battle-cry of the opposition, in Ireland it had a basis in truth. Corruption of this type was probably inevitable, considering that the executive was imposed from the outside, and was under pressure from the English, and not from the Irish Parliament.

It is hardly necessary to elaborate on the justice of Montesquieu's remarks on the penal code. Though often these laws were a dead letter it remained true that Catholics were disfranchised, forbidden to sit in Parliament, excluded from corporations, forbidden certain professions, especially law, forbidden to establish schools, and excluded from the university and the army. It was because of the hardships at home that so many Irishmen were found on the Continent in the eighteenth century.

It was in this eighteenth-century Ireland that Burke first tasted practical politics, as secretary to W. G. Hamilton. It was during these years (1761–5) that Burke appears to have been actively interested in Irish history, and to have been in touch with historians like Leland and O'Conor.¹ Burke was active in connection with the injustices of the penal code, as can be seen from his relations with O'Conor and Curry—both members of the Catholic Committee— and from his literary work, the *Tracts on the Popery Laws*.² He also took some part in the attempt to pass a bill enabling Catholics to join the British army in Portugal, but this attempt failed.³ Burke's services as Hamilton's secretary gained him a pension of £300 per annum; but, on his quarrel with Hamilton, he refused the pension.⁴ It is interesting that Burke had thus a short career as a supporter of the government in Ireland. During this time he appears to have approved, on the whole, of the Irish constitution, and had no sympathy with Irish radicalism.⁵ He was interested in large issues such as the problem of the penal code; but, apparently, not in details of the structure of government. At this time he is less interested in practical questions than in general problems which lend themselves to literary and philosophical treatment. Thus he deals with the penal system in terms of Natural Law, and supports his opinions with quotations from Cicero.

After his appointment as Lord Rockingham's secretary, Burke had very little to do with Irish politics before 1773, when the Irish Parliament, encouraged by the Lord Lieutenant, Lord Harcourt, initiated legislation to tax absentee landlords. This raised, among other things, the question whether Ireland had the right to decide on its own taxes, which was, in fact, the American question. It was thus naturally supported by Chatham and Shelburne, on the principle that a state had the right to decide on its own internal taxes. But the Rockinghams, who had passed the Declaratory Act, were against this doctrine, and held that it was the English Parliament that should decide on imperial questions. Besides, the Rockinghams owned property in Ireland, and this was perhaps the fundamental reason why Burke took an active part in opposing the proposed tax. Burke's arguments on this subject are given their clearest expression in *A Letter to Sir Charles Bingham on the Irish Absentee Tax*,⁶ and stress especially the practical difficulties that such a proposal entailed. These arguments owe nothing to Montesquieu or political theory,

¹ See above, pp. 31–2.   ² *Idem.*   ³ Lecky, op. cit., ii, p. 69.
⁴ *Corr.*, i, pp. 62–64.   ⁵ See Vincitorio, op. cit.
⁶ Oct. 30, 1773: *Works*, v, pp. 437–45.

and their source is to be found mainly, no doubt, in the personal discussions between the Rockinghams.[1]

For some time after this Burke took little or no part in Irish affairs, and in October 1777 we find him writing to Fox to the effect that he has lost contact with Ireland:

> It is within a few days of eleven years since I was in Ireland, and then after an absence of two. Those who have been absent from any scene for even a much shorter time, generally lose the true practical notion of the country, and of what may or may not be done in it.[2]

However, in the following year Irish politics were beginning to assume importance for England: Ireland, following America, was now demanding commercial freedom. The American revolt had had an important effect on the minds of the Irish, especially among the Dissenters of the north, who were at this time extremely radical. The Irish imperial problem was in essentials the same as the American one, and the success of the Americans emboldened the Irish. Besides, the American revolt had other important repercussions in Ireland: the war reduced outlets for Irish smuggled goods, thus causing great hardship among the Irish. The Lord Lieutenant warned the English government of the dangerous state of Ireland, and in response Lord North introduced measures designed to give some relief to Irish trade. These measures, introduced in April, 1778, caused furious opposition from English trading towns, and the bills were passed only in a mutilated form. Burke played an active part in supporting North's propositions, going so far as to press for free trade between the two islands. His ideas on this subject are given in his *Two Letters to Gentlemen in the City of Bristol*, written in April and May, 1778, where he replies to objections raised by his constituents to his support of relief for Irish trade.[3] In these letters Burke expresses his belief in the imperial supremacy of England over Ireland, in which he is simply continuing the Rockingham faith in the Declaratory Act of 1766. He also appeals for free trade, and his ideas on this subject sound like an echo of what was by this time a commonly discussed idea.[4] Burke's ideas here owe nothing to Montesquieu, though Montesquieu's remarks on the injustice of the commercial restrictions imposed on Ireland would have lent support to Burke.

In 1779 the cause of Ireland was seriously adopted by the opposition. Ireland had been left practically stripped of defence at a time

---

[1] See J. E. Tyler, 'A Letter from the Marquis of Rockingham to Sir William Mayne on the proposed absentee tax on 1773', *Irish Historical Studies*, viii (1952-3), pp. 362-9.
[2] *Works*, v, pp. 451-2.   [3] Ibid., ii, p. 43 seq.   [4] See Lecky, op. cit., ii, p. 172.

when England was at war with America, France and Spain; and it was in response to this emergency that the Irish Volunteers were formed. The Volunteers, though under the impeccable leadership of Lord Charlemont, were, strictly speaking, an illegal organization, and greatly feared by the Lord Lieutenant, for the country was discontent with the failure of the North propositions of 1778, and the Irish had retaliated by imposing a non-importation agreement. There were riots in Dublin, and in Parliament a strong opposition of patriots under Henry Grattan were harassing the government, who were finding that in this time of national emergency the system of having a Court 'interest' in the Commons was insufficient to discipline the House. Thus placemen like Henry Flood and Hussey Burgh went over to opposition, placing patriotism higher than their pensions. In October 1779 the Irish Parliament passed a short money bill for six months. These signs were not missed by the opposition in England, who pressed for timely concessions before Ireland followed the example of America. Lord Rockingham and Burke played an active part in these debates.[1] The outcome was that North introduced in December 1779 a number of measures which gave Ireland something not far short of free trade.

The ministers hoped that Ireland, having won free trade, would now be content, and make no further demands. Ireland was, however, now more fully aware of the shortcomings of its constitution, and the Irish were aspiring to a constitution more closely modelled on that of England. Montesquieu was quoted often by Irish politicians who wanted such liberties as a Habeas Corpus Act.[2] By 1780 Ireland, like America in 1776, had reached the stage of demanding legislative and judicial independence from England, maintaining the imperial connection through the Crown alone. Thus in April, 1780, Grattan introduced a declaration of independence into the Irish Commons, asking if Great Britain would refuse to the loyal subjects of Ireland what she had offered to the rebels of America. After a debate of fifteen hours the motion was indefinitely adjourned.[3] Burke did not approve of Grattan's motion, and is reported to have said: 'Will no one speak to this madman? Will no one stop this madman Grattan?'[4] However, the Irish patriots continued to press for independence, without making any greater

---

[1] P.H., xx, pp. 635–51; 651–57.   [2] See *Parliamentary Register*, i, pp. 52, 168, 248.
[3] *The Speeches of the Right Honourable Henry Grattan*, edited by his Son, 4 vols., 1822, i, p. 38 seq.
[4] *Memoirs of the Life and Times of the Rt. Hon. Henry Grattan by his Son, Henry Grattan, Esq.*, M.P., 5 vols., 1839–46, ii, p. 36.

gain than a Habeas Corpus Act early in 1782. The attitude of the
Rockinghams at this time was cautious, since they had to be 'consistent' and maintain the principles of the Declaratory Act of 1766.
Thus, speaking in February 1781, Fox said,

> In better times than these he should have talked of the superintending power of
> the British Parliament over Ireland, and over every part of the British monarchy;
> but such was the miserable situation to which the King's servants had reduced
> this country, that the question was of a very delicate nature indeed, and it was by
> no means a matter easy to be handled without disturbing what ought not to be
> disturbed.[1]

In Ireland, however, the government was getting more and more
out of touch with public opinion, and the Volunteers were becoming
more exasperated. On December 28, 1781, there was a meeting of
the first Ulster Regiment at Armagh, which summoned a Convention. The Convention met at Dungannon on February 15, 1782,
and demanded independence. It was in the following month, under
pressure from many sides, that the North government collapsed,
and Lord Rockingham became head of the new administration in
March. The Rockinghams were thus faced with the Irish problem,
and the Duke of Portland was sent to Dublin as Lord Lieutenant.

The Rockinghams were eager to find a remedy to the Irish problem, which would retain as much as possible of the 'superintending
power' of Great Britain, and the Duke of Portland worked to achieve
this end. The ministry asked Grattan and Lord Charlemont to delay
their demands while a solution was being worked out. But to their
surprise this was refused, and they found themselves confronted with
an ultimatum. On April 16 Grattan presented his amended address to
the Crown for independence, and this passed unanimously. Portland
tried hard to get the Irish to accept a treaty which would regulate
the external affairs of the two countries, but this was to no avail.
The ministry was therefore forced to yield and the offending Act of
6 George I giving England the right to legislate for Ireland was
repealed, without any treaty to take its place. The argument of the
Irish patriots was that no treaty was needed:

> Bind us to you by the only chain that can connect us,—*the only chain we will ever
> consent to wear,—the dear ties of mutual love and mutual freedom.*[2]

These words of Lord Charlemont read very like Burke on the
nature of the imperial link with the American colonies;[3] but Burke,
like his colleagues, was not happy to see Ireland held to England by

---

[1] P.H., xxi, p. 1295.   [2] *Memoirs of Grattan*, ii, pp. 242 (April 17, 1782).
[3] See above, p. 99.

such slender bonds. When on April 8, 1782, William Eden had moved for the independence of Ireland, without any treaty to bind the two countries, Fox and Burke had violently opposed, and Burke went so far as to say,

> The motion before the House went, in some measure, to tear asunder the connection between England and Ireland.[1]

But Burke was forced to bow before the inevitable, and we find him writing to Lord Charlemont in June 1782:

> I assure you my Lord, that I take a sincere part in the general joy, and hope that mutual affection will do more for mutual help and mutual advantage between two kingdoms than any ties of artificial connection whatever. . . . I am convinced no reluctant tie can be a strong one, and that a natural cheerful alliance will be a far securer link of connection than any principle of subordination borne with grudging and discontent.[2]

The 'natural cheerful alliance' mentioned here is the treaty which the Rockinghams hoped for—in vain—between the two islands. Lord North had likewise hoped, too late, for a treaty between Great Britain and the American colonies. This was the eighteenth-century vision of the imperial relationship when the older mercantile system had broken down. The idea of a treaty was an idea stumbled on by eighteenth-century politicians dealing with the essentially new problem of imperial relations, and was not to be learned from political theorists. Burke does not therefore turn to Montesquieu for help on the Irish imperial problem. Burke's idea of granting independence to Ireland and linking the two countries by a treaty was learned from experience. At the same time we find him anxious to preserve the Rockingham idea of 'consistency', which leads to some curious face-saving, as when he says, that the imperial power 'knew no bounds but such as its own discretion made it agree to prescribe to it'.[3]

The events which followed the Revolution of 1782—the movement for Renunciation, and Pitt's Irish Propositions of 1785—need not be dealt with here, as these are essentially problems arising out of the settlement of 1782, and are beyond the scope of Montesquieu's ideas on imperial relationship. Again, it will not be necessary to deal with the Regency crisis of 1788-9, which is a special constitutional problem on which the authority of Montesquieu was irrelevant. There is, however, an important constitutional problem after 1782 to which the authority of Montesquieu was felt very much

---

[1] P.H., xxii, p. 1257.   [2] *Memoirs of Grattan*, ii, p. 301.   [3] P.H., xxiii, p. 34.

N

relevant. After 1782 it seemed to many that Ireland had gained all the liberties of the renowned British constitution, except that the Lord Lieutenant replaced the King. However, it was soon felt by Grattan and the patriot opposition that the constitution was being corrupted by the patronage of the Crown. Thus the constitution of Ireland was felt to be liable to the malady that Montesquieu had prophesied as that which would destroy the British constitution: the legislative power would become more corrupt than the executive. Indeed, the attitude of the opposition was very like that of Burke and his friends when the *Present Discontents* was being composed. But the problem in Ireland was graver, since the corruption was real, and probably inevitable, since the executive power was imposed from without, and had at all costs to keep the Irish Parliament in harmony with Westminster. At the same time matters were becoming more complicated with the increase of radicalism at the time of the French Revolution, and the emergence of the Catholic question.

The culmination of Irish discontent was in the years of the French Revolution. In 1790 the Earl of Westmoreland became Lord Lieutenant, and, served by men like John Fitzgibbon, he was to stand for resistance to all reform: he was eager to retain Ireland as an inferior to England, to see that the Irish executive power, taking orders from the English government, would carry these orders in the Irish Parliament. In 1790 the opposition responded to this challenge by introducing a place bill and a bill for disfranchising revenue officers, but these were defeated. Meanwhile, outside Parliament discontent was spreading rapidly, and extra-parliamentary opinion was becoming militant. In June 1789 a Whig Club had been formed, composed of Grattan, Charlemont, and other men of similar sympathies. These men were eager to maintain the constitution of 1782 in its purity, i.e. free from the corrupt influence of the executive power. Burke saw a close affinity between the Whig Club and the Rockinghams, between the situation of the Irish Whigs of 1789 and the Rockinghams of 1769–70: the Irish Whigs, like the Rockinghams, resisted the power of the Crown by having recourse to 'party'.[1] The Whig Club were aristocratic, and had no sympathy with radicalism; the measures they supported were place bills, pension bills, and measures to disfranchise revenue officers. They were thus pressing for a greater separation of powers. But the Whig Club was not the only organization eager for reform: there were radicals, taking inspiration

[1] F. Hardy, *Memoirs of Charlemont*, ii, pp. 219–20.

largely from the French Revolution. In July 1791 the anniversary of the fall of the Bastille was celebrated at Belfast, and an address sent to the French. In the same town the United Irishmen were formed: a union between Protestants and Catholics to secure parliamentary reform. The members of the Whig Club were opposed to the French Revolution, which Grattan referred to as 'that plant of Gaelic growth; its taste is death, though 'tis not the tree of knowledge'.[1] At the same time Catholic reformers were becoming more radical, passing under the leadership of John Keogh; but they were hostile to the French Revolution, and—partly as an indication of this—engaged Burke's son Richard in August 1790 as their agent. Burke himself approved of the activities of the Catholic Committee so long as they were not republican, for he had always approved of Catholic emancipation.

Burke's opinions on the Irish problems of this time are expressed notably in his *Letter to Sir Hercules Langrishe* written in 1792. Langrishe was an independent member of the Irish House of Commons, friendly to the Catholics, but, in Burke's view, not sufficiently liberal. Burke had taken part in measures for Catholic relief in 1778 and 1782, and had written to Lord Kenmare (then head of the Catholic Committee) on the same subject.[2] But it is in the letter to Langrishe that we find the clearest expression of Burke's ideas on this problem. The arguments which Burke uses can be dealt with here very rapidly, as they owe nothing to Montesquieu. Burke sees the problem as a practical one, and argues in favour of the removal of incapacities at that time while it could be done without necessitating parliamentary reform as well. He believes that the constitution of 1782 was not made for 'great, general, and prescriptive exclusions'.[3] He also mentions the importance of respecting the feelings of the people, and the obligation we have to be just; but his terms are vague and general, with no trace of any direct influence of political theorists. At the same time he expresses his opinion on the idea of a legislative union between Great Britain and Ireland:

I have heard a discussion concerning such an union amongst all sorts of men ever since I remember anything. For my own part, I have never been able to bring my mind to anything clear and decisive upon the subject. There cannot be a more arduous question. As far as I can form an opinion, it would not be for the mutual advantage of the two kingdoms.[4]

[1] *Memoirs of Grattan*, iv, p. 36.
[2] See *Works*, v, pp. 486–90; iii, pp. 282–97.
[3] Ibid., iii, p. 305.
[4] Ibid., p. 337.

Thus on this fundamental point he differs from Montesquieu, though it must be remembered that in 1792 circumstances were very different from the time when Montesquieu gave his opinion on legislative union to Lord Charlemont. Burke did not live to take part in the great controversy on the Union; but in the debates on this subject Burke's literary executor, French Laurence, said that it was Burke's opinion,

> that the two countries had now grown up, under circumstances which did not admit of such an incorporation. But what he desired was, that the connection of the sister kingdoms should be reduced to a positive compact; that the manner should be explicitly defined, in which Ireland, with the entire and absolute power of local legislation, as far as she now enjoys it, should be bound on impartial questions of peace and war . . . to stand or fall with the fortunes of Great Britain.[1]

This is simply a reformulation of the solution proposed by the Rockinghams to the Irish imperial problem in 1782; and we have noted that this solution was arrived at through experience and trial and error, not from political theorists.[2]

The attempt in 1792 to enfranchise the Catholics failed, not so much because of the policy of England as on account of the hostility of the Lord Lieutenant and his Anglo-Irish advisers, who were eager to retain power in the hands of a Protestant oligarchy. Richard Burke had taken some part in negotiations between the Catholic Committee and the government, but had done little but antagonize Lord Westmoreland and his supporters, and in September 1792 the Committee dispensed with his services. Burke saw the failure of his son's attempts to obtain Catholic relief as the result of the policy of the Lord Lieutenant and his friends, whose corrupt means of government was perverting the spirit of the constitution.[3] However, the result of the failure of the Irish government to respond to public opinion was an increase in radicalism in Ireland. An association called the Friends of the People was formed, with Grattan as a conspicuous member, and they demanded not only Catholic emancipation, but also parliamentary reform, thus associating two problems which Burke, in his letter to Langrishe, had wanted to see kept apart. The outcome of this was that Westmoreland, under pressure from the English government as well as from Irish radicalism, was forced to reverse his policy and countenance a relief bill, which was passed in 1793, conceding the county franchises to the Catholics, who for the first time were now mentioned in a speech from the

---

[1] P.H., xxxiv, p. 311 (Jan. 23, 1799).   [2] See above, p. 75.   [3] *Corr.*, iii, p. 378.

throne. At the same time a motion was introduced to admit Catholics to Parliament; but this was defeated. The failure of this motion was regretted by Burke, who was of opinion that if representatives of a Catholic aristocracy were admitted to the Irish Parliament this would help to stem the progress of radicalism among the Irish Catholics.[1]

When in the summer of 1794 the Portland wing of the opposition joined Pitt's ministry, leaving Fox and his friends in isolation, this had important consequences for Ireland. It was understood by Portland that Irish affairs would be handled by him and his supporters, Lord Fitzwilliam (Lord Rockingham's heir) going to Ireland as Lord Lieutenant to replace Westmoreland. This, however, caused a great deal of friction between Pitt and Portland, when it was understood that Fitzwilliam was in favour of admitting Catholics to the Irish Parliament and of dismissing the old staunch placemen who had supported Westmoreland. Fitzwilliam went to Ireland without a clear understanding of the extent of his powers in these matters; and when he accompanied his dismissal of John Beresford and other placemen with an expression of the view that further Catholic relief was a matter of urgency, he was recalled. This was a great blow to Grattan and the patriots, who had hoped to see Fitzwilliam expel 'corruption' from the constitution and return to what they conceived to be the pure system of 1782. If Fitzwilliam had had his way there would have been a greater separation of powers, though he does not seem to have had any understanding of how—in the absence of modern political parties—to avoid deadlock between separate executive and legislative powers. The essential problem, as he saw it, was the problem which had always been most important for the Rockinghams: to purge 'corruption' and 'influence' from the constitution. Burke followed the events of 1794–5 with the greatest interest, and no one was more dismayed than he when Fitzwilliam was recalled. However, at this time Burke was an old man, broken with grief on the death of his son in August 1794, and in his letters where he frequently comments on Irish affairs he has no coherent plan to offer for Ireland.[2]

With the recall of Fitzwilliam the last chance to placate the discontent of the Irish had passed. It is perhaps fortunate that Burke did not live to see the result of the mishandling of Irish affairs: the

---

[1] Ibid., iv, p. 125 seq.
[2] See letters of 1794–5 in the *Correspondence of E. Burke and William Windham*, ed. J. P. Gilson, Cambridge, 1910; and in *The Epistolary Correspondence of the Right Hon. E. Burke and Dr. French Laurence*, 1828.

Rebellion and the Union. It is ironical that Burke spent his last days, before his death in 1797, in a task which was to reduce future contacts between Ireland and France. He played an important part in helping to found the college at Maynooth, where henceforth Catholic priests were to be educated instead of being sent abroad to Irish colleges on the continent.[1]

This brief survey of Burke's participation in Irish politics has revealed little influence of Montesquieu. If Burke did not apply Montesquieu's historical method to the problem of Ireland in the way he applied it to America and India, this may be because the Irish question became of major importance after 1789, at a time when he had reacted against the determinism of Montesquieu's method. Besides, on many aspects of the Irish problem—a problem of imperial relations—Montesquieu had no guidance to offer. We have seen, however, that Montesquieu had been in favour of a legislative union between Ireland and England, an opinion not shared by Burke. On the question of the Irish penal code Burke and Montesquieu thought alike; but here there is no question of Montesquieu's influence, Burke having in the years 1761-5 drawn his ideas on this subject from older classical sources.

---

[1] See Burke's correspondence with Dr. Hussey, *Corr.*, iv, pp. 266 seq.

CONCLUSION

AT the beginning of this study we noted that it was a common-place of Burke studies to speak of him as a disciple of Montesquieu. It is now possible for us to understand to what extent this is true. We have seen that at every period of his career, whether writing as a literary man, political propagandist, or philosopher, or speaking in the House of Commons, Burke is to some degree influenced by Montesquieu. We have seen that the men of the eighteenth century felt that the wisdom of Montesquieu was relevant to the main political problems of their time, and that Burke's writings and speeches on the British constitution, America, India, the French Revolution and Ireland all owe something to Montesquieu. At the same time, while examining the influence of Montesquieu on Burke, our study has—paradoxically, one might think—helped to affirm the originality and the essential Englishness of Burke's mind. We have seen that he is not a servile imitator of Montesquieu: what he learns from Montesquieu he adapts to a new purpose, and this is often for the purpose of political propaganda.

Burke spent the first twenty years of his life in his native country; but, in spite of the intimate links between Ireland and France, French culture does not seem to have had much importance for him at this time. His reading appears to have been mainly the classics and English literature, and his opinion of France was a poor one. It would seem that it was not until he went to England to keep law terms that Burke 'discovered' Montesquieu; and the early literary works of Burke, written between 1750 and 1765, show an intense admiration for Montesquieu combined with a dislike of Rousseau. In the *Abridgment of English History* (1757) Burke proclaims Montesquieu the greatest genius of the age, and copies his historical method as well as his theory of the origin of the British constitution. In this work Burke takes the writing of history seriously, and had thought of writing a history of English law, a task which Hale had attempted. It was Burke's interest in English Common Law and its traditions which led him to dislike the unhistorical reasoning of Rousseau, and led him to admire the achievement of Montesquieu. In him Burke found a competent legal historian who had succeeded in a field where the English—even Hale—had failed. The English legal historians were better antiquarians than historians; but in Montesquieu Burke found that the genetic method, which the English had used in a fumbling way, was raised to the status of an historical method, making history a scientific discipline. Burke's attempt to apply this method to English history is rather unsure, leading him into rather vague hypotheses; but the *Abridgment* is a work of promise, and if Burke had not deserted scholarship for politics his achievement in this field might have been very great indeed.

As a politician Burke was confronted with various practical issues demanding solutions not normally to be found in works of political theory. However, Burke proved an excellent propagandist, and was clever in adapting the wisdom of Montesquieu to the purposes of propaganda for the Rockinghams. In the years 1765–70 Burke was concerned with the problem of the working of the British constitution, and the relationship between the King and Parliament. The sources of his ideas on this we found in the friction which came about, for various reasons, between George III and Lord Rockingham; and we have seen that the Rockinghams were led to assume an attitude contrary to the letter and spirit of the constitution as described by Montesquieu. Nevertheless, in his pamphlet, *The Present Discontents*, Burke makes use of ideas he found in Montesquieu: ideas on the importance of governing a people according to their temper and character, and ideas on the nature and principle of despotism. In his speeches on America we found a further use of Montesquieu's ideas, Burke applying to the American colonies the historical method he had learned while writing the *Abridgment*. However, at the same time, Burke's ideas on the British constitution were developing in a way which led him into unconstitutional doctrines certainly owing nothing to Montesquieu. In his speeches on India and on the impeachment of Warren Hastings we find a further application of Montesquieu's historical method for a political end.

It is in his works on the French Revolution that Burke reaches his full stature as a thinker. We have seen that it is difficult to find precise sources for his writings at this time, as he was drawing mainly on a rich and fertile mind which had accumulated political wisdom over years as writer and politician. Burke, confronted with arguments of natural right, turned to arguments which appeal to history and tradition, and most of these arguments, in one form or another, had been used in the seventeenth century against the exponents of absolute monarchy. Burke's spiritual ancestors are the exponents of English Common Law who believed that political systems should be based not on theories of the sovereign will or social contract, but on the ancient constitution and tradition. In Montesquieu Burke found a thinker whose mind was of this same historical and legal cast, who despised theories of social contract and natural right, who revered the ancient institutions and laws of France. The similarity of Burke's ideas in his writings on the French Revolution to the ideas of Montesquieu is to be explained not entirely in terms of direct influence, but also, and especially, by the similarity of English and French conservative and legal thought. Burke's only direct debt to Montesquieu at this time is when he analyses the spirit of the French constitution. In Montesquieu he saw not so much a writer to be imitated, as a fellow-worker in the great cause of defending civilization and the old order against theories which would sweep all established institutions away. The enemies of Montesquieu were the enemies of Burke; and the criticisms levelled against Montesquieu by the revolutionaries were also applicable to Burke. Above all both Burke and Montesquieu revered the British constitution, which the revolutionaries considered a monument of superstition and ignorance. It is chiefly as the defender of the British constitution that Burke, at this time, admires Montesquieu. Montesquieu had spent twenty years writing the *Esprit des lois*, and his considered judgement was that the British constitution was the greatest monument to liberty. Burke had spent twenty years in politics, and he likewise puts the British form of government before all others. His political theory is, in the last resort, a defence of this constitution.

Burke's last political cause was the cause of his native country, and here the influence of Montesquieu is slight. Burke did not apply Montesquieu's historical method to an analysis of the Irish problem in the same way as he had applied it to America and India. This may be because after 1789 he no longer believed that human affairs could be explained in this way. The Irish problem was essentially one of imperial relationships, on which Montesquieu was not an authority at this time. Burke shared Montesquieu's views on the injustice and cruelty of penal laws; but he did not share the views on legislative union which Montesquieu had expressed to Lord Charlemont.

Without the influence of Montesquieu the works of Burke would certainly be poorer. In his early literary period it is mainly the *Abridgment of English History* which we owe to the inspiration of Montesquieu. Between 1765 and 1789 the influence of Montesquieu helped Burke to become a great propagandist, especially when dealing with the problems of America and India. After 1789 the direct influence of Montesquieu is slight, but he was in Burke's eyes a model of all that was greatest in the *Ancien régime* discredited at the time of the Revolution. In France Montesquieu was being attacked because he had defended the French and British constitutions. It is Burke who, in a sense, defends Montesquieu and continues the tradition for which the great French thinker stood.

BIBLIOGRAPHY OF BOOKS AND MANUSCRIPTS CITED

I. MANUSCRIPTS

AUXERRE. Archives départementales de l'Yonne, Auxerre: the following documents, relative to the families of Parisot and Sparre, and to the household of the bishop of Auxerre, J.-B.-M. Champion de Cicé: Conclusions capitulaires, G. 1812, fol. 29–31. Coste (legal documents), 73, 74, 76. Enregistrements, bureau d'Auxerre, 23 Feb., 1819. Guimard (legal document), 3, no. 29. Registre des provisions, G. 1606, fol. 167. Register of Saint Eusèbe, 15 April, 1776. Tribunal criminel, An V, L. 1259.

BELFAST. Note Books and papers of John Black, in the Public Record Office of Northern Ireland.

DUBLIN. Burke Manuscripts in the National Library of Ireland.

LONDON. Will, dated 24 April, 1772, of Thomas Nugent, proved 27 April, 1772, in the Principal Probate Registry, Somerset House.

NORTHAMPTON. Correspondence of E. Burke deposited by Earl Fitzwilliam with the Northamptonshire Record Society, Delapré Abbey, Northampton.

SHEFFIELD. Correspondence of E. Burke and of the second Marquis of Rockingham deposited by Earl Fitzwilliam in the Central Library, Sheffield.

II. MONTESQUIEU

1. WORKS OF MONTESQUIEU

a. Complete Works.

Œuvres de M. de Montesquieu, 3 vols., Amsterdam and Leipzig, 1758.

Œuvres de Montesquieu, 3 vols., London, 1767.

Œuvres de M. de Montesquieu, 5 vols., An IV–1796.

Œuvres complètes, ed. Roger Caillois (Bibliothèque de la Pléiade), 2 vols., 1949–51.

Œuvres complètes de Montesquieu, ed. André Masson (Les Editions Nagel), 3 vols., 1950–55.

b. Individual Works and smaller collections.

Considérations sur les causes de la grandeur des Romains et de leur décadence, Amsterdam, 1734.

Considérations sur les causes de la grandeur des Romains et de leur décadence, nouvelle édition, à laquelle on a joint un Dialogue de Sylla et d'Eucrate, 1748.

Défense de l' 'Esprit des loix', à laquelle on a joint quelques éclaircissements, Geneva, 1750.

Dialogue de Sylla et d'Eucrate, in Mercure de France, 1745.

Discours prononcé par M. le président de Montesquieu à la rentrée du parlement de Bordeaux ... 1725, Geneva and Paris, 1772.

Discours prononcé par M. le président de Montesquieu, lorsqu'il fut reçu a l'Académie françoise, 1728.

Ebauche de l'éloge historique du maréchal de Berwick, in FITZJAMES, J., Duke of Berwick, *Mémoires ... écrits par lui-même*, 1778.
De l'Esprit des loix, 2 vols., Geneva [1748].
De l'Esprit des loix, 3 vols., London, 1751.
De l'Esprit des lois, nouvelle édition, 4 vols., London, 1757.
Essai sur le goût, part of article GOUT in *Encyclopédie ou Dictionnaire raisonné des sciences, des arts et des métiers*, ed. D. Diderot and J. L. d'Alembert, 17 vols., 1751-65.
Lettres familières du président de Montesquieu à divers amis d'Italie [Florence], 1767.
Lettres persanes, 2 vols., Cologne[= Amsterdam], 1721.
Lysimaque, in *Mercure de France*, 1754.
Œuvres posthumes de M. de Montesquieu, London and Paris, 1783.
Pensées de Montesquieu adressées à son fils, Brussels, 1786.
Projet d'une histoire physique de la terre ancienne et moderne, in *Mercure de France*, 1719; *Journal des savants*, 1719.
Le Temple de Gnide, in *Bibliothèque française*, Amsterdam, 1724.
Le Temple de Gnide [*Céphise et l'Amour*], 1725.
Traité des devoirs, in *Bibliothèque française*, Amsterdam, 1726.
Voyage à Paphos, in *Mercure de France*, 1727.

c. Translations into English.

The Complete Works of M. de Montesquieu, 4 vols., 1777.
The History of the Troglodytes translated from the French, Chelmsford, 1766.
The Miscellaneous Pieces of M. de Secondat, 1759.
Persian Letters, translated by John Ozell, 1722.
Persian Letters, translated by John Ozell, 6th edition, Edinburgh, 1773.
Reflections on the Causes of the Grandeur and Declension of the Romans, 1734.
A Sketch of an Historical Panegyric of the Marshal of Berwick by the President Montesquieu, in FITZJAMES, J., Duke of Berwick, *Memoirs ... written by himself*, 2 vols., 1779.
The Spirit of the Laws [translated by Thomas Nugent], 2 vols., 1750.
The Temple of Gnidus, 1767.
Two Chapters of a Celebrated French Work intitled 'De l'Esprit des lois', Edinburgh, 1750.
A View of the English Constitution, by Baron de Montesquieu, being a translation [by F. Maseres] *of the sixth chapter of the eleventh book of his L'Esprit des Loix*, 1781.

2. WORKS ON MONTESQUIEU

Actes du Congrès Montesquieu réuni à Bordeaux du 23 au 26 mai 1955, Bordeaux, 1956.
ALEMBERT, J. Le R. d', *Éloge de Montesquieu*, in *Encyclopédie ou Dictionnaire raisonné des sciences, des arts et des métiers*, ed. D. Diderot and J. Le R. d'Alembert, 17 vols., 1751-65, v, pp. iii-xviii.
Anonymous, *Le Disciple de Montesquieu à MM. les députés aux Etats Généraux*, 1789.
BARRIERE, Pierre, *Un grand Provincial : Charles-Louis de Secondat, baron de La Brède et de Montesquieu*, Bordeaux, 1946.
BERLIN, Sir Isaiah, 'Montesquieu', *Proceedings of the British Academy*, 41 (1955).
BEYER, C. J., 'Le problème du déterminisme social dans l'*Esprit des lois*', *Romanic Review*, 39 (1948), pp. 102-6.
BONNO, Gabriel, *La Constitution britannique devant l'opinion française de Montesquieu à Bonaparte*, 1931.

CARCASSONNE, Elie, *Montesquieu et le problème de la constitution française au XVIIIe siècle* [1927].

COLLINS, J. C., *Voltaire, Montesquieu and Rousseau in England*, 1908.

CRANE, R. S., 'Montesquieu and British thought', *Journal of Political Economy*, 49 (1941), pp. 592–600.

CRISAFULLI, A. S., 'Montesquieu's story of the Troglodytes: its background, meaning and significance', PMLA, 58 (1943), pp. 372–92.

DAVY, G., 'Sur la méthode de Montesquieu', RMM, 46 (1939), pp. 571–86.

DEDIEU, Joseph, *Montesquieu*, 1913.

——, *Montesquieu et la tradition politique anglaise en France*, 1909.

——, *Montesquieu, l'homme et l'œuvre*, 1943.

DELPIT, Jules, *Le Fils de Montesquieu*, Bordeaux, 1888.

*Deuxième Centenaire de l'*Esprit des lois' *de Montesquieu, 1748–1948: Conférences organisées par la ville de Bordeaux*, Bordeaux, 1949.

DIMOFF, P., 'Cicéron, Hobbes et Montesquieu', *Annales Universitatis Saraviensis*, 1 (1952), pp. 19–47.

DODDS, Muriel, *Les Récits de voyages, sources de l'*Esprit des lois *de Montesquieu*, 1929.

DURKHEIM, E., *Quid Secundatus politicae scientiae instituendae contulerit*, Bordeaux, 1892.

FLETCHER, F. T. H., *Montesquieu and English Politics, 1750–1800*, 1939.

FOLKIERSKI, W., 'Montesquieu et Vico', *Actes du Congrès Montesquieu*, Bordeaux, 1956.

[GROUVELLE, P.-A.], *De l'Autorité de Montesquieu dans la révolution présente*, n.p., 1789.

KOEBNER, R., 'The authenticity of the letters on the "Esprit des lois" attributed to Helvétius', *Bulletin of the Institute of Historical Research*, 24 (1951), pp. 19–43.

LANSON, Gustave, 'Le déterminisme historique et l'idéalisme social dans l'*Esprit des lois*', RMM, 23 (1916), pp. 177–202.

LEVI-MALVANO, E., *Montesquieu e Machiavelli*, Paris, 1912.

LEVIN, L. M., *The Political Doctrine of Montesquieu's* Esprit des lois: *its Classical Background*, New York, 1936.

MASSON, André, 'Naissance et fortune de l'"Esprit des lois"', *Revue des deux mondes*, October 15, 1948.

MIRKINE-GUETZEVITCH, Boris, 'De l'"Esprit des lois" à la démocratie moderne', in MIRKINE-GUETZEVITCH (Ed.), *La Pensée politique et constitutionelle de Montesquieu*, 1948.

——, (Ed.), *La Pensée politique et constitutionelle de Montesquieu : bicentenaire de l'*Esprit des lois', 1748–1948, 1948.

OAKE, Roger B., 'Montesquieu's analysis of Roman history', *Journal of the History of Ideas*, 16 (1955), pp. 44–59.

PRICE, E. H., 'Montesquieu's historical conception of the fundamental law', *Romanic Review*, 38 (1947), pp. 234–42.

REGNAULT, Théodore, *Tableaux analytiques de l'*Esprit des lois' *suivis de la comparaison de plusieurs passages de Montesquieu et de Blackstone*, 1824.

SECONDAT, Jean-Baptiste de, *Mémoire pour servir à l'éloge historique de M. de Montesquieu*, in L. VIAN, *Histoire de Montesquieu*, 1878.

SHACKLETON, Robert, 'Montesquieu, Bolingbroke, and the separation of powers', FS, 3 (1949), pp. 25–38.

——, 'Montesquieu et Doria', *Revue de littérature comparée*, 29 (1955), pp. 173–83.

SHACKLETON, Robert, 'Montesquieu in 1948', FS, 3 (1949), pp. 299–323.
——, 'Montesquieu's correspondence: additions and corrections', FS, 12 (1958), pp. 324–45.
——, 'La religion de Montesquieu', *Actes du Congrès Montesquieu*, Bordeaux, 1956.
——, 'Les secrétaires de Montesquieu', *Œuvres* (Nagel), ii, pp. xxv–xliii.
STEWART, William, 'Montesquieu et l'Angleterre', *Deuxième Centenaire de l'"Esprit des lois"*, Bordeaux, 1949.
STRUCK, W., 'Montesquieu als Politiker', *Historische Studien*, vol. 228, Berlin, 1933.
TAYLOR, O. R., 'Bernard Routh et la mort de Montesquieu', FS, 3 (1949), pp. 101–21.
VIAN, Louis, *Histoire de Montesquieu*, 1878.

III. BURKE

1. WORKS OF BURKE

a. Complete Works

The Works of the Right Honourable Edmund Burke, 8 vols., 1792–1827.
The Works of Edmund Burke (Bohn's British Classics), 8 vols., 1854–89.

b. Individual Works and Correspondence.

Correspondence of Edmund Burke, ed. T. W. Copeland and others, Cambridge, 1958– (in progress, vols. 1–3 published).
Correspondence of Edmund Burke and William Windham, ed. J. P. Gilson, Cambridge, 1910.
Correspondence of the Right Hon. Edmund Burke, ed. Charles William, Earl Fitzwilliam, and Sir Richard Bourke, 4 vols., 1844.
The Epistolary Correspondence of the Right Hon. Edmund Burke and Dr. French Laurence, 1827.
An Essay towards an Abridgment of the English History [1757].
A Note-Book of Edmund Burke, ed. H. V. F. Somerset, Cambridge, 1957.
A Philosophical Enquiry into the Origin of Our Ideas of the Sublime and Beautiful, ed. J. T. Boulton, 1958.

c. Works to which Burke contributed.

The Annual Register, 1758–66.
[BURKE, William, and BURKE, Edmund], *An Account of the European Settlements in America*, 1757.

d. Sale Catalogue of Burke's Library.

Catalogue of the Library of the late Right Hon. Edmund Burke [1833].

2. WORKS ON BURKE

BRYANT, D. C., *Edmund Burke and His Literary Friends*, Washington University, 1939.
——, 'New Light on Burke', *The Quarterly Journal of Speech*, 39 (1953), pp. 351–2.
COBBAN, Alfred, *Edmund Burke and the Revolt against the Eighteenth Century*, 1929.

Cone, C. B., *Burke and the Nature of Politics*, Lexington, Kentucky, 1957.

Copeland, T. W., 'Burke's *Vindication of Natural Society*', *Library*, 4th series, 18 (1937–8), pp. 461–2.

——, *Edmund Burke, Six Essays*, 1950.

——, and Smith, M. S., *A Checklist of the Correspondence of Edmund Burke*, Cambridge, 1955.

Enaudi, Mario, 'The British Background of Burke's Political Philosophy', *Political Science Quarterly*, 49 (1934), pp. 576–98.

Hoffman, Ross J. S., *Edmund Burke, New York Agent*, Philadelphia, 1956.

MacCunn, John, *The Political Philosophy of Burke*, 1913.

Magnus, Sir Philip, 'The character and private life of Edmund Burke', *English Studies*, 1949, pp. 25–42.

——, *Edmund Burke*, 1939.

Morley, John, *Burke*, 1879.

Murray, Robert H., *Edmund Burke: a Biography*, Oxford, 1931.

Newman, Bertram, *Edmund Burke*, 1927.

Osborn, A. M., *Rousseau and Burke*, Oxford, 1940.

Parkin, Charles, *The Moral Basis of Burke's Political Thought*, Cambridge, 1956.

Parrel, C. de, 'Burke and Calonne', *French Quarterly*, 11 (1929), pp. 11–18.

Prior, Sir James, *Memoir of the Life of Edmund Burke*, 2nd edition, 2 vols., 1826.

——, *Life of Edmund Burke*, 5th edition, 1891.

Samuels, A. P. I., *Early Life, Correspondence and Writings of Edmund Burke*, Cambridge, 1923.

Skalweit, Stephan, *Edmund Burke und Frankreich*, Cologne and Opladen, 1956.

Somerset, H. V. F., 'A Burke discovery', *English*, 8 (1951), pp. 171–8.

Stanlis, P. J., *Edmund Burke and the Natural Law*, Michigan, 1958.

Sutherland, L. S., 'Edmund Burke and the first Rockingham administration', *EHR*, 47 (1932), pp. 46–72.

Vincitorio, G., 'Edmund Burke and Charles Lucas', *PMLA*, 68 (1953), pp. 1047–55.

Wecter, Dixon, 'The Missing Years in E. Burke's Biography', *PMLA*, 53 (1938), pp. 1102–25.

——, *Edmund Burke and His Kinsmen*, Boulder, Colorado, 1939.

Weston, J. C., 'The ironic purpose of Burke's *Vindication* vindicated', *Journal of the History of Ideas*, 19 (1958), pp. 435–441.

Young, G. M., 'Burke', *Proceedings of the British Academy*, 29 (1943).

IV. GENERAL WORKS

Acton, J. E. E. Dalberg, Baron Acton, *Essays on Church and State*, ed. Douglas Woodruff, 1952.

Albemarle, George Thomas, Earl of, *Memoirs of the Marquis of Rockingham*, 2 vols., 1852.

Aulard, F.-A., *Histoire politique de la Révolution française*, 5th ed., 1921.

Bagehot, W., *The English Constitution, Reprinted from the 'Fortnightly Review'*, 1867.

Barker, Sir Ernest, *Essays on Government*, Oxford, 1945.

——, *Natural Law and the Theory of Society, 1500 to 1800, by Otto Gierke*, 2 vols., Cambridge, 1934.

Barnes, D. G., *George III and William Pitt, 1783–1806*, Stanford University, 1939.

BATESON, Mary, *A Narrative of the Changes in the Ministry, 1765–67, told by the Duke of Newcastle*, 1898.

BAYLE, Pierre, *Dictionnaire historique et critique*, 2 vols., Rotterdam, 1697.

BLACK, J. B., *The Art of History*, 1926.

BLACKSTONE, Sir William, *Commentaries on the Laws of England*, 4 vols., Oxford, 1765–69.

BLAMPIGNON, E.-A., *Le Duc de Nivernais, ou un grand seigneur au XVIIIe siècle*, n.d.

BOLINGBROKE, Henry Saint John, Viscount, *Letters on the Study and Use of History*, 2 vols., 1752.

——, *Works*, ed. David Mallet, 5 vols., 1754.

BOND, E. A., *Speeches of the Managers and Counsel in the Trial of Warren Hastings*, 4 vols., 1859–61.

BOULAINVILLIERS, Comte Henri de, *Essais sur la noblesse de France*, 1732.

——, *Histoire de l'ancien gouvernement de la France*, 3 vols., 1727.

BOYLE, Patrick, *The Irish College in Paris from 1578 to 1901*, 1901.

BROOKE, John, *The Chatham Administration, 1766–1768*, 1956.

BROWN, P. A., *The French Revolution in English History*, 1918.

BUTTERFIELD, Herbert, 'Charles James Fox and the Whig opposition', *Cambridge Journal of History*, 9 (1949), pp. 293–330.

——, *George III, Lord North and the People, 1779–1780*, 1949.

——, *Man on His Past*, Cambridge, 1955.

CARTWRIGHT, John, *Take Your Choice*, 1776.

CASSIRER, Ernst, *The Philosophy of the Enlightenment*, translated by F. C. A. Koelln and J. P. Pettegrove, Princeton, 1951.

CHARLEMONT, James Caulfeild, Earl of, *The Manuscripts and Correspondence of James, first Earl of Charlemont*, Historical Manuscripts Commission, Twelfth Report, Appendix, Part x, 1891; Thirteenth Report, Appendix, Part viii, 1894.

CHESTERFIELD, Philip Dormer Stanhope, Earl of, *The Letters of Philip Dormer Stanhope, 4th Earl of Chesterfield*, ed. Bonamy Dobrée, 6 vols., 1932.

CLARK, Sir George, *The Later Stuarts*, Oxford, 1934.

COBBAN, Alfred, *The Debate on the French Revolution, 1789–1800*, 1950.

COBBETT, W. and WRIGHT, J., *The Parliamentary History of England*, 36 vols., 1806–20.

[COLEPEPPER, Sir John], *His Majesties Answer to the XIX Propositions*, 1642.

COMTE, Auguste, *Cours de Philosophie positive*, 6 vols., 1835–52.

Courier de Londres, London, 1789–90.

COURTENAY, John, *Philosophical Reflections on the Late Revolution in France*, 1790.

Critical Review, 1789–90.

DALRYMPLE, John, *An Essay towards a General History of Feudal Property in Great Britain*, 1757.

DAVIES, A. Mervyn, *Warren Hastings, a Maker of British India*, 1935.

DIDEROT, D., and ALEMBERT, J. Le R. d', *Encyclopédie ou Dictionnaire raisonné des sciences, des arts et des métiers*, 17 vols., 1751–65.

DODWELL, H. H., *British India*, vol. 5 of *The Cambridge History of India*, Cambridge, 1929.

DUBOS, abbé Jean-Baptiste, *Histoire critique de l'établissement de la monarchie française dans les Gaules*, 3 vols., 1734.

——, *Réflexions critiques sur la poésie et sur la peinture*, 2 vols., 1719.

Du Deffand, Marie-Anne, marquise, *Correspondance complète*, ed. le marquis de Sainte Aulaire, 3 vols., 1866.

Dumont, E., *Souvenirs sur Mirabeau*, 1832.

Durry, M.-J., *Autographes de Mariemont, première partie : avant 1800*, 2 vols., 1955.

Echard, Laurence, *The History of England from the First Entrance of Julius Caesar and the Romans*, 3 vols., 1707–18.

Entreves, A. P., d', *Natural Law*, 1951.

Farington, Joseph, *The Farington Diary 1793–1821*, ed. J. Greig, 8 vols., 1922–28.

Feiling, Keith, *Warren Hastings*, 1954.

Fieldhouse, H. N., 'Bolingbroke and the idea of non-party government', *History*, 23 (1938–39), pp. 41–56.

Fitzjames, J., Duke of Berwick, *Mémoires du maréchal de Berwick, écrits par lui-même*, 2 vols., 1778.

——, *Memoirs of the Marshal Duke of Berwick, written by himself*, 2 vols., 1779.

Forrest, G. W., *Selections from the State Papers of the Governors-General of India: Warren Hastings*, 2 vols., Oxford and London, 1910.

Fortescue, Sir John, (Ed.), *The Correspondence of King George the Third*, 6 vols., 1927–28.

Fueter, Eduard, *Geschichte der neueren Historiographie*, Munich and Berlin, 1936.

Garrick, David, *The Private Correspondence of David Garrick*, 2 vols., 1831–32.

Gentleman's Magazine, 1789–90.

Giannone, Pietro, *The Civil History of the Kingdom of Naples*, translated by James Ogilvie, 2 vols., 1729–31.

Gibbon, E., *The History of the Decline and Fall of the Roman Empire*, 6 vols., 1776–88.

Grattan, Henry, *Memoirs of the Life and Times of the Rt. Hon. Henry Grattan by his son, Henry Grattan, Esq.*, M.P., 5 vols., 1839–46.

——, *The Speeches of the Right Honourable Henry Grattan*, edited by his son, 4 vols., 1822.

Grimm, F. M., Baron, *Correspondance littéraire, philosophique et critique, par Grimm, Diderot, Raynal, Meister, etc.* ed. M. Tourneux, 16 vols., 1877–82.

Grotius, Hugo, *Le Droit de la guerre et de la paix*, translated by Jean Barbeyrac, 2 vols., Leyden, 1759.

Guicciardini, Francesco, *History of Italy translated by Austin Parke Goddard*, 10 vols., 1753.

Guttridge, G. H., *David Hartley, M.P., An Advocate of Conciliation, 1774–83*, Berkeley, California, 1926.

——, *English Whiggism and the American Revolution*, Berkeley, California, 1942.

Halhed, N. B., *A Code of Gentoo Laws*, 1776.

Hardy, Francis, *Memoirs of the Political and Private Life of James Caulfield, Earl of Charlemont*, 2 vols., 1812.

Harlow, Vincent T., *The Founding of the Second British Empire, 1763–1793*, vol. 1, 1952.

Hayes, Richard, *Biographical Dictionary of Irishmen in France*, Dublin, 1949.

——, *Ireland and Irishmen in the French Revolution*, 1932.

——, *Irish Swordsmen of France*, Dublin, 1934.

——, *Old Irish Links with France*, Dublin, 1940.

The History of the Trial of Warren Hastings, Esq., 1796.

Holdsworth, Sir William, *A History of English Law*, 6th edition, 13 vols., 1938–52.

HUME, David, *Enquiries Concerning the Human Understanding*, ed. L. A. Selby-Bigge, 2nd edition, Oxford, 1951.

——, *Essays Moral, Political and Literary*, ed. T. H. Green and T. H. Grose, 2 vols., 1875.

——, *History of England*, 6 vols., 1754–62.

——, *Letters of David Hume*, ed. J. Y. T. Greig, 2 vols., Oxford, 1932.

KIRK, Russell, *The Conservative Mind*, 1954.

LALLY-TOLENDAL, T.-G., comte de, *Mémoire de M. le comte de Lally-Tolendal ou seconde lettre à ses commetans*, 1790.

LAPRADE, W. T., *England and the French Revolution*, 1789–97, Baltimore, 1909.

——, *Parliamentary Papers of John Robinson*, 1774–1784, 1922.

[LA ROCHE, M.-L. de], *Lettres de M. Helvétius au président de Montesquieu et à M. Saurin relatives à l'aristocratie et la noblesse*, 1789.

LECKY, W. E. H., *A History of Ireland in the Eighteenth Century*, 5 vols., 1892.

LEE, Grace, *Huguenot Settlements in Ireland*, 1936.

LEMAIRE, André, *Les Lois fondamentales selon les parlementaires*, 1907.

LEVY-SCHNEIDER, L., *L'Application du Concordat par un prélat d'ancien régime, Mgr Champion de Cicé*, 1921.

LOLME, Jean-Louis de, *La Constitution de l'Angleterre*, Amsterdam, 1771.

——, *Constitution of England*, 1775.

London Chronicle, 1789–90.

LYTTELTON, George, Baron, *Letters from a Persian in England to His Friend at Ispahan*, 1735.

MACCOBY, S., *English Radicalism*, 5 vols., 1935–55.

MACHIAVELLI, N., *The Works of the Famous Nicolas Machiavel*, 3rd edition, 1720.

——, *The Works of Nicolas Machiavel Newly Translated by E. Farneworth*, 2 vols., 1762.

MCILWAIN, C. H., *The American Revolution*, New York, 1923.

MAVIDAL, J.; LAURENT, E.; and others, *Archives parlementaires*, 82 vols., 1862–1913.

MAXWELL, Constantia, *Dublin under the Georges*, 1714–1830, 1936.

MEINECKE, Friedrich, *Die Entstehung des Historismus*, 2 vols., Munich and Berlin, 1936.

Minutes of the Evidence taken at the Trial of Warren Hastings, 11 vols., 1788–94.

MONCKTON-JONES, M. E., *Warren Hastings in Bengal*, 1772–1774, Oxford, 1918.

MORELLET, abbé André, *Lettres de l'abbé Morellet à Lord Shelburne*, ed. Lord Fitzmaurice, 1898.

MOUNIER, J.-J., *Nouvelles observations sur les Etats généraux de France*, n.p., 1789.

NAMIER, Sir Lewis, *England in the Age of the American Revolution*, 1930.

——, *Monarchy and the Party System*, Oxford, 1952.

——, *The Structure of Politics at the Accession of George III*, 2nd edition, 1957.

O'CONOR, Charles, of Balenagar, *Dissertations on the History of Ireland*, 2nd edition, Dublin, 1766.

O'CONOR, Charles, D. D., *Memoirs of the Life and Writings of the Late Charles O'Conor of Balenagar*, vol. i, Dublin [1796].

OWEN, J. B., *The Rise of the Pelhams*, 1957.

PAINE, Thomas, *Common Sense*, 1776.

——, *The Rights of Man*, 1791.

——, *The Rights of Man, Part II*, 1792.

Pares, Richard, *King George III and the Politicians*, Oxford, 1954.

——, *Limited Monarchy in Great Britain in the Eighteenth Century*, 1957.

——, Review of Brooke, John, *The Chatham Administration*, 1956, EHR, 72 (1957), pp. 333–37.

Pargellis, S., 'The theory of balanced government', *The Constitution Reconsidered*, ed. Conyers Read, New York, 1938.

Parkes, J. and Merivale, H., *Memoirs of Sir Philip Francis*, 2 vols., 1867.

The Parliamentary Register: or History of the Proceedings and Debates of the House of Commons of Ireland (1781–1800), 20 vols., Dublin, 1784–1800.

Plumb, J. H., *Sir Robert Walpole*, vol. i, 1956.

Pocock, J. G. A., *The Ancient Constitution and the Feudal Law*, Cambridge, 1957.

Popper, Karl, *The Poverty of Historicism*, 1957.

Porritt, E. and A. G., *The Unreformed House of Commons*, 2 vols., Cambridge, 1909.

Price, Richard, *A Discourse on the Love of Our Country*, 1789.

——, *Observations on the Nature of Civil Society*, 1776.

Rapin-Thoyras, Paul de, *Histoire de l'Angleterre*, 13 vols., The Hague, 1724–36.

——, *The History of England . . . Done into English with Notes, by N. Tindal*, 15 vols., 1725–31.

Read, Conyers, (Ed.), *The Constitution Reconsidered*, New York, 1938.

Reports from Committees of the House of Commons reprinted by Order of the House, 1803, vols. v–viii.

Ritcheson, C. R., *British Politics and the American Revolution*, Oklahoma, 1954.

Robertson, C. Grant, *Select Statutes, Cases and Documents to illustrate English Constitutional History, 1660–1832*, 1904.

Robertson, William, *History of Scotland*, 2 vols., 1759.

Robson, E., *The American Revolution in its Political and Military Aspects, 1763–1783*, 1955.

Roche, James, *Critical and Miscellaneous Essays of an Octogenarian*, 2 vols., Cork, 1851.

Romilly, Sir Samuel, *Memoirs of the Life of Sir Samuel Romilly*, 2nd edition, 3 vols., 1840.

Rousseau, Jean-Jacques, *The Political Writings of J. J. Rousseau*, ed. C. E. Vaughan, 2 vols., Cambridge, 1915.

Russell, Lord John, *Memorials and Correspondence of Charles James Fox*, 4 vols., 1853.

St. James's Chronicle, 1789–90.

Schuyler, R. L., *Parliament and the British Empire*, New York, 1929.

Sedgwick, Romney, (Ed.), *Letters from George III to Lord Bute*, 1939.

Sewall, R. B., 'Rousseau's second Discourse in England from 1755 to 1762', *Philological Quarterly*, 17 (1938), pp. 97–114.

Sieyes, Emmanuel-J., *Qu'est-ce que le Tiers Etat?* ed. Edme Champion, 1888.

Smith, Adam, *The Wealth of Nations*, 2 vols., 1776.

Smith, W. J. (Ed.), *The Grenville Papers*, 4 vols., 1852–53.

Stephen, Sir Leslie, *History of English Thought in the Eighteenth Century*, 2 Vols., 1876.

Straus, R., *Robert Dodsley*, 1910.

Strauss, Leo, *Natural Right and History*, Chicago, 1953.

Strickland, W. G., *A Dictionary of Irish Artists*, 2 vols., Dublin, 1913.

Stuart, Gilbert, *An Historical Dissertation concerning the Antiquity of the English Constitution*, 1768.

STUBBS, J. W., *The History of the University of Dublin*, Dublin, 1889.

SULLIVAN, Francis Stoughton, *An Historical Treatise on the Feudal Law and the Constitution and Laws of England*, 1772.

SUTHERLAND, L. S., *The East India Company in Eighteenth Century Politics*, Oxford, 1952.

TEMPLE, Sir William, *The Works of Sir William Temple*, 4 vols., 1757.

TYLER, J. E., 'A letter from the Marquis of Rockingham to Sir William Mayne on the proposed absentee tax of 1773', *Irish Historical Studies*, 8 (1952-3), pp. 362-9.

VAUGHAN, C. E., *Studies in the History of Political Philosophy*, 3 vols., Manchester, 1925.

VEITCH, G. S., *The Genesis of Parliamentary Reform*, 1913.

VOLTAIRE, Marie Arouet de, *Œuvres complètes de Voltaire*, ed. Louis Moland, 52 vols., 1877-85.

WALPOLE, Horace, *Letters*, ed. Paget Toynbee, 16 vols., Oxford, 1903-5.

——, *Memoirs of the Reign of King George the Third*, ed. G. F. R. Barker, 4 vols., 1894.

——, *The Yale Edition of Horace Walpole's Correspondence*, ed. W. S. Lewis, New Haven, 1937- (in progress).

WALSH, T. J., 'The Irish College at Bordeaux: some Cork associations with the Gironde', *Journal of the Cork Historical and Archaeological Society*, 52 (1947).

WEITZMAN, Sophia, *Warren Hastings and Philip Francis*, Manchester, 1929.

The Whisperer, 1770-72.

Whitehall Evening Post, 1789-90.

WINDHAM, WILLIAM, *The Windham Papers* [Ed. by Lewis Melville], 2 vols., 1913.

WINSTANLEY, D. A., *Lord Chatham and the Whig Opposition*, Cambridge, 1912.

——, *Personal and Party Government*, 1760-1766, Cambridge, 1910.

WOODBRIDGE, H. E., *Sir William Temple, the Man and His Work*, New York, 1940.

WRIGHT, John, *Sir Henry Cavendish's Debates of the House of Commons*, 1768-71, 2 vols., 1841-43.

INDEX

195